Precarious Enterprise on the Margins

Jessica Gerrard

Precarious Enterprise on the Margins

Work, Poverty, and Homelessness in the City

Jessica Gerrard
University of Melbourne
Melbourne Graduate School of Education
Melbourne, Victoria, Australia

ISBN 978-1-137-59482-2 ISBN 978-1-137-59483-9 (eBook)
DOI 10.1057/978-1-137-59483-9

Library of Congress Control Number: 2017945216

© The Editor(s) (if applicable) and The Author(s) 2017
This work is subject to copyright. All rights are solely and exclusively licensed by the Publisher, whether the whole or part of the material is concerned, specifically the rights of translation, reprinting, reuse of illustrations, recitation, broadcasting, reproduction on microfilms or in any other physical way, and transmission or information storage and retrieval, electronic adaptation, computer software, or by similar or dissimilar methodology now known or hereafter developed.
The use of general descriptive names, registered names, trademarks, service marks, etc. in this publication does not imply, even in the absence of a specific statement, that such names are exempt from the relevant protective laws and regulations and therefore free for general use.
The publisher, the authors and the editors are safe to assume that the advice and information in this book are believed to be true and accurate at the date of publication. Neither the publisher nor the authors or the editors give a warranty, express or implied, with respect to the material contained herein or for any errors or omissions that may have been made. The publisher remains neutral with regard to jurisdictional claims in published maps and institutional affiliations.

Cover illustration: © donatas1205

Printed on acid-free paper

This Palgrave Macmillan imprint is published by Springer Nature
The registered company is Nature America Inc.
The registered company address is: 1 New York Plaza, New York, NY 10004, U.S.A.

Preface

This book is the product of a convergence of desires. At one level, it represents my ongoing commitment to engage in research that addresses the deep abiding inequalities that pattern our social world. It therefore marks a continuation of my interest in understanding power, culture and identity and the intersections of education and work. It also represents my desire to better understand the multifaceted everyday experiences of poverty: experiences that cannot, as I reflect in Chaps. 1 and 2, be simplistically rendered as 'excluded', or worse still, as 'in lack', 'depraved' or 'out of joint'. The everyday contours of poverty are not expressions of deficiency or laziness in an otherwise functional capitalism. They are expressions of the dysfunctionality of contemporary capitalism, of the social relations of inequality and injustice, felt and lived in diverse ways. There is a need therefore to resist simplistic explanations, categorisations and labels. We know well that the dynamic powerful practices of class, gender, sexuality and race spill over, intersect, and frame social experience in multifarious, and sometimes unexpected, ways. With this impetus in mind, my hope is that this book contributes meaningfully to the ongoing academic and public discussions on how to create politically engaged research attuned to the constantly changing—but nevertheless deeply embedded—structures of social injustice.

At the same time, at least in part, this is a book also born out of frustration. The idea for this book emerged whilst I was in the midst of completing a different reserach project for my doctoral thesis at the University of Cambridge, UK 2007–2011. Here, whilst living and studying in one of the most elite educational institutions in the world, I was troubled by the homelessness and poverty on the streets of Cambridge. My own feelings about studying at Cambridge were mixed. On the one hand, having worked previously as a school teacher and having never aspired to an 'Ivy League' education, I could never shake the sensation of being an (incredibly beholden) fish out of water. This provided ample fuel to feed ambiguous feelings of gratitude and an urgency to work hard. Yet, on the other hand, these feelings were countered by a political awareness of— and frustration over—the past and present inequalities that puncture the hallowed halls of an elitist institution such as Cambridge. This privilege appeared to jump out and grab me, keeping a firm hold as I inevitably compared the stark differences in the educational ethos and history of Cambridge and the subject of my doctoral research: the history of radical working-class and Black educational movements (see Gerrard 2014).

Perhaps this political frustration was heightened for me as an Anglo Australian studying in England, aware of the colonial roots and ties stained with Empire my home country has with England. I could not help but feel the paradoxical tentative embrace of the central educational arteries of mother Empire. Educational institutions and intellectual traditions are of course central to nation and Empire building. As an Australian studying in England I was travelling a well traversed and worn down path with roots in colonisation. Long-held traditions of pilgrimages from Empire's outposts to its heartland educational institutions have brought many from the 'South' in search of social mobility (or affirmation), and (for some) an authoritative nod of recognition from Empire's heartland institutions (see also Connell 2007). These journeys are also centrally implicated in the histories of resistance and critique from 'the colonies' (see Schwartz 2003). More recently, student activism surrounding racist colonial links to colleges and university scholarships, have sharpened analyses of the relationship between institutions like Cambridge and Oxford University and Empire (see Newsinger 2016).

Nevertheless, the symbolic and material importance of this authoritative nod of recognition cannot be understated. Many challenges to university elitism have demanded expansion and augmentation of the nod: from the push for women to be fully included into the University (finally realised in 1988 when the last all-male college, Magdalene College, opened its doors to women, infamously marked on the day by some male students wearing Black arm bands in protest [see Dyhouse 2006]), to the complex biographies of migration and diaspora that underlie the history of colonisation and education. Yet, at the same time, such journeying is deeply imbricated in the social processes of global mobility that have ultimately strengthened and deepened the grooves of class, race and gendered distinctions (see Mirza 2015). Despite various policies and programmes, Cambridge remains an elite, largely white, institution (see e.g. Vasagar 2010).

Moreover, just a very gentle scratch of the surface of Cambridge reveals the wealth of labour that creates the 'student experience': the cleaners who clean students' college rooms and houses, the servers who deliver four-course meals to students in grand eating halls, the cooks who prepare these meals, and the countless other workers who were having a very different 'Cambridge experience' to that of students and academic staff. Cambridge is also a city with notable poverty and homelessness, and it is here that the seeds of this book began. The homeless sellers of the homeless street press, *The Big Issue*, particularly brought this poverty and homelessness to the fore on the streets of Cambridge city. Positioned on bustling street corners and filling the air with their sales pitches, sellers appeared to interrupt business-as-usual university life. In a city known for its manicured lawns, imposing college buildings and quaint cobbled stone streets this poverty and homelessness could be interpreted as 'out of joint', visually, culturally and materially.

It is this seeming contradiction in elitism and poverty that first sparked the idea for the research for this book. Yet, it is a contradiction that is far from being 'out of joint'; it is intimately intertwined with the ways in which inequalities are created under capitalism. As this book illustrates, homeless street presses such as *The Big Issue* in Melbourne and London and *Street Sheet* in San Francisco are important contemporary examples of informal economies and work. At a time with stubborn chronic and long-term unemployment, dramatic shifts in work conditions and availability, and growing under-employment, these sorts of work practices have growing significance. To state it plainly, for many women and men this is the only form of work available. As a work practice reliant on the enterprising spirit and motivation of the sellers, homeless street press work also highlights the messy interconnections of contemporary labouring and learning. Sellers must cultivate the right skills and dispositions in order to attract sales and generate income, in precarious conditions.

And so, a doctoral thesis completed and another research project on, I finally embarked on the research for this book through a McKenzie Postdoctoral Research Fellowship at the University of Melbourne, 2012–2015. Over three years, I spent many hours passing time and talking with sellers of homeless street press predominantly in Melbourne (*The Big Issue*), but also in San Francisco *(Street* Sheet) and London (*The Big Issue*) as my research took me to the places in which homeless street press first began and was made popular. In addition, a significant proportion of my preparation for this book was following the archive traces of these homeless street presses internationally. As I document in Chap. 3, homeless street press are connected to a long history of homeless self-help and activism in the US (such as in the *Street Sheet*), which was then taken up and re-born as a 'social enterprise' (a business with a social purpose) through *The Big Issue* first in London and then in Melbourne, and now in multiple cities internationally. In this book, rather than document and describe the experience of homeless street press sellers as extraordinary to life under capitalism, I set out to place the politics of the working and learning lives of sellers in the context of wider social relations of inequality and injustice.

References

Connell, R. W. (2007). *Southern Theory: The Global Dynamics of Knowledge in Social Science*. Crows Nest: Allen & Unwin.

Dyhouse, C. (2006). *Students: A Gendered History*. London/New York: Routledge.

Gerrard, J. (2014). *Radical Childhoods: Schooling and the Struggle for Social Change*. Manchester: Manchester University Press.

Mirza, H. S. (2015). Decolonizing Higher Education: Black Feminism and the Intersectionality of Race and Gender. *Journal of Feminist Scholarship, 7/8*, http://www.jfsonline.org/issue7-8/articles/mirza/

Newsinger, J. (2016). Why Rhodes must Fall. *Race & Class, 58*(2): 70–78.

Schwartz, B. (Ed.). (2003). *West Indian Intellectuals in Britain*. Manchester: Manchester University Press.

Vasagar, J. (2010, December 7). Twenty-one Oxbridge Colleges Took No Black Students Last Year. *The Guardian*. http://www.theguardian.com/education/2010/dec/06/oxford-colleges-no-black-students

ACKNOWLEDGEMENTS

Thanks must first go to the sellers of homeless street press across Melbourne, San Francisco and London. I am indebted to sellers for the time they took out of their busy days to talk with me and their willingness to have me tag along whilst they worked. I have a tonne of gratitude, appreciation and respect for these sellers. Of course, I can lay no claim to fully understanding their experience and feelings, but my hope is that what I have written here faithfully reflects the stories that they wanted to be told and the everyday experiences of their work. I am also truly thankful to the workers and volunteers at *The Big Issue* offices in Melbourne and London and the Coalition on Homelessness' *Street Sheet* office in San Francisco. They too took time out of demanding schedules to talk with me about their work and the work of homeless street press, and I am sincerely grateful.

Thanks to my many colleagues and students at the University of Melbourne and beyond: academic work is really a collective endeavour, and I feel grateful for the support I have had over the past four years, and to the many conversations that have prompted me to think again, and think deeper. Thanks particularly to my colleagues and friends at MGSE and beyond, the members of the 'Politics, power and policy' reading group, Lesley Farrell, David Farrugia, Shelley Mallett, Julie McLeod, Shaun Rawolle, Fazal Rizvi, Sophie Rudolph, Glenn Savage, Arathi Sriprakash, Juliet Watson, Peter Woelert, and Lyn Yates. I also offer my heartfelt thanks to those who read sections of the draft monograph as I approached the deadline. Annette Allerding, David Farrugia, Emma Partridge, Sophie

Rudolph, Arathi Sriprakash, Amanda Thompson and Juliet Watson: thank you for taking time to read and offer helpful feedback. And thanks too to Patrick Liem, who offered invaluable assistance with preparing the photographs for publication.

Finally, thanks to my family and friends for your support and patience. Thank you for graciously enduring endless discussions about book titles and updates on the progress of the book, but also for your love, care, lightness and dance. As Emma Goldman said, "it's not my revolution if I can't dance!" And to Amanda, for your insight, compassion, smiles, hotcakes, and adventures, I am truly grateful.

Contents

1 Introduction: Work, Poverty and Capitalism 1
   Enterprise on the Margins *Themes* 5
   Poverty in Urban Spaces: Homeless in Melbourne
   San Francisco and London 11
   Chapter Overview 19
   Notes 22
   References 22

2 Marginality Reconsidered 27
   Writing About Marginality: Ants, Skyscrapers,
   Maps and Walking the City 28
   Margins: "The Silent, Silenced, Centre" 36
   Everyday Working and Learning Lives 40
   Confessionals, Testimonies and Everyday Life:
   Notes on the Research 42
   References 49

3 Homeless Street Press: Historical and Contemporary
   Connections 53
   Homeless Street Press: Histories of Homelessness and Work 54
   Street Sheet *and* The Big Issue: *Activism, Self-Help*
   and Social Enterprise 60
   The Informal (Moral and Entrepreneurial)
   Economies of Homeless Street Press 67

Researching The Big Issue *and* Street Sheet 72
References 75

4 **Time Is Money** 79
  Keeping Busy, Getting By 81
  A Day's Work 89
  References 105

5 **Being Productive: Working, Not Begging** 107
  Gabby and Rob 108
  Working on the Margins 112
  Distinguishing (Marginalised) Work: Not Begging 117
  Entrepreneurial Identities at Work 123
  References 128

6 **Learning to Entrepreneurially Labour** 131
  From the Work Ethic to the Learning Ethic 132
  The Hope of Learning/Working 137
  Learning to Labour 140
  Lessons of the Trade: Sales, Smiles and Self-Reliance 142
  References 150

7 **Working in Public: Value, Exchange and Performance** 153
  Amber and Jeffrey 154
  The Value of Exchange 161
  Performing for the Public: Working in Urban Spaces 166
  References 176

8 **Moving On?: Aspirations, Pathways and Stasis** 179
  'Pathways': Becoming a Seller 183
  Perpetual Transition/Stasis 189
  Dom 196
  References 200

9 **Epilogue: Enterprise on the Margins** 203

Index 207

List of Images

Image 1	Rachel's photo	90
Image 2	Andrew—Superman doorway	92
Image 3	Stacey—First $20 for the day	94
Image 4	Matt—Parliament Station pitch	96
Image 5	Tony—TAB	97
Image 6	Oli—The view of trees from his pitch	101

CHAPTER 1

Introduction: Work, Poverty and Capitalism

The ringing in of the twenty-first century was pockmarked by events highlighting the embedded inequalities of capitalism. Both the Global Financial Crisis and the Occupy movement, for instance, prompted sustained political attention towards unemployment, homelessness and inequality. More recently, the feverish popularity of Thomas Picketty's *Capital* in 2013 demonstrates, at the very least, a longing for better and deeper explanations of the disproportionate distribution of resources under capitalism. Crucial to deeper understandings of inequality is the examination of the contemporary conditions of work. Work is central to the production of inequality, marginality and poverty: work organises our time, influences our identities, reflects and produces the cultural and social dynamics of gender and race, and ultimately is an expression of status, class and economic capacity.

In the current context, the impact of the shifting precarious conditions of work on those already struggling to get by, maintain or obtain employment is a key challenge transnationally (see Shildrick et al. 2012; Kalleberg 2013). This includes the increasing imperative for 'adaptable' and 'flexible' workers capable of learning new forms of work for the changing needs of the labour market. There is a new cohort of marginalised poor—young and old—who are excluded from the 'knowledge economy' and 'information age', but who are expected to participate in education in order to obtain work (see Castells 2010). Thus, contemporary work cultures and conditions are keenly felt by both those who are in work and those who

© The Author(s) 2017
J. Gerrard, *Precarious Enterprise on the Margins*,
DOI 10.1057/978-1-137-59483-9_1

are out of work. As Kathi Weeks writes, "Work is crucial not only to those whose lives are centred around it, but also, in a society that expects people to work for wages, to those who are expelled or excluded from work and marginalised in relation to it" (2011: 2).

Enterprise on the Margins seeks to contribute new understanding of these contemporary conditions of marginality and work transnationally. It takes as its focus the historical emergence and contemporary practice of one of the most informal, insecure and precarious forms of work on the margins: homeless street press—the magazines and papers sold on street corners by the homeless, unemployed and poor. Drawing on in-depth ethnographic research, and building upon theories of marginality, work, and learning, *Enterprise on the Margins* investigates the expectations and experiences of work, and learning to work, by those living in poverty and homelessness. At the centre of this book are the women and men engaged in selling homeless street press across three cities: *The Big Issue* in Melbourne and London and *Street Sheet* in San Francisco.

Internationally, particularly since the late 1990s, sellers or vendors[1] of homeless street press have become a common sight on urban street corners (e.g. *The Big Issue, Street Sheet, Real Change, StreetWise*). Part of a longer tradition of public journalism (see e.g. Danky and Wiagand 1992), homeless street press distinguishes itself as a paper or magazine sold specifically by women and men living in homelessness or poverty. For many, it represents the only form of work available, providing an important avenue for legitimate and legal income. Sellers earn their living either off donations or on commission per sale, depending on the business model of the street press. In the case of *The Big Issue*—now the largest global franchise of homeless street press—sellers buy the magazines at half price, thereby making half of every sale. *Street Sheet* sellers obtain the paper for free from the grass-roots campaign organisation The Coalition on Homelessness and 'sell' it by asking for a donation.

This book purposefully moves across the three cities in order to demonstrate how homeless street press constitutes a form of work that has developed transnationally, connected to global shifts in work conditions and culture. San Francisco is home to the longest-running activist homeless street press—*Street Sheet*, which both predates *The Big Issue* and has very different organisational practices and aims; London is home to *The Big Issue*, arguably the first social enterprise—a business with a 'social conscious' or a 'social goal' established in 1991;

whilst Melbourne (where the bulk of the research was undertaken) is one of the first international expansions of *The Big Issue* beyond the UK, initiated in 1996. In examining across these three sites, *Enterprise on the Margins* investigates homeless street press as connected to the informal economy and the growing social enterprise sector, representative of important contemporary shifts in how homelessness and poverty is lived, understood and responded to.

By focusing on the accounts and experiences of homeless street press sellers, *Enterprise on the Margins* examines how the contemporary imperative to work and to develop oneself for work, is felt, navigated, and understood by those excluded from mainstream employment and education. This book demonstrates that those who are unemployed and seemingly 'unproductive' are in fact highly productive. Work is—as these lives attest—a powerful experience, brewing with feelings of dignity, recognition and worth. Homeless street press sellers engage in a range of enterprising activities in their attempt to feel and be productive and to manage the bleak material reality of poverty and homelessness within wealthy nations and cities. Yet, these women and men do so in difficult contexts. As *Enterprise on the Margins* reveals, in addition to managing poverty and in some cases homelessness, sellers must contend with the harsh conditions of working in all weather through summer and winter on city streets, days with few or no sales, the exhaustion of working 'on show' in public, and the struggle of cultivating the 'right' sales tactic in order to attract buyers.

In large part, this book emerges from my concern to contribute to the understanding of lives on the margins that does not fall prey to the familiar popular narratives of failure and stigma (see also Peel 2003). As Dillabough and Kennelly (2010) reflect, there is a need to address how marginalisation comes to be represented as 'trauma', 'lack' and 'other', and ultimately to resist such representations. As one of the most visible forms of poverty, homelessness is an easy target for simplistic interpretations of poverty, and is repeatedly equated with unproductivity or failure. Of course, homelessness is, as I note below, far more diverse than what is 'visible' on the streets, including couch surfing, in overcrowded conditions, and refuges. Nevertheless, explanations of homelessness often collapse into collections of individual 'risk factors', as if poverty can be explained by a shopping list of determinants: family breakdown, drug and alcohol abuse, mental illness and work-shy mentalities

(Farrugia and Gerrard 2016; see also Parsell and Marston 2012). Such explanations compound the false perception that poverty is an individual failing that can be eradicated if people just try hard enough, work hard enough, learn enough and better themselves enough.

Thus, in writing this book my aim is not only to 'surface' the experience of homeless street press sellers. Just to focus in on the lives of those who are excluded without consideration of the ways in which inequality, poverty and marginalisation is constituted through wider social relations can replicate problematic narratives of the poor as 'other' and 'lacking', and thereby replicate the notion that poverty is an individual failing. Simply giving 'voice' to the marginalised and oppressed does not rectify much weightier and powerful social and economic processes of inequality within capitalism. Rather, we need—now more than ever at a time of increasing global social inequalities—accounts of inequality that squarely face the moral, political, social, economic and cultural processes through which inequality is created, understood and made possible to intervene into. At the very least, it is necessary to acknowledge the ways in which marginalisation (and with this homelessness) is constituted—as a social, economic and policy category.

Therefore, the approach taken in *Enterprise on the Margins* is to offer an in-depth account of the working lives of homeless street press sellers, alongside a consideration of the ways in which these lives are knitted into the fabric of our social relations: not a world apart. To do so, *Enterprise on the Margins* gives significant space to the rich accounts of sellers, including thick description of my research field notes, alongside theoretical development—moving across experience to theory and back again. Across the chapters of this book are four interwoven thematic objectives, which aim to contextualise the experiences of the homeless street press sellers within wider social relations and expectations, and which point to the overarching conceptual contributions this book aims to make.

In what follows in this chapter, first, I explicate each of these four themes: (1) becoming productive—working and learning lives on the margins; (2) social enterprise, the welfare state and informal work; (3) visible lives—homelessness, morality, performance and public space; and (4) precarious lives—stasis and mobility. I then turn to the context of this book and reflect on the city as a space and practice in relation to urban poverty and inequality. Here, I offer some brief notes on my research in Melbourne, San Francisco and London to provide the reader with some orientation. Finally, I provide an overview of the chapters in this book.

ENTERPRISE ON THE MARGINS THEMES

Becoming Productive: Working and Learning Lives on the Margins

First, *Enterprise on the Margins* outlines the ways in which being productive—being engaged in (informal, highly marginalised and precarious) work—shapes the lives of those who are excluded from the formal labour market. Here, my motivation is to examine the cultural, moral and social dimensions of contemporary work. The presumption that work is a self-affirming activity, tying us morally and subjectively to our work, underpins the fabric of capitalist social relations (see Weber 1984; Weeks 2011). A 'work ethic' has long defined the ways in which capitalism creates and maintains cultures of work discipline. With this it creates a range of social relations that frame experiences and judgements of inclusion and exclusion, success and failure, and productive and unproductive citizenship (Weeks 2011).

Correspondingly, there are deep connections between the practices and institutions of—and moral attachments to—learning and working, which are undergoing significant transformation in the contemporary context. In 1977, Paul Willis explored the gendered and classed social codes that extend across schooling and work for working-class 'lads' in England in his ground breaking ethnography *Learning to Labour*. In 2017, amidst transformation in learning and labouring practices which extend well beyond school-to-work 'pathways', it is necessary to analyse anew the intersections between education and work (see also Dolby and Dimitriadis 2004: 6). *Enterprise on the Margins* takes up this challenge by examining the intersections of learning and labouring beyond the formal educational and work institutions most often associated with the post-war welfare states. In doing so, it situates work on the margins—in informal economies and social enterprises—as sites of both earning and learning.

The continued, if at times arguably rhetorical, embrace of the 'learning society' and 'knowledge economy', along with the shifting needs and precarious nature of the labour market certainly accentuates the need for development, learning citizen selves (see Coffield 1999; Seddon 2004; Crowther 2004). Current government policies attempt to cultivate agile and adaptable workers able of responding to the shifting needs of the labour market. In *Enterprise on the Margins*, I draw on my previous development of the notion of a 'learning ethic' in order to explore the connections between learning and work, where learning is narrowly shackled to the world of work, and with this the inequalities of capital accrual (see Gerrard 2014). As with the work ethic, the learning ethic is morally charged, and creates a host of social relations and practices of inclusion/exclusion and success/failure. As I explore in *Enterprise on the Margins*, these ethics operate in correspondence—supporting the ideal productive learning citizen self. In contemporary society, to be worthy and good is to demonstrate willingness to develop oneself for, and engage in, work.

It is within this context that homeless street press represents both a work and learning practice on the margins. Through selling magazines and newspapers on the street, sellers are engaging in a form of work that addresses their fundamental need for income. Yet, as a work practice created for those outside of formal employment, it also is invariably educative. Part of my contention is that underpinning a large part of the informal economy of homeless street press is a moral—and institutional—imperative to demonstrate self-development and learning for work. As the motto of *The Big Issue* puts it—it is a 'hand up, not a hand out'. Of course, these expectations differ significantly depending on the organisational ethos of the street press. *Street Sheet*, for instance, takes a very different—and more activist—approach than *The Big Issue*. Yet, these street presses cannot be separated from the broader social expectations of aspirational entrepreneurial subjectivities, and work on the self, in aid of finding, obtaining and maintaining work (see Rose 1992). Thus, there are both subtle and not so subtle expectations to be learning to do better and be more productive.

Enterprise on the Margins, then, explores the everyday work cultures of precarious workers and the ways learning to work are interwoven in the very practice of this marginal work. At the same time, this book also examines the past and present social understandings of and expectations for 'productive citizenship', operating within the dynamics of gender, race and class. In doing so, I endeavour to tease out some of the taken-for-granted moral judgements made about idleness and productivity, and the ways in which these invariably colour interventions into the lives of those who are deemed to be 'unproductive' are justified and practised.

Social Enterprise, the Welfare State and Informal Work

Second, this book develops new understanding of an emerging, but currently under-researched, field of practice: social enterprise. Transnationally, debates surrounding the nature of, and what to do about, inequality, poverty and homelessness are waged amidst considerable shifts towards market-based approaches in the delivery and governance of welfare, health and education (see Newman and Clarke 2009). As the roles and responsibilities of the welfare state shift, there is significant innovation and growth in private partnerships and quasi-private/not-for-profit initiatives, such as social enterprise.

This is shaped by the expansive—if varied—international embrace of a neoliberal politics. In this embrace, market and business models are viewed as the correct innovative antidote to the so-called slow-moving bureaucracies of the welfare state (Mazzucato 2014). Governments have actively encouraged the involvement of a range of private actors in social services, such as education, employment assistance, welfare, housing and health. This has led to the regrowth of long traditions of philanthropy, and the emergence of a range of market-based responses to social problems including microfinance and social enterprise, such as the homeless street press, *The Big Issue* (see Roy 2010; Teasdale 2010; Gerrard 2017a). Both academic and public treatment of social enterprise tends to pull towards polar opposite analytic positions: unquestioning celebration of the market and its innovative potential, versus fervent critique of the incursion of corporatisation and marketisation in the community sector. Missing from these accounts is, first, a consideration of the complex historical relationship between the state, the market and private interests in the provision of goods and services to the poor, and, second, the lived experiences of those most effected by the mergence of this field of practice. This is what *Enterprise on the Margins* aims to contribute.

Connected to this is the import of informal work and the informal economy (see Sassen 1994). As a range of significant ethnographic and sociological research has already established, the poor and homeless have long engaged in a range of informal means to generate income and get by (see Gaber 1994; Gowan 2010; Turner and Schoenberger 2012; Adriaenssens and Hendrickx 2011). In the context of the subject of this book, this has involved the creation of a commodity (the homeless street press), and an associated market and exchange relations, for the purposes of creating work (Cockburn 2014). This is a commodity that is morally charged, granting sellers a note of distinction from, for instance, beggars by denoting them with judgements of deservingness and productivity. At the same time, its 'selling point' still rests on sellers being understood and recognised as homeless by potential buyers (Lindemann 2006). In other words, it is commodity that is not necessarily bought for its utility, but for its meaning. This is, as Zizek points out, a purchase that is not merely about buying and consuming, but is about "doing something meaningful, showing our capacity for care and our global awareness, participating in a collective project" (2009: 35). This book seeks to unpick how this moral culture of the work and the commodity is lived and felt by those at the centre of its market: the sellers.

Visible Lives: Homelessness, Morality, Performance and Public Space

Third, *Enterprise on the Margins* is concerned with reflecting on the intersections of public urban space with homelessness and visible poverty. As one of the most visible forms of poverty, homelessness has long attracted attention and intervention. Images and photographs of homelessness are routinely used in the media, academic texts, policy and advocacy papers, and in popular culture as a means to incite concern, action, and judgement (see Gerrard and Farrigua 2015). There has long been a desire to look, to visually document, and to use as a means to shock or prompt action about, social suffering: as Susan Sontag reflects, "The iconography of suffering has a long pedigree" (2003: 40). Within this desire are complicated and, at times, contradictory gendered, racialised and classed moral concerns.

In the case of visible homelessness, the 'sight and scene' of homelessness is also visceral in that it is experienced, and viewed, in public space (Gerrard and Farrugia 2015). Homeless street press extends and augments this viewing, provoking interaction through the exchange process between seller and buyer. In this book, I examine the practices of performance and exchange that occur in the everyday work practices of homeless street press sellers. Here, this book points to the complex—and oft-times difficult—experiences of needing to be visible for sales, whilst managing the exposure of being on view in city streets. Underpinning this is the moral dynamics of the exchange: vendors 'perform' and demonstrate their worthiness and productivity in various ways, and to varying degrees of success, in order to attract sales.

Precarious Lives: Stasis and Mobility

Fourth, *Enterprise on the Margins* demonstrates the difficult position many in poverty face, when managing both the expectations and aspirations to be socially mobile and prolonged poverty. Here, I aim to tease open popular pronouncements surrounding the fluidity of our contemporary times, to examine that which is both 'immobile' and 'precarious' at once. Contemporary social analysis is awash with terms and concepts pronouncing insecurity and mobility. From the 'risk society' (Beck 1992) to 'liquid modernity' (Baumann 2000), the 'reinventing self' (Elliott 2013) and now the 'precariat' (Standing 2011), primacy is given to notions of fluidity, uncertainty, movement and flux: high-status globetrotters; the aspirational and mobile middle class; the shifting experiences of the precarious poor. Sometimes it is hard not to feel a little motion sick amidst all this perpetual movement: identities in constant performative flux; the withering of traditional divisions of labour; and the apparent destabilisation of 'nation' and 'state' and 'citizen self' in contemporary global(ising) capitalism all emphasise a perspective of change.

In this book, I bring forward the lives of those that have long been punctured by precariousness: the lives of the homeless, unemployed and poor. Sellers of homeless street press could be understood to be a part of what has been described as the contemporary 'precariat' (see Standing 2011): what Wacquant suggests are "(sub)proletarians of the margins", existing outside of the "conventional sphere of regulated waged work" and identified by what they do not have—homes, jobs, official papers (2007: 72–73). To be sure, the form of work sellers engage in is highly precarious.

Yet, to depict these lives only in terms of 'risk', 'flux' and 'uncertainty' would belie a concurrent, and associated, experience of stasis. The current scholarly attention given to contemporary precarity lends itself to ahistorical understandings of precariousness, insecure work and homelessness (see Neilson and Rossiter 2008). Lying underneath—or perhaps rather at the centre—of the undeniable transformations in contemporary social relations are many continuities and experiences of immobility, past and present. Inequality remains a persistent presence in capitalist societies, despite the dynamic and multifarious ways it is lived and felt.

Moreover, 'precarious lives' are as much characterised by routine and monotony as they are by flux. To be poor is to experience everyday mundane suffering occupied by a constant anxiety about money. "To understand what poverty is," Mark Peel (2003: 70) states, "you have to be able to imagine worrying about money all the time." Whilst livelihoods and lives may be 'precarious', they are also anchored in routines that are required to manage the everyday experience of getting by. Sustained marginalisation and poverty has long cultivated (spatial, temporal, affective) monotony and is of course characterised by immobility (see Wacquant 2008a, b). There is a kind of friction therefore between the expectation of social mobility and advancement and the experience of stasis and poverty. Internationally, the poor are expected to demonstrate how they are alleviating themselves from their poverty, and then are often disciplined for not doing so through punitive welfare systems (see Shildrick et al. 2012).

When aspiration, mobility and self-development are at the core of modern citizenship expectations, the routines of poverty can be a source of discomfort and shame for those whose lives are at the pointy end of social inequality. Morally cloaking these feelings are the markings of a range of oppositional judgements: deserving/underserving; lazy/aspirational; productive/idle; success/failure. Such judgements nestle upon and stick to the bodies and biographies of the poor and unemployed, often coming to rest with a host of gendered, racialised, classed and ablest assumptions. These are double-edged judgements. People in poverty are seen to have shamed themselves *and* their communities for supposedly not fulfilling their role in being productive citizens. Indeed, at times those who are deemed failures are positioned as failing and shaming the nation state (see DePastino 2003; Gerrard 2017b). Often those who refuse or resist these judgements are then seen to be shameless: as destructive, desperate, depressed or depraved (see Walker 2014).

The effects of this, though, are not universal. Whilst 'the poor', 'the homeless' and 'the unemployed' are collectivising terms, there is no singular monochrome narrative of these experiences. As Raymond Williams writes, "There are in fact no masses, but only ways of seeing people as masses" (2002 [1958]: 98). Poverty and inequality may be permeated by common experiences of hardship, but it is also at its heart characterised by difference: there is no one way of being poor. Moreover, difference and 'otherness' is embedded in the experience of poverty and inequality: those who are poor are routinely made to feel that they are different and 'other than'. Judgments made about those experiencing poverty can sharpen feelings of distinction. Perceptions of deservingness and expectations of appropriate code of conduct can weigh heavily. North American writer Dorothy Allison (1994) puts it this way in her biographical essay 'A question of class':

> *My family's lives were not on television, not in books, not even comic books. There was a myth of the poor in this country, but it did not include us. No matter how hard I tried to squeeze us in. There was an idea of the good poor—hard-working, ragged but clean, and intrinsically honorable. I understood that we were the bad poor: men who drank and couldn't keep a job; women, invariably pregnant before marriage, who quickly became worn, fat, and old from working too many*

hours and bearing too many children; and children with runny noses, watery eyes, and the wrong attitude. ... We were not noble, not grateful, not even hopeful. We knew ourselves despised. My family was ashamed of being poor, of feeling hopeless. What was there to work for, to save money for, to fight for or struggle against? We had generations before us to teach us that nothing ever changed, and that those who did try to escape failed.

Here, Allison calls attention to the sharp edges of shame cultivated in the face of moral judgements surrounding the poor, and what they should, or should not, be doing.

In this book I explore the ways in which the expectation and aspiration to move beyond, be 'productive' and develop is lived and felt by sellers of homeless street press. In doing so, I critically examine two of the most morally charged and taken-for-granted ideals of modern citizenship practices: that we must work and that we must develop and educate ourselves for work. I argue for the need for renewed analysis of the interweaving techniques of education and work, learning and labouring in relation to poverty and inequality.

POVERTY IN URBAN SPACES: HOMELESS IN MELBOURNE SAN FRANCISCO AND LONDON

Tracing the everyday working experiences of the sellers of homeless street press, this book explores the lived reality of poverty and precarious work. In writing this book, throughout 2012–2014 I spoke and spent time with approximately 65 sellers of homeless street press in Melbourne, San Francisco and London. In the main location for the research, Melbourne, I spent over a year interviewing and spending time with 40 *Big Issue* sellers. The vast majority of these sellers are, have been, or live in fear of becoming, homeless. I explicate in more detail the research approach in Chap. 2, but to give a brief overview here: this book is based on over 100 interviews with sellers, and hundreds of hours spent with sellers as they worked, as well as interviews with organisers of homeless street press in the three cities.

All of these cities have significant homelessness. The most recent statistical Australian census data from 2011 suggests that there are over 100,000 people homeless on any given night in Australia, which amounts to approximately 1 in 200 Australians (Australian Bureau of Statistics 2011). Of these, close to 23,000 reside in Victoria, an increase of 20% in homeless people since 2006. A significant number of these are in the Melbourne area. US federal estimates suggest that there are just under 120,000 homeless people in California, accounting for 22% of homelessness across the US (U.S. Department of Housing and Urban Development 2016). 6,996 of these are noted as living in the San Francisco area (*ibid*; Fisher et al. 2015). While in England, research suggests approximately 185,000 adults experience homelessness every year (Fitzpatrick et al. 2015), and at least 7500 sleep rough each year in London (Crisis 2015).

It is important to note, however, the difficulty in the enumeration of homelessness and the likelihood of higher actual rates of homelessness. Australia relies significantly on deriving statistical results from analysis of the national census, relying on "assumptions" and inferences from the data (Australian Bureau of Statistics 2011). The US national estimates, described as a 'point-in-time' estimate, draws on the data collection of different districts and regions concerning rough sleepers and counts of beds in shelters and supported and transitional housing (U.S. Department of Housing and Urban Development 2016). Similarly, in the UK, any statistical claim on homelessness is made using a combination of counts of rough sleeping, temporary accommodation placements, and homeless applications for housing (see Fitzpatrick et al. 2015).

Moreover, across all these nations and the cities for this research it is well recognised that there is a 'hidden homelessness' that eclipses much of this data analysis, such as overcrowding, couch surfing in the homes of friends and family, and insecure or undocumented homelessness. It is also recognised that a large number of this 'hidden homeless' are women and children (whose experiences are often characterised by family violence), young people, and gay, lesbian, transgender and queer people (see McLoughlin 2013; Miller and Du Mont 2000; Ecker 2016). For this research, however, the vast majority of sellers were well into adulthood, with the youngest seller I interviewed being 25 years of age. In addition, only two sellers mentioned being gay or queer, and only in the context of more informal discussions with me about their lives. With regards to gender, all sellers I spoke with identified within a binary woman–man definition of gender identity, and thus I use the language of women and men throughout—though I recognise the significance of trans- and non-gender-binary experiences of homelessness (see e.g. Shelton 2015).

Thus, experiences of homelessness are diverse *within* and *across* these three cities. Indeed, whilst Australia, the US and England are often used as comparative international sites, or used as nation state markers of the global 'North', comparison and analysis across these cities here is not intended to imply cultural, social or political correspondence. At the very least, there are clear differences in political governance structures between the constitutional monarchy of England (and devolved governments of the UK) and the federal (and relatively decentralised) system of the US, and the federal (but comparatively centralised) system of Australia. Each of these nations and cities has different approaches, services, governance practices and past and present understandings of homelessness (see Minnery and Greenlagh 2003). Moreover, in each, the state is not the only agency involved in the delivery of services and in development of proposals surrounding homelessness. Not-for-profit, charitable and philanthropic sectors have long created their own practices and initiatives in response to homelessness.

Nevertheless, it is also important to recognise the ways in which these cities and nations are connected. Comparison across these cities offers a unique and salient opportunity to understand experiences of homelessness and the transformation of work on the margins transnationally. As major cities of the global capitalist North, these cities and nations have undergone differing, but parallel, developments in government throughout the twentieth century and into the twenty-first century. Australia and the US, both settler colonial states, and England, share a past and present connection to the practices of Empire. Australia, nestled amidst the global South, has maintained an unequivocal firm orientation first to England as its (still continuing) formal governing monarch, and more recently to the US as its geopolitical ally. By exploring across these sites, it is possible to develop understanding of the transnational experiences of homelessness and work in 'advanced capitalist' contexts, and the different approaches to, and experiences of, homeless street press.

In all of these countries, the economic crises in the 1970s, along with significant social and cultural unrest, were a catalyst for a major crisis in the trust of the nation state, and in the welfare states created in response to the Great Depression and the Second World War (Harvey 2005). At this time, across these nations, there was a combined reconfiguration of the state towards privatised, corporatized, managerial and marketised modes of governance (what is now referred to as 'neoliberalism'), and a concurrent "re-discovery" of poverty (Hobsbawm 1994). Thus, as governments explored ways to increasingly marketise public services, there was increased public and political attention surrounding poverty and homelessness.

As a result, throughout the 1970s and 1980s there was a parallel development of the understanding of 'homelessness' as a particular policy 'problem'—in the sense that governments constituted particular meanings about homelessness as problematic and in need of intervention (see Bacchi 2009). Consequently, there emerged a (still-growing) policy suite and service sector surrounding it (see Gerrard 2017a; Farrugia and Gerrard 2016). In the UK, the 1977 Housing (Homeless Persons) Act offered a direct legislative response to homelessness, and has been subsequently followed by a number of Acts and policy directives (O'Connell 2003). In Australia, the 1985 Supported Accommodation Assistance Program marked the first targeted policy aimed at reducing homelessness, with more recent 'National Plans' (see Gerrard 2015). While in the US, the McKinney-Vento Act, originally adopted by Congress in 1987 with various amendments since, has worked to instate homelessness as a key policy area (Miller 2011).

Comparison across Melbourne, San Francisco and London thus has significance not only for the development of homeless street press and the informal economies of social enterprise. In addition, Australia, the US and England are connected through transnational flows of capital, people, and policy ideas steeped in the cultural politics of Empire and the global North. This assists to contextualise and position homelessness as bound to the contingencies and particularities of each city and nation, but also as an experience that has correspondences across advanced capitalist nations (Farrugia and Gerrard 2016).

Researching in the City

Melbourne, San Francisco and London constitute both the site and the context for this book. The research for this book was conducted on the street corners, curbs, cafes, parks and shopping malls of these cities, and based on conversations had amidst the sounds and smells of the city hustle and bustle. The importance of this context cannot be overstated. Whilst homelessness and poverty are not only urban or city-bound concerns (see Cuervo 2014; Farrugia 2014; Farrugia 2015), the city—as a space, place, practice and imagining—has powerful effects for the ways in which homelessness and poverty is lived and felt, particularly for homeless street press sellers. Cities, as networks of diverse and complex practices, have long been understood as representing points of convergence, diversity, multiplicity and possibility. In his seminal *The Country and the City*, Raymond Williams (1973), for instance, writes powerfully on the ways in which country and city evoke particular culturally taken-for-granted meanings and assumptions. He writes, "The city has gathered the idea of an achieved centre: of learning, communication, light", whilst the country represents "a natural way of life: of peace, innocence and simple virtue" (1973: 1).

Thus, large metropolitan cities such as Melbourne, London and San Francisco can take on metaphoric or symbolic meaning. Such cities often come to be understood as 'world cities' representing a "global sense of place" through their close proximity to global and national power, cultural diversity, and their role in transitory movements of capital, trade, people and culture (see Massey 2007). Cities, therefore, are first and foremost a practice. Whilst they may have a geographic reference, their meaning and significance lies in constantly changing practices that extend beyond any postcode or definitive mappings.

Saskia Sassen suggests cities are spaces that transcend the scalar hierarchy of national–regional–local: cities are not bounded units, but a "node in a grid of cross-boundary processes" (2000: 146). They are pivotal spaces when it comes to the lived experience and social meanings of homelessness and poverty. Cities are often considered spaces in which worlds collide, where cultures rub up against each other, and social space becomes condensed, forcing interactions and encounters otherwise avoided. Because of their diversity, cities are often understood as spaces of 'encounters' with 'strangers' and the 'other'. For some, this means that they represent a potential social space of cosmopolitanism and cultures of hospitality, whilst for others they represent spaces of danger, fear and anxiety (see Rundell 2014).

Certainly, the portrayal of homelessness often draws on the incidental and inevitable encounter with homelessness in cities (Gerrard and Farrugia 2015). Most often, these sorts of encounters are interpreted as unwelcome and uncomfortable interruptions in city life. In his study on homeless shelters, Robert Desjarlais, for instance, suggests that homelessness is a "ghostly presence" threatening the "peaceful, artful air of cafes, libraries and public squares" (1997: 2). More recently, in her ethnography of homeless men in San Francisco, Teresa Gowan describes, "Emaciated panhandlers display their sores and amputations, genial hustlers simultaneously entertain and disturb, and haggard men and bundled-up women stare off into space, jarring the sensibilities of more comfortable passersby" (2010: 3).

This apparent discordance is exacerbated by the ways in which cities—particularly in countries like Australia, England and the US—are central symbols for capital and consumerism. Cities are emblematic spectacles of consumer capitalism through the cultivation of pseudo-public grand shopping malls, and the constant movement of people in and through space to accommodate the commute to work and consumerism (see Gerrard and

Farrugia 2015). In this sense, homelessness can appear as 'out of joint' with the demands, culture, aesthetic and temporal logics of capitalism in cities (*ibid.*). Yet, this 'out of joint' positioning of homelessness belies the interrelationship that poverty and homelessness has with the growing inequalities shaped by consumer capitalism (*ibid.*). Homelessness and poverty in the city, in other words, cannot be separated from the city's growth of wealth and consumption.

Ben Highmore states cities have traditionally been understood as bodylike, evoking a bird's-eye view of the city from up above, in which the city becomes "composed of arteries and veins" (2005: 4). He writes this metaphor is "a small step from claiming that the health of a city depends on efficient circulatory systems, to suggesting forms of aggressive surgery (slum clearance, new arterial roads and so on) when these systems appear blocked" (*ibid.*). Sociologist Loic Wacquant suggests that there are increasing attempts to 'ghettoize' poverty and homelessness and to create city-living that can avoid encounters with homelessness through the creation of wealthy 'gated communities' and the often violent policing of homelessness through move-on policies and laws (2007). In such divided practices, some districts or parts of cities "become national symbols and namesakes for all the ills of the cities" (Wacquant 2008b: 116).

Considering the relationship of homelessness to cities inevitably means considering the relationship of cities to nations, as well as transnational movements of people. As 'world spaces', cities do appear to have a particular meaning transcending the boundaries of the nation state through their diversity and their place in migratory movements of people. In this way, cities often are taken to have their own cultural and social forms and logics; they are a "distinctive form of civilisation" (Williams 1973: 1). London, for instance, is often joked to be its own country or city state, apart from England. Yet, they also have particular and often emblematic meanings for countries; important places that mark a particular version (imagined or otherwise) of aspiration, achievement and culture.

Cities both blur and sharpen the 'imagined communities'—to borrow from Benedict Anderson (1983)—of nation state, national identity, transnational connections. This blurring and sharpening occurs in and through the transitory and migratory patterns of people, capital and goods, alongside. continued (and recently growing and accentuated) inequalities; the experience of stasis and capture for many within the city; and the recent re-emergence of nationalist politics in the wake of the mass global migration of refugees and asylum seekers. Cities are practices/spaces both of transition and movement and of stasis and immobility. The social meaning and experience of homelessness cannot be considered outside of these dynamics. Globally, homelessness is connected to both national and international inequality and migration—migration often (though not always) prompted by inequality, lack of opportunity and injustice.

The visible presence of homelessness in cities has certainly prompted a range of interventions, from charitable services to laws against loitering, and move-on policies in the lead-up to 'urban renewal' or major international events such as the Olympics (e.g. Kennelly and Watt 2011). It is important, therefore, to be careful in representations of homelessness in cities as being constitutively 'out of joint'. Globally in both the past and present homelessness and destitution has been a wavering, but constant, presence in cities. This is not to suggest that, as the often-quoted maxim goes, "the poor will always be with us"; rather, in countries such as England, the US and Australia, capitalism has long created stark inequities.

In order to provide context to the specific sites of this research, I offer below brief overviews of the three cities that form the basis of this book. These brief contextual descriptions aim to bring to the surface the spatial dynamics that invariably framed the research upon which this book is based, as well as the everyday experiences of the sellers.

Melbourne

Melbourne is where the research for this book was predominantly based. The capital city of the state of Victoria, and the second largest city in Australia (after Sydney), Melbourne—including its sprawling suburbs—is home to over four million people. The inner city—where the research was carried out—consists of criss-crossing grid streets and laneways fanning up from the banks of the Yarra River. As a geographically small city centre, it was relatively easy for me to walk up and down Melbourne's gridded streets throughout the days and weeks to recruit, chat, keep in touch and spend time with sellers of *The Big Issue* magazine.

Nestled North of the City is the University of Melbourne, my workplace, and often the starting point for my walks into the city. Also to the North are the suburbs of North Melbourne, Carlton, Fitzroy and Collingwood—traditionally working-class and poor suburbs, now fast gentrifying, but still defined by the towering presence of council estate flats. Past and present, these suburbs have particular significance to Aboriginal people, Melbourne's many migrant communities, and the homeless and poor. Previously the 'slums' of Melbourne, they have often been considered the shameful shadowy side of the city and hence have experienced waves of interest, intervention and projects of renewal (see Birch 2004). More recently, these suburbs were also home to some of the first homeless services including refuges and family violence services.

San Francisco

San Francisco, with an estimated population of just under 900,000 is one of California's largest cities. Pushed into the San Francisco Peninsula, and carved up by its well-known hills, the city is incredibly dense. When in San Francisco, it was the streets of The Mission, The Castro, Haight-Ashbury and, most particularly, The Tenderloin that eventually became familiar as I spoke and spent time with sellers of the *Street Sheet*. The Tenderloin is home to San Francisco's 'skid row', with high levels of rough sleeping and a high density of homeless refuges, services, low-rent hotel rooms and low-cost restaurants. This area is also home to the Coalition on Homelessness, the organisation which publishes *Street Sheet*, and which provides a vehicle for homeless campaigning and advocacy. I spent many days at the Coalition, chatting with the activists that worked within the organisation, and the sellers who would drop by to collect the *Street Sheet*. I met other sellers walking the streets of Tenderloin, who would then take me for walks around the city into the Castro, Haight-Asbury or down Market Street on their attempts to sell the *Street Sheet*.

London

London, by far the largest of the three cities with over 8.5 million residents, lays the strongest claim to status as a 'global city'. Its tremendous size meant that my usual tactics of walking the city were made much harder. Less contained than Melbourne and San Francisco, the winding sprawl of central London along and outwards from the river Thames, became the main site of the study: from Vauxhall, to Kings Cross, Covent Garden, Waterloo, Liverpool Street and Victoria station. I concentrated at first on highly dense tourist areas, such as Covent Garden, where I would bump into sellers during their workday. I also spent time at *The Big Issue* offices at Vauxhall. Perched on a busy corner intersection this office is where sellers could come to stock up on magazines or speak to *The Big Issue* staff.

In addition, I spent time with sellers at key distribution points of the magazine. *The Big Issue* in London has a devolved franchise-based distribution structure, in which a small handful of sellers now run their own businesses of magazine distribution around the city. Other sellers come to them to purchase the magazine to sell, and the distribution sellers receive a cut from the sale.

CHAPTER OVERVIEW

The book is organised thematically, and each chapter draws on the research conducted across Melbourne, San Francisco and London.

Chapter 2, 'Marginality Reconsidered', provides a reflection on writing about, and researching on, marginality. Starting with a reflection of a research encounter with a seller in Melbourne, this chapter explicates the ethical and political dimensions of the book, highlighting the methodological dilemmas that lie at the heart of researching—and representing—marginality. Teasing out the concept of 'margins', I consider what it means to research and write about marginality in the context of ongoing poverty and inequality in affluent capitalist societies. Here the cultural and social presumptions bound to notions of marginality, and in particular the operations of 'the other' and 'the normal' are critically examined. Drawing on postcolonial scholar Gayatri Chakravorty Spivak's (1988) notion of the 'margins' as the "silent, silenced centre", and surveying recent theorisations of precarity, poverty and expulsion, this chapter argues the importance of centring analysis on the 'margins' in ways that acknowledges the constitution of marginality—epistemologically and ontologically—through wider practices of power in social relations. Here, I also outline some of the methodological decisions made, and challenges faced, in conducting this research. In particular I describe how I attempted to avoid the 'confessional' culture of social research that seeks to mine the experience of 'others', and provide some context to the sellers whose working lives I attempt to faithfully represent here.

Chapter 3, 'Homeless Street Press: Historical and Contemporary Connections', starts with a contextualisation of this sociological research within the much longer interconnected history of homelessness and work (see also Gerrard 2017b). Here, I outline the historical development of homeless street press, connecting contemporary versions with the history of 'hobo' publications in the early twentieth century and radical activist street press cultures in the US. This chapter then examines the particular emergence of *Street Sheet* and *The Big Issue*, tracing the diverging interests in activism (*Street Sheet*) and empowerment through work (*The Big Issue*). This discussion points to the diversity of homeless street press, and the various intents of the street press: from activism to advocacy, self-help, informal work and social enterprise. Here, the historical interconnections between practices of self-help, work, learning and initiatives for the unemployed are examined.

From Chap. 4, *Enterprise on the Margins* turns more concertedly to the experiences of homeless street press sellers. Chaps. 4, 5, 6, 7 and 8 purposefully bring in a range of conceptual tools as a means to analyse the accounts of homeless street press sellers traversing across theory, field notes and interview transcripts from the research. These chapters utilise in-depth and rich research extracts as a means to give space to the experiences and accounts of the sellers. This approach aims to offer contextualised accounts of sellers' working lives and of the research undertaken, rather than brief 'snippets' that reveal little of the research encounter (Gowan 2010). As Gowan reflects in the writing of her ethnography of homeless men in San Francisco, there is a danger that decontextualized accounts, "smooth over contradictions, losing the uneven texture of the specific in the service of the generalization and oversimplifying complex relationships" (2010: xxiv). Thus, in moving across theory and experience in each chapter, and drawing heavily on extended research extracts, my hope is to avoid neat and secure narrative explanations. Rather, I hope the reader is left with a sense of the complexity and uncertainty that characterises sellers' everyday working lives (as it does all our lives).

Chapter 4, 'Time is Money', draws predominantly on Melbourne sellers' own photographs of a 'typical day's work', as a means to explore the everyday routines and rituals that characterise sellers' work. Starting with a brief reflection on time and the work ethic, in this chapter I first discuss the everyday practices of work time in the entrepreneurial work carried out by sellers across the three cities. The discussion then turns to Melbourne sellers' photographs to tease out the everyday practices of working as a homeless street seller.

Chapter 5, 'Being Productive: Working, Not Begging', examines the effects of the expectation to be productive and working for sellers of homeless street press, and the tension between begging and working for the sellers and organizations across the three cities. Two themes in particular are highlighted in this chapter: first, the importance of mitigating the experience of idle unemployment with activities and work, and, second, the effects of feeling judged as either productive or unproductive.

Here, I outline how significant lines of distinction are made by sellers between themselves and beggars, including between their current work as sellers and their previous experience as beggars. Drawing on literature on marginal work and unemployment (e.g. Adkins 2017; Weeks 2011), including George Orwell's (1975) reflections on the work of beggars, this chapter discusses the ways in which selling homeless street press is a precarious form of work, interconnected with various other forms of labour undertaken in the supposedly 'bare' and 'idle' space of unemployment.

In Chap. 6, 'Learning to Entrepreneurially Labour', the intersections between learning and working are examined. Here, social enterprise and the informal work of homeless street press selling are examined as a contemporary site of learning to work. This chapter works with theories of learning and working in order to explicate the ways in which informal and work-based learning constitutes an important site of self-making in contemporary societies (e.g. Illich and Verne 1976; Seddon 2004; Solomon 2005; Kelly 2013; Gerrard 2014). Within the chapter, I explore the ways in which different homeless street presses aspire for sellers to engage in self-work, learning and self-transformation, and how sellers experience these expectations. Here in particular, differences in approaches between the self-help activist *Street Sheet* and the social enterprise *The Big Issue* are analysed.

Chapter 7, 'Working in Public: Value, Exchange and Performance', delves into the experience of working in sales in public. Here, the value of the exchange for sellers of homeless street press is explored, focusing in particular on the aspirations for, and fulfilment of, social relationships and income accrual. Drawing on the ethnographic research, this chapter explores the tensions in the desire for and experience of social relationships with buyers and the struggle many sellers face in 'performing' themselves in order to attract sales. In doing so, this chapter reflects on the morally charged and public nature of the exchange market created by homeless street press, and the ways in which this relates to social and cultural expectations for employment and self-help for those who are poor.

Chapter 8, 'Moving On?: Pathways, Aspirations and Stasis', *Enterprise on the Margins* considers the desire and imperative to 'move on'. Ending with the thorny question of what next for homeless street press sellers, *Enterprise on the Margins* purposefully stresses the absence of any neat conclusions. The chapter reveals the very difficult negotiations made by those attempting to engage in self-help and self-development for productive work, whilst at the same time negotiating long-term poverty. Many of the sellers across Melbourne, London and San Francisco must manage disabilities, serious health conditions and the effects of long-term poverty whilst also engaging in entrepreneurial work. I start with a reflection on 'pathways' and 'aspirations' in the context of the inequalities of advanced capitalism (see Appadurai 2013; Raco 2009; Sellar 2015). In particular I examine the ways in which stasis and mobility is lived as a perpetual ontological state. The chapter then explores sellers' diverse considerations of their possible futures, including aspirations and plans for future work and education and the common experience of not being able to plan amidst the everyday struggle to get by. Finally, in Chap. 9 I end *Enterprise on the Margins* with a brief reflective epilogue on writing this book.

Notes

1. Sellers of homeless street press are referred to throughout this book as 'sellers', though, particularly for *The Big Issue*, they are also commonly referred to as 'vendors' as reflected in some of the quotes.

References

Adkins, L. (2017). Disobedient Workers, the Law and the Making of Unemployment Markets. *Sociology, 51*(2), 290–305.
Adriaenssens, J., & Hendrickx, S. (2011). Street-Level Informal Economic Activities: Estimating the Yield of Begging in Brussels. *Urban Studies, 48*(1), 23–40.
Allison, D. (1994). *Skin: Talking about Sex, Class and Literature*. New York: Open Road Integrated Media.
Anderson, B. (1983). *Imagined Communities: Reflections on the Origin and Spread of Nationalism*. London/New York: Verso.
Appadurai, A. (2013). *The Future as Cultural Fact: Essays on the Global Condition*. London: Verso.
Australian Bureau of Statistics. (2011). *Census of Population and Housing: Estimating Homelessness, 2011*. http://abs.gov.au/ausstats/abs@.nsf/Latestproducts/2049.0Main%20Features22011
Bacchi, C. (2009). *Analysing Policy: What's the Problem Represented to Be?* Frenchs Forest: Pearson Australia.
Baumann, Z. (2000). *Liquid Modernity*. Cambridge: Polity Press.
Beck, U. (1992). *Risk Society*. London: Sage.
Birch, T. (2004). These Children Have Been Born in an Abyss': Slum Photography in a Melbourne Suburb. *Australian Historical Studies, 123*, 1–15.
Castells, M. (2010). *End of Millennium* (2nd ed.). Oxford: Blackwell Publishing.

Cockburn, P. J. L. (2014). Street Papers, Work and Begging: 'Experimenting' at the Margins of Economic Legitimacy. *Journal of Cultural Economy, 7*(2), 145–160.

Coffield, F. (1999). Breaking the Consensus: Lifelong Learning as Social Control. *British Educational Research Journal, 25*(1), 479–499.

Crisis. (2015). *About Homelessness.* London: Crisis.

Crowther, J. (2004). In and Against Lifelong Learning: Flexibility and the Corrosion of Character. *International Journal of Lifelong Education, 23*(2), 125–136.

Cuervo, H. (2014). Critical Reflections on Youth and Equality in the Rural Context. *Journal of Youth Studies, 17*(4), 544–557.

Danky, J. P., & Wiagand, W. A. (Eds.). (1992). *Print Culture in a Diverse America.* Urbana/Chicago: University of Illinois Press.

DePastino, T. (2003). *Citizen Hobo: How a Century of Homelessness Shaped America.* Chicago/London: The University of Chicago Press.

Desjarlais, R. (1997). *Shelter Blues: Sanity and Selfhood Among the Homeless.* Philadelphia: University of Pennsylvania Press.

Dillabough, J., & Kennelly, J. (2010). *Lost Youth in the Global City: Class, Culture and the Urban Imaginary.* New York/London: Routledge.

Dolby, N., & Dimitriadis, G. (2004). Learning to Labor in New Times: An Introduction. In N. Dolby, G. Dimitriadis, & P. Willis (Eds.), *Learning to Labor in New Times* (pp. 1–14). London: RoutledgeFalmer.

Ecker, J. (2016). Queer, Young and Homeless: A Review of the Literature. *Child and Youth Services, 37,* 325–361, ifirst.

Elliott, A. (2013). *Reinvention.* London/New York: Routledge.

Farrugia, D. (2014). Towards a Spaitalised Youth Sociology: The Rural and the Urban in Times of Change. *Journal of Youth Studies, 17*(3), 293–307.

Farrugia, D. (2015). *Youth Homelessness in Late Modernity: Reflexive Identities and Moral Worth.* Singapore: Springer.

Farrugia, D., & Gerrard, J. (2016). Academic Knowledge and Contemporary Poverty: The Politics of Homelessness Research. *Sociology, 50*(2), 267–284.

Fisher, N., Miller, N., & Walter, L. (2015). *California's New Vagrancy Laws: The Growing Enactment and Enforcement of Anti-Homeless Laws in the Golden State.* Berkeley: Policy Advocacy Clinic, Berkeley Law, University of California.

Fitzpatrick, S., Pawson, H., Bramely, G., Wilcox, S., & Watts, B. (2015). *The Homelessness Monitor: England 2015.* London: Crisis.

Gaber, J. (1994). Manhattan's 14th Street Vendors' Market: Informal Street Peddlers' Complementary Relationship with New York City's Economy. *Urban Anthropology and Studies of Cultural Systems and World Economic Development, 23*(4), 373–408.

Gerrard, J. (2014). All that Is Solid Melts into Work: Self-Work, the 'Learning Ethic' and the Work Ethic. *The Sociological Review, 62,* 862–879.

Gerrard, J. (2015). The Limits of Learning: Homelessness and Educating the Employable Self. *Discourse, 36*(1), 69–80.

Gerrard, J. (2017a). Welfare Rights, Self Help and Social Enterprise. *Journal of Sociology, 53*(1), 47–62.
Gerrard, J. (2017b). The Interconnected Histories of Homelessness and Labour. *Labour History, 112*, 155–174.
Gerrard, J., & Farrugia, D. (2015). The 'Lamentable Sight' of Homelessness and the Society of the Spectacle. *Urban Studies, 52*(12), 2219–2233.
Gowan, T. (2010). *Hobos, Hustlers and Backsliders: Homeless in San Francisco.* Minneapolis: University of Minnesota Press.
Harvey, D. (2005). *A Brief History of Neoliberalism.* Oxford: Oxford University Press.
Highmore, B. (2005). *Cityscapes: Cultural Readings in the Material and Symbolic City.* Basingstoke: Palgrave Macmillan.
Hobsbawm, E. (1994). *Age of Extremes.* London: Abacus.
Illich, I., & Verne, E. (1976). *Imprisoned in the Global Classroom.* London: Writers and Readers Publishing Cooperative.
Kalleberg, A. L. (2013). Globalization and Precarious Work. *American Sociological Association, 42*(5), 700–706.
Kelly, P. (2013). *The Self as Enterprise.* Furnham: Gower Publishing.
Kennelly, J., & Watt, P. (2011). Sanitizing Public Spaces in Olympic Host Cities: The Spatial Experiences of Marginalized Youth in 2010 Vancouver and 2012 London. *Sociology, 45*(5), 765–781.
Lindemann, K. (2006). A Tough Sell: Stigma as Souvenir in the Contested Performances of San Francisco's Homeless *Street Sheet* Vendors. *Text and Performance Quarterly, 27*(1), 41–57.
Massey, D. (2007). *World City.* Cambridge: Polity Press.
Mazzucato, M. (2014). *The Entrepreneurial State: Debunking the Public vs Private Sector Myths.* London/New York/Delhi: Anthem Press.
McLoughlin, P. J. (2013). Couch Surfing on the Margins: The Reliance of Temporary Living Arrangements as a Form of Homelessness Amongst School-Age Home Leavers. *Journal of Youth Studies, 16*(4), 521–545.
Miller, P. M. (2011). An Examination of the Mckinney-Vento Act and Its Influence on the Homeless Education Situation. *Educational Policy, 25*(3), 424–450.
Miller, K., & Du Mont, J. (2000). Countless Abused Women: Homeless and Inadequately Housed. *Canadian Women Studies, 20*(3), 115–122.
Minnery, J., & Greenhalgh, E. (2003). Approaches to Homelessness Policy in Europe, the United States and Australia. *Journal of Social Issues, 63*(3), 641–655.
Neilson, B., & Rossiter, N. (2008). Precarity as a Political Concept, or, Fordism as Exception. *Theory, Culture & Society, 25*(7–8), 51–72.
Newman, J., & Clarke, J. (2009). *Publics, Politics and Power: Remaking the Public in Public Services.* London: Sage.
O'Connell, M. E. (2003). Responding to Homelessness: An Overview of US and UK Policy Interventions. *Journal of Community & Applied Social Psychology, 13*(2), 158–170.

Orwell, G. (1975). *Down and Out in Paris and London*. London: Penguin Books.
Parsell, C., & Marston, G. (2012). Beyond the 'At Risk' Individual: Housing and the Eradication of Poverty to Prevent Homelessness. *The Australian Journal of Public Administration, 71*(1), 33-44.
Peel, M. (2003). *The Lowest Rung: Voices of Australian Poverty*. Cambridge: Cambridge University Press.
Picketty, T. (2013). *Capital in the Twenty-First Century*. Harvard: Harvard University Press.
Raco, M. (2009). From Expectations to Aspirations: State Modernisation, Urban Policy and the Existential Politics of Welfare in the UK. *Political Geography, 28*, 436-444.
Rose, N. (1992). Governing the Enterprising Self. In P. Heelas & P. Morris (Eds.), *The Values of Enterprise Culture: The Moral Debate* (pp. 141-164). London: Routledge.
Roy, A. (2010). *Poverty Capital: Microfinance and the Making of Development*. New York/London: Routledge.
Rundell, J. (2014). Imagining Cities, Others: Strangers, Contingency and Fear. *Thesis Eleven, 121*(1), 9-22.
Sassen, S. (1994). The Informal Economy: Between New Developments and Old Regulations. *The Yale Law Journal, 103*(8), 2289-2304.
Sassen, S. (2000). New Frontiers Facing Urban Sociology at the Millennium. *British Journal of Sociology, 51*(1), 143-159.
Seddon, T. (2004). Remaking Civic Formation: Towards a Learning Citizen? *London Review of Education, 2*(3), 171-186.
Sellar, S. (2015). 'Unleashing Aspiration': The Concept of Potential in Education Policy. *Australian Educational Researcher, 42*, 201-215.
Shelton, J. (2015). Transgender Youth Homelessness: Understanding Programmatic Barriers Through the Lens of Cisgenderism. *Children and Youth Services Review, 59*, 10-18.
Shildrick, T., MacDonald, R., Webster, C., & Garthwaite, K. (2012). *Poverty and Insecurity: Life in Low-Pay, No-Pay Britain*. Bristol: The Policy Press.
Solomon, N. (2005). Identity Work and Pedagogy: Textually Producing the Learner-Worker. *Journal of Vocational Education and Training, 57*(1), 95-108.
Sontag, S. (2003). *Regarding the Pain of Others*. New York: Picador.
Spivak, G. C. (1988). Can the Subaltern Speak? In C. Nelson & L. Grossberg (Eds.), *Marxism and the Interpretation of Culture* (pp. 271-313). Bassingstoke: Macmillan Education.
Standing, G. (2011). *The Precariat: The New Dangerous Class*. Bloomsbury Academic.
Teasdale, S. (2010). Models of Social Enterprise in the Homelessness Field. *Social Enterprise Journal, 6*(1), 23-34.
Turner, S., & Schoenberger, L. (2012). Street Vendor Livelihoods and Everyday Policies in Hanoi, Vietnam: The Seeds of a Diverse Economy? *Urban Studies, 49*(5), 1027-1044.

U.S. Department of Housing and Urban Development. (2016, November). *Part 1: Point-in-Time Estimates of Homelessness*. The 2016 Annual Homeless Assessment Report (AHAR) to Congress.
Wacquant, L. (2007). Territorial Stigmatization in the Age of Advanced Marginality. *Thesis Eleven, 91*, 66–77.
Wacquant, L. (2008a). *Urban Outcasts*. London: Polity Press.
Wacquant, L. (2008b). Ghettos and Anti-Ghettos: An Anatomy of the New Urban Poverty. *Thesis Eleven, 94*, 113–118.
Walker, R. (2014). *The Shame of Poverty*. Oxford: Oxford University Press.
Weber, M. (1984 [1930]). *The Protestant Ethic and the Spirit of Capitalism*. London Unwin.
Weeks, K. (2011). *The Problem with Work: Feminist, Marxist, Antiwork Politics, and Postwork Imaginaries*. Durham/London: Duke University Press.
Williams, R. (1973). *The Country and the City*. Oxford: Oxford University Press.
Williams, R. (2002 [1958]). Culture is Ordinary. In Ben Highmore (Ed.), *The Everyday Life Reader* (pp. 91–100). London/New York: Routledge.
Willis, P. (1977). *Learning to Labour*. Hampshire: Gower.
Zizek, S. (2009). *First as Tragedy Then as Farce*. London: Verso.

CHAPTER 2

Marginality Reconsidered

Margins and marginality are key concepts for this book. Homeless street press sellers are engaged in highly marginalised work, and are themselves marginalised from mainstream formal education and employment. Inequality and poverty, in other words, are experienced in and through margins. However, writing about marginality is invariably fraught. The language and terms used to describe, the narratives told and concepts used to depict marginality have effect. Margins—and marginalities—are created in and through social relations that perpetuate particular dynamics of power and privilege and which are based on particular normative presumptions of the 'good life'. This is not to say that the experience of marginality is a discursive creation: it is a material reality created through the power dynamics of class, colonisation, race, gender and sexuality. Margins are created in and through historically contingent material operations of power, in which particular lives are pushed to the margins, deemed marginalised and excluded. Global and national social relations are permeated by divisive inequities, exclusions and practices of exploitation that create margins (see e.g. Sassen 2014). To write about marginality, therefore, is not a simple undertaking of pointing out and putting under the microscope the experience of marginality. There is a need to address the social dynamics that create such marginality, including the ways in which research can replicate representations of the dysfunctional and marginal 'other'.

© The Author(s) 2017
J. Gerrard, *Precarious Enterprise on the Margins*,
DOI 10.1057/978-1-137-59483-9_2

In this chapter, I explore the tensions inherent in researching marginality and poverty in the context of the research undertaken for this book. This is done in full acknowledgement that there are no easy answers to such tensions: they are in many ways irresolvable. Yet, it is imperative to reflect and prise apart the politics and power at play in the narratives created in and of the lives of 'others'. First, drawing on an extended reflection of a research encounter and theories on the construction of 'knowing', I consider how research instantiates points of view: the implicit and explicit ways research positions itself as authorial text over and of the lives of others. Second, I outline a conceptual approach to marginality, which attempts to address—or at least recognise and make explicit—the tensions and difficulties of this research space, and which has informed the writing of this book. Third, I discuss how centring the everyday lives of homeless street press sellers provides a means to focus on the social relations of marginality within contemporary capitalism. Finally, I turn to the specific ethical and political dilemmas that arose in this research. Here, I outline my approach in researching homeless street press sellers' working lives, when these women and men are already so often compelled to narrate their life stories to medical practitioners, social workers, housing workers and employment consultants for access to basic services.

Writing About Marginality: Ants, Skyscrapers, Maps and Walking the City

Well, they have subways where you have people coming out and they look like ants' nests, they go in all directions, and if you are in the road they run over you. (Matt, 38 years old, Melbourne)

Perched next to me on a wall ledge on a busy Melbourne street corner, Matt's description of the city as an ants' nest resonated. It is a sunny day, and this is the second recorded interview we had done together. The first time I met him, Matt was standing on one of the busiest pitches in Melbourne hurriedly attempting to sell his last two *The Big Issue* magazines for the day. I had approached him to see if he would be interested in being interviewed for the research, and he asked me to sit and wait until he had sold the magazines. I sat on a nearby bench and watched as shoppers and workers hurried past Matt averting eye contact as he smiled and searched for signs of someone who might be interested in buying—someone walking a little slower, someone rummaging through their bag perhaps in search of change, someone willing to meet his eyes. He described these tactics later to me; the ways he had learnt to read the subtle (and sometimes not so subtle) body language of people walking towards him. In that moment, I was struck by how earnestly he engaged with everyone who walked past him. Matt moved his body to follow people as they walked past him, leaning in saying hello, moving his last two copies of *The Big Issue* so that they were in prime viewing position, calling out and trying to engage each and every person with at least a greeting ('Hello!', Good afternoon!', 'How are you?'), if not a sales pitch ('Get your *Big Issue*!', 'Help the homeless!').

A surprise $50 tip from a passer-by prompted him to finish up for the day, magazines unsold. He suggested we go to the shopping centre food court across the road to sit and chat. In this first interview, Matt spoke in hushed mumbling tones of the journey to becoming a seller, of having to address shyness and aggression in order to be able to sell, of his concern that his Aboriginality would invite racism and racist slurs as he sold magazines on the street. Listening back to the tape later I could only just make out much of the conversation. He spoke of the economic and practical difficulty of living day-to-day, and of needing to fix the leak in his car—where he was living—before it next rained. He marvelled at the $50 tip, the best he had ever received in his seven years on and off of being a *Big Issue* seller. After this first conversation, I was unsure if I would see Matt again. He had agreed to participate further in the research, and he told me his usual pitches and the times when he usually worked, but as he did not have a phone and was living out of his car, I was not hopeful that I would be able to track him down. As it turned out, over the next six months I saw Matt regularly—almost every week.

This second interview, having spent more time together, he is more relaxed and jumps up and down from sitting chatting with me to serenading people with attempted sales as they walk past. At this quieter less busy pitch, Matt has a milk crate for sitting on, a homemade sign advertising *The Big Issue* and a portable radio beaming out tinny pop songs into the expansive city air. We are in the midst of talking plans. Matt has just had word from a university lecturer that he has once again failed a course he has twice attempted before. He is determined to enrol again, but reckons this will mean giving up *The Big Issue*, as his income from the magazine is just enough to survive with no saving possible. Matt refuses to go on government welfare benefits, saying it is easier to manage himself by himself and that he does not want to be tied to the government. This is perhaps unsurprising, given the complicated, overly stringent and culturally inappropriate bureaucratic procedures, as well as racism, that Aboriginal and Torres Strait Islander people often face in navigating the Australian welfare system (see Paradies and Cunningham 2009; Baldry et al. 2006). Matt has decided that once the good weather in Melbourne has passed, he will go north to work with some friends on a fishing boat, where he could save some of his income to re-enrol at university.

His comment about the city as an ants' nest is brief. He is talking about how he feels okay about leaving the city for a while, and how he finds working in the city challenging. This is something sellers bring up with me again and again: working on the streets of the city takes its toll, from feeling hyper-vigilant towards possible dangers, to the trials of managing the constant hustle and bustle as well as the often unforgiving Melbourne weather. For Matt, the challenge of the city is the '9-5' 'suit culture' of office work. His comparison of people to ants is a vivid interpretation of this culture, from the point of view of someone who witnesses much of the movement of the city.

Matt's description prompted me to reflect on the multidimensions of the 'gaze' in the act of selling *The Big Issue*. To be sure, being a homeless street press seller renders Matt visible: subject to the viewing and judgement of the hundreds and thousands of people who walk past him, and those who stop to chat or buy a magazine. At the same time though, Matt is also an active, reflective and critical purveyor of the city and the people who walked past. As I explore in Chap. 7, there are complex encounters, interrelationships and performances created in the act of the exchange of homeless street press. The presence of homelessness and sellers of homeless street press on city streets is not simply an opportunity for 'the public' to view or gaze 'the homeless'—it is an encounter; and like any encounter, it is "multi-directional and dynamic" and "actively constructed" (Gerrard and Farrugia 2015: 2223).

Matt's description of people as ants also powerfully pulls into view the taken-for-granted position-taking that can plague academic writing on marginality. Academic knowledge often finds its authoritative voice through positioning itself as exterior to the subject of the research. Like detectives or cartographers, researchers will often speak of 'unearthing', 'uncovering', 'mapping' or 'surveying'. French sociologist and theorist Pierre Bourdieu observes that 'mapping' "is the analogy which occurs to an outsider who has to find [their] way around in a foreign landscape and who compensates for [their] lack of practical mystery" (1977: 2). "Knowledge does not merely depend," Bourdieu continues, "on the particular standpoint an observer 'situated in space and time' takes up on the object". Rather, "in taking up a point of view on the action, withdrawing from it in order to observe it from above and from a distance, [they] constitute practical activity as an *object of observation and analysis, a representation*" (*ibid.*, original emphasis).

Mapping, detecting and surveying metaphors are more than descriptive methodological verbs: they capture one of the deepest tensions in research—that of analytic judgement and distance. For some, analytic distance is the authoritative and methodological base for research. American sociologist Kai Erikson puts it this way (2008a: 405):

Sociologists can be said to look at social life from the peculiar vantage of a 14th floor. The individual qualities of persons seem less distinct and even less interesting at that height, for one can sense that there are forces out there in the world that give shape and direction to the flows of everyday behaviour in somewhat the same way that they give shape and direction to the flows of traffic on the sidewalk. When we sociologists speak of "society", then, we are usually speaking of tides, currents, forces, pulls—something in the organisation of social life that induces people to act in reasonably predictable ways. It seems obvious when one views the world from a 14th floor that there are consistencies in the way people think and act; consistencies in the way they move from place to place; consistencies in the way they see the universe around them, relate to one another, and even negotiate a path through the moving swarms of pedestrians on a sidewalk. Human life is subject to social forces that give it form and pattern.

In this quote, Erikson determines the work of the sociologist through the capability to view, describe, catalogue and judge 'tides', 'currents', 'flows' and 'swarms'.

Yet, responding to Erikson, feminist sociologist Dorothy Smith (2008) problematises the 14th-floor metaphor. She argues, "When [Erikson] suggests that the sociologist looking down on the street from above may be able to discern "tides, currents, forces, pulls" at work among people, he does not attend to how the terms he uses objectifies" (Smith 2008: 418). Smith's response highlights the long-held debates surrounding the creation of knowledge about others. Smith points to the ways in which looking *upon* marginalisation can take for granted the position of researcher-as-purveyor. In his rejoinder to Smith, Erikson however makes the point, "Whether one is 'above' or 'to the side of' or 'underneath' the social scene one is looking at makes no difference at all. These are all ways of establishing a kind of conceptual distance" (2008b: 438).

French scholar and philosopher Michel de Certeau also reflects on the presumed authorial judgement afforded by an elevated vantage point.

In his 'Walking the city', he muses on the "voluptuous pleasure" "of looking down on" the city, in this case from the great heights of the no-longer 110th floor of New York's World Trade Centre (1988: 92). This pleasure, de Certeau suggests, is derived from being "lifted out of the city's grasp". "When one goes up there, [one] leaves behind the mass that carries off and mixes up in itself any identity of authors and spectators" (*ibid.*). From such a perspective, the 'city' can be constructed as a space of a "finite number of stable, isolatable, and interconnected properties" (*ibid.*: 94). In this construction, de Certeau suggests, the myriad footsteps that 'walk the city' are overlooked. He writes, "Their swarming mass is an innumerable collection of singularities. Their intertwined paths give their shape to spaces. They weave spaces together" (*ibid.*: 97).

Thus, the principal problematic with the potential for reification and objectification in analytic distance is the ways in which such singularities are understood. 'Tides', 'currents', 'forces' and 'pulls' do not simply arise as objective truths out of the busy entangled activities of the street. Rather, they are judged, surmised, evaluated and often at times assumed to be present from various standpoints. There is danger in assuming authority from the space of spectatorship.

The history of the social sciences is mired in problematic pseudo-scientific judgements about tides and currents: from the neuroticism, hysteria and low intelligence of women as an explanation for their apparent relative absence from public life, to the biological and cultural deficiencies of the working class and the Irish, and the non-European majority world, as an explanation for inequality, slavery, colonisation and imperialism (see also Gerrard et al. 2017). Sociology, anthropology, ethnography and the academy more generally, all have shadowy pasts. All, for instance, have rested on knowledge and research practices that presume the superiority of masculinist and class-based elitist knowledge and traditions of the global North (Connell 2008; Bhambra 2009). All, therefore, have created a range of troublesome 'representations' of the 'margins', from women, to Indigenous peoples, the poor, the working class, and homosexual, queer and gender-diverse people.

Research that burrows so vigorously to 'get to the bottom' of marginality, difference and inequality can forget to look up, look around and question the way in which this marginality is constituted. This is, as postcolonial scholar Franz Fanon identifies, the danger of research that aims only to objectively and narrowly describe. Drawing on the analogy of "anatomists who are all surprised when, in the midst of a description of a tibia, they are asked how many fibular depressions *they* have", Fanon highlights how research of this nature "is never a question of themselves but of other" (2008: 129). Embedded within research representation is an authorial position, which is as Fanon so powerfully reminds us, steeped in the cultural politics of contemporary authority. "To speak", Fanon argues, "means to be in a position to use a certain syntax, to grasp the morphology of this or that language, but it means above all to assume a culture, to support the weight of a civilization" (2008: 8).

Marginality, oppression and difference, as social processes, cannot be analysed neutrally. Even in research that claims to distance itself from, or to critically engage with, experiences of oppression and disadvantage, academia—and the cultures of knowledge production within academic research—is invariably entangled within the instantiation of political authority. The politics of representation is particularly troublesome within research that takes as its focus marginalised people. This research focus can occur with such energy and determination that researchers can forget to look up and look around to examine the wider, and often taken-for-granted, practices of power and authority which contextualises academic research. As with Fanon's anatomists, to turn or flip the research gaze beyond the 'other' can appear utterly startling. The challenge, therefore, is generating research agendas that do not create objective categories of 'research subjects' to be tallied and pronounced, as if separate from the rest of the social world and the research (see Farrugia and Gerrard 2016).

This has direct repercussions for the representation of experience and the construction of research agendas. When sitting with Matt, at that stage in the research I had spent a lot of time thinking about, and talking to sellers about, what it felt like to be visible and open to the gaze of the public in their everyday work. The central premise of homeless street press work is visibility: visibility and awareness of homelessness in the public's mind's eye, and visibility of sellers in order to promote sales. Sellers of *The Big Issue*, for instance, wear branded high-visibility vests, caps and bags in order to attract attention. Yet, Matt's comment reminded me that understanding sellers as subject to the gaze and surveillance of the public only gets halfway there in terms of understanding their experience. Indeed, to talk solely about experiences of marginality in terms of social processes done *to them* may problematically reproduce normative judgements and distinctions between us/them, functional/dysfunctional, normal/strange.

This is not to obfuscate the very real experiences of marginality. To be sure, sellers' experiences are in many ways marginal. Most are, or have been, homeless, and many still live in fear of becoming homeless. At the same time, they are engaging in highly precarious, marginal forms of employment. As the chapters of this book explore, the experience of being a homeless street press seller is one deeply marked by feelings and experiences of marginality. Yet, by constantly positioning sellers as subject to power, subject to surveillance, subject to dominance, I was in danger of replicating the normative boundaries of mainstream and marginal (see also Farrugia and Gerrard 2016).

With British sociologist Beverley Skeggs (2011), I suggest there is a need to reconceptualise social activity that appears to exist on the margins of the relations of production: people, for instance, who are not involved in formal work or education, and whose activities Pierre Bourdieu would consider as 'failing' to play the game. Even in analyses that seek to understand the wider social and structural processes that create inequality, marginality and disadvantage are often still described in terms of what people are not doing, or what they do not have. A common misinterpretation arising from a representation of lack (and of Bourdieu's theories of social capital, for instance) is a presumption—however well intentioned—that the solution to inequality is to simply address this lack (see Skeggs 2004; Gerrard 2013; Reay 2007). As such, those on the margins are often constitutively represented as 'in lack', lacking, for instance, the right social or cultural capital in which to make the right choices.

By focusing attention on what people do not have, we may fuel a fantasy that inequality and injustice can be solved if people experiencing marginality simply become more like the 'mainstream'. The problem here is that what constitutes 'right' cultural or social capital—the so-called mainstream or norm—never comes into critical view, and remains an unproblematised out-of-focus background. The very power dynamics and social relations that create inequality slip from analytic scrutiny. To counter this, there is a need to research, understand and theorise 'marginal' experiences without simply noting that they fail in the neoliberal capitalist model of the "proper person": we need to think beyond understanding these people, as Skeggs argues as persons who are "non-propelling-future accruing subject[s] with the wrong capitals, and who cannot access the fields of exchange to convert, accrue, or generate value for themselves" (2011: 501)

In research on homelessness and disadvantage, for instance, there is significant attention devoted to identifying, enumerating and describing the individual characteristics that determine one's social position: from alcoholism to family breakdown, unemployment and domestic violence

(Farrugia and Gerrard 2016). Such research attention—however well intentioned—can replicate the perception that disadvantage, marginality and inequality are synonymous with failure, dysfunction and depravity in distinction from an unproblematic 'successful' 'mainstream' social experience (*ibid.*). As such, the experiences of homelessness, poverty and inequality can appear constitutively and deterministically 'out of joint', and perhaps even 'extraordinary' and 'strange' from an unexamined 'mainstream' 'norm' (see Gerrard and Farrugia 2015). Obfuscated are the social and economic relations of disadvantage, marginality and inequality: these are conditions created through capitalist social relations and therefore cannot be fully understood unless analysed in relation to the successful, the normal, and the privileged and advantaged (*ibid.*).

This is particularly significant in the context of popular accounts of poverty that emphasise the peculiarities and extremities of the poor 'other'. Here, moralised accounts of hyper-sexualised working-class women, for instance, or out-of-control, angry Black young men, or indolent Indigenous young people, or deviant homeless people allow judgements of difference, deficit and excess from the comforts of the couch (see Skeggs 2005; Gerrard and Ball 2013; Gerrard and Farrugia 2015; see also Back 2007; Peel 2003). This intensity of moral judgement of the 'other' has significant repercussions for how popular and political judgements are made, and debates are waged, in relation to those who are deemed different or 'other' (see Boltanski 2003). Representations of the poor can feed a desire to look upon the 'other' and gasp at differences, deficiencies and defects, whilst never troubling the social relations that create poverty (see Gerrard and Farrugia 2015).

In response, Les Back (2007) argues the worth of sociological understanding made neither in haste nor with moral or political authoritative certainty. He suggests the need for sustained listening and reflection that acknowledges the tensions and limits, but also possibilities for understanding of the lives lived in our current world along with the social relations, norms and understandings that surround and make them. "In a sense", Back writes, "the task is to link individual biographies with larger social and historical forces and the public questions that are raised in their social, economic and political organization" (2007: 23).

In this book, therefore, whilst the focus is on the experiences of those who are homeless and marginal, the aim is not to document their lives via an inventory of personal characteristics, nor as tragic or heroic evidence of poverty. As Mark Peel (2003: 32) suggests, "Describing disadvantage is a dangerous game, for their stories, tragic, despairing, heroic or humorous, may come to be all that is known about their places and all that is true about their lives." This book is concerned with understanding marginality in the context of the capitalist social relations that create it. Marginal experiences are therefore not extraordinary to the norm, but central to the constitution of what we deem to be economically, socially or culturally normal or successful. To explicate the approach taken in this book further, in what follows, drawing on theoretical contributions on inequality, precariousness and exclusions, I explore the conceptualisation of margins and marginality, before then turning to the particular methodological decisions made for the research for this book.

Margins: "The Silent, Silenced, Centre"

In her groundbreaking essay 'Can the subaltern speak', Gayatri Chakravorty Spivak reflects on the margins as 'the silent, silenced centre' (1988: 78). Spivak prises open the presumptions made about margins and marginality from the point of view of 'Western' scholarship. Her problematisation troubles the ways 'Western' knowledge practices—including the academy—can depict, categorise and reify 'marginalisation'. In particular, Spivak's reflections call into question how marginality is constructed as peripheral. There is, for instance, nothing 'minority' or 'periphery' about women's experiences or the experiences of the colonised majority South.

The concept of margins and marginality is therefore concerned with understanding the operations of power and the practices that make people marginalised (see e.g. te Riele 2006). It is an attempt to conceptually grapple with the ways in which particular experiences and voices are marginalised in and through the creation of normative and dominant knowledge and cultural practices. It does not, therefore, presume that what is marginalised is marginal in the sense that it is unimportant or inconsequential, but that these experiences are rendered marginal. This is a tricky, but important, distinction. To term an experience as being marginal is to label the dynamics of power that create marginality: what is marginalised is not marginal to social relations; it is in fact central.

This conceptualisation of marginality draws on a common Marxist, feminist and postcolonial radical inversion: a challenge to the notion that the everyday lives of the excluded, marginalised and disadvantaged are relatively insignificant to the creation of social relations. As Marx (1972: 437) wrote, "We make [our] own history, but [we] do not make it as [we] please; [we] do not make it under self-selected circumstances, but under circumstances existing already, given and transmitted from the past." Thus, those who are marginal are not marginal to history or social relations, but must make their way within an existing set of social and power relations pitted against them. This conceptualisation understands social relations as created by ordinary actions of women and men. This is not to 'flatten' all power relations in the conceptual framing of marginality. There is a danger that marginality is used to collectivise multiple experiences of oppression and inequality— describing all power relations of oppressions as expressions of experience on the margins. The conceptual utility of marginality lies in its capacity to both recognise diverse relations of power (including class, gender, race and sexuality) and destabilise the taken-for-grantedness of the norms produced by these relations of power. Marginality points to the ways in which some people are rendered marginal through the operations of power within which normative judgements and categories are made.

This approach is at the heart of the many attempts to understand the contemporary experiences of marginality in advanced capitalist nations. Recently, Guy Standing (2011) developed the notion of the 'precariat', a new *class-in-the-making* in the Marxist sense, to emerge out of the conditions of global neoliberalism. Standing connects the precariat to the withering of post-war liberal ideals of the 'good life' and salaried work: home ownership, jobs for life, pensions and paid holidays. According to Standing the emergent 'precariat' describes not only the experience of the contemporary working poor and insecure employment, but also an overarching "lack of a secure work-based identity" (2011: 9). The precariat refers to the constitutive experience of insecurity, including, for instance, labour market insecurity, employment insecurity, income insecurity, skill reproduction insecurity and representational insecurity (Standing 2011: 10).

Undoubtedly, for the sellers who I spoke with, their incomes, homes, futures and social relationships were precarious. Yet, Standing's particular assertions surrounding the emergence of the 'precariat' as a new class arguably represents an analytic stretch. Using the post-1945 work landscape of the global North as his point of contemporary comparison, Standing overlooks a much longer (and global) history and experience of employment insecurity in capitalism that has long been central to class relations (see Breman 2013; Neilson and Rossiter 2008). Nevertheless, at the very least Standing's contribution indicates the centrality of marginal work and workers in the establishment of new work orders.

New work orders, however, are also characterised by profound exclusions and expulsions. Saskia Sassen's (2014) recent account of the multiple forms of 'expulsions' in global capitalism connects new work orders with a broader account of global inequality. Sassen contends that contemporary global realities are characterised by a brutal and complex practice of expulsion. Expulsions, Sassen suggests, are part of a new contemporary dynamic, which must be understood and examined anew in the wake of fundamental shifts in global relations. Here, Sassen (2014: 1) investigates "the complex notes of expulsion, because they can function as a window into major dynamics of our epoch." Sassen's exploration points to the multiple forms of expulsions under capitalism: from the expulsion of unemployed workers from social welfare, to the creation of 'dead land and dead water' through intensive mining, and the eviction of farmers and communities from land for capital gain. Sassen's development of expulsions is a useful means to connect the experiences of inequality and injustice with diverse (broad and particular) global pursuits for capital gain.

This understanding is reflected also in sociologist Lois Wacquant's (1996) description of the growing 'underclass' constituting 'advanced marginality'. Focusing on the spatial logics of inequality, in which the 'poor' are 'ghettoized' along lines of race and class, Wacquant suggests that a new urban marginality is constituted by the collapse of the welfare state and associated institutions (Wacquant 2008). In *Urban Outcasts*, he suggests that entrenched marginality is being supported by "state policies of urban abandonment", leading to the effective "punitive containment of the Black (sub-)proletariat" (2008: 3–4). For Wacquant, reflecting in particular on the US context, modern marginality is put to work in the ways in which people and populations are contained, and abandoned, underpinned by the structured and historically embedded politics of race and class.

These varying attempts to capture and understand the contemporary experiences of being 'outcast', 'expelled' and 'precarious' are all attempts to represent the contemporary dynamics of inequality. Undoubtedly, it is important not to complacently invoke historical explanations for contemporary realities. Nevertheless, there are aspects of historical conditions that do persist, albeit in transformed ways. This includes the ways in which memories and experiences of industrialisation (and associated social structures) endure and 'haunt' the present (see Strangleman 2017). The continued importance of work—and of associated class relations—is undeniable in the contemporary context. The sustaining impact of class and the modalities of race, gender and sexuality, are being reconstituted anew (see e.g. Warren 2015; Breman 2013; Sudbury 2005).

For instance, the intersections of race and class have profound implications for those who are poor and marginalised. Certainly, the vast majority of sellers I spoke with in San Francisco were Black, as were the many visibly homeless people on the street—a familiar phenomenon across the US (see Jones 2016; Wagner and White 2015). Race also punctures the social relations of class and poverty in Australia and the UK. In the context of this study, for example, there has been significant recent press coverage in Britain concerning an apparent rise in the number of Romani and Eastern European *Big Issue* sellers. This came to the fore in 2012 when Romani seller Firuta Vasile successfully contested a local authority ruling that she was not entitled to housing benefits because she did not have a 'real job' (Morris 2012). This prompted *The Daily Mail* newspaper to "launch an investigation" which claimed that one in three *The Big Issue* sellers were from Romania, with many organised by "luxury" "gangs" (Constable 2012). Here, public debates about deservingness circle around race and class, as well as gender, demonising and questioning the deservingness of those who 'come to' England.

To consider marginality, therefore, is to consider the ways in which poverty and class is sutured with the politics of race. This is true in relation to the contemporary fear of migration and refugees that is fuelled by the rise of far-right politics transnationally. It is also true in relation to settler colonialism and imperialism that provide both the past and present context of both the US and Australia. To consider the very notion of 'home' and 'homelessness' for instance, in the context of the history of colonialism and forced displacement of Indigenous peoples, raises a number of complexities (see Wilson 2003; see also Gerrard 2017). Imperial expansion brought with it a fundamental disjuncture in social and cultural meanings of home and land. As Lowitja O'Donoghue (1998) points out, in order to understand Indigenous relations to land, to country and ultimately to home, "You need to discard notions of real estate, titles and deeds. Forget about notions of ownership. Forget about land as a commodity to be bought and sold."

Indigenous experiences of colonial invasion cannot be simply encapsulated in the terminology of 'homelessness': rather, they indicate a fundamental undermining of Aboriginal ontology "based on spiritual and physical connectedness to their land and sea country" (Havemann 2005). These histories are not simply written out of existence, neither by a new policy initiative or by a government apology for taking Indigenous children away from their parents – also known as the stolen generation (in the case of Australia). From the continued lack of services for, and marginality of, First Nations peoples, to the continued neglect to recognise their sovereignty and rights, Indigenous politics are central to marginality and homelessness.

The social relations of power that surround gender and sexuality also underpin marginality, poverty and class. This has particular importance when considering the experience of 'homelessness': a term that hides so much diversity in its seemingly simplistic notion of those without a home. As already noted, there is a significant number of 'hidden homeless' who are most often women, fleeing family violence, often with their children, sleeping on the floors and couches of friends (see McLoughlin 2013; Miller and Du Mont 2000; Ecker 2016), and whose experiences of homelessness are invariably gendered (see Watson 2016). There is also a significant number of homeless lesbian, gay, intersex, queer and transgender young people who must struggle with an ongoing global political context—across nation states—steeped in moral normative judgements (which often spill over to violence) about what it is to be a man, a woman, a family, and to be loved (e.g. see Australian Human Rights Commission n.d.).

These myriad experiences indicate the need to tread carefully with the representations, and claims, made about marginality. This recognition of diversity is based in an understanding of the interconnections of the relations of power, not its divisions. As Sara Suleri argued in 1992, to claim one particular standpoint can gloss over the relationships and connections of power. Marginality, then, is both the conditions produced by neoliberal global capitalism and the space from which to challenge its basis.

Everyday Working and Learning Lives

Enterprise on the Margins focuses on the everyday practices and experiences of sellers of homeless street press. The focus on the everyday, the ordinary and perhaps even banal, has significant conceptual and methodological underpinnings and effects, and is connected to the understanding of marginality outlined in this chapter. Taking the conceptual and methodological standpoint of the everyday focuses attention on the taken-for-granted, routinised and 'common sense'. It is, in other words, about understanding "the most repeated actions, the most travelled journeys, the most inhabited spaces that make up, literally, the day to day" (Highmore 2002: 1; see also Back 2015). Focus on the everyday provides the opportunity to prise open and rethink all of the seemingly small day-to-day moments, moments that may appear trivial, but which are in fact the 'bread and butter' of marginality in capitalist social relations. Importantly, this conceptualisation of the everyday is not guided by determinist logics, in which the everyday is understood as a mirror reflection of, or absolutely determined by, the dominant orders of social relations. Rather, this is about understanding the both as steeped in social orders and as spontaneous, full of potential and difference.

Sociologists and philosophers have approached this kind of conceptualisation in a range of ways. French philosopher Henri Lefebvre, for instance, talks of the 'rhythmed organisation' of everyday life (2004). In this conceptualisation, that which is relative to social relations appears authentic and necessary. Yet, every repetition of the mundane creates the possibility for disruption. In this way disruption is inevitable within the ordinary, as each repetition of the everyday mundane is different and potentially transgressive. He writes, "When it concerns the everyday, rites, ceremonies, fetes, rules and laws, there is always something new and unforeseen that introduces itself into the repetitive: difference" (2004: 6). This insistence on the constitutive presence of difference in what appears to be mundane is centrally about resisting a view of the 'banal' as insignificant and, consequently, of the 'masses' as 'monolithic'. As with de Certeau (1988), this focus on the everyday connects singularities, multiplicities and potentialities within the temporal, spatial, interrelational, subjective and day-to-day habits, routines and events.

A focus on the everyday is also born out of feminist theorising: on the insistence that what is seemingly private is in fact political and imperative. Feminist sociologist Dorothy Smith, for instance, develops a methodology based on the 'problematics' of the 'everyday/everynight' (2005). For Smith, the critical task of research is to take a 'woman's standpoint'. Such a standpoint, according to Smith, starts from the understandings and problems of the everyday, and rejects essentialist or determinist categories or assumptions of practice (*ibid.*). Again, her concern is to understand the multiplicity of experience, in connection to wider social relations, or what she terms 'ruling relations'. Notwithstanding criticisms for her reification of a 'woman's standpoint', Smith's centring of the everyday—and in particular the everyday of work—points to the significance of investigating how people make "life liveable", as Back (2015) puts it.

Ultimately, it is in and through the tacit everyday routines and practices that we live out our understandings, and through which we feel the world. The orientation towards the everyday in this book also offers a means to recognise the profound import of encounters in the working lives of homeless street press sellers. This is a work practice that is premised on opening an opportunity for encounters between the sellers and 'the public'. Moreover, as sellers walk through or stand on city streets, they are in this act creating encounters with homelessness (see Gerrard and Farrugia 2015).

In addition, placing the everyday at the centre of this book is an attempt to develop understanding of the diversity of lived reality as a multiplicity of capitalist social relations and the marginality contained within/cultivated by it. It is an attempt to understand the everyday lived reality of social relations that are so often categorised, and then reified—categories like 'the poor', 'woman', 'Black', 'working class', 'unemployed', 'homeless'.

Relatedly, it is also an attempt to examine that which is so often glossed over—the taken-for-granted and the routinised. This is about recognising not only that the 'mundane' (including people who are considered mundane) is central, but also that everything (and everybody) is mundane. "Everyday life" Felski writes, "does not only describe the lives of ordinary people, but recognises that every life is an element of the ordinary. We are all ultimately anchored in the mundane" (1999: 15).

This has particular significance in the case of this book. As discussed above, there is a tendency to treat the lives of the marginalised and poor as exceptional, as constitutively different from the rest of society. A focus on the everyday—in this case the working lives of homeless street sellers—enables a consideration of the particularities of homelessness and poverty in the context of wider social relations. This way, 'the poor' and 'the homeless' are not treated as exotic and ultimately reified social categories or descriptions. Rather, they reference a state of existence that is tightly interwoven into the fabric of social relations. They are not 'apart' from the 'mainstream', but constitutive to it.

CONFESSIONALS, TESTIMONIES AND EVERYDAY LIFE: NOTES ON THE RESEARCH

As I have outlined, academic research on marginality wrestles with the politics of representation. The authorial claim 'to know' is implicitly and explicitly asserted in the writing on the lives of 'others', and comes with inexorable tensions surrounding the representation of experience. The many attempts to address these tensions, and the power dynamics at play in research relationships, are never really able to shake off the inevitable difficulties in writing on the experience of 'others'. This is an irreconcilable tension, but a tension that must be carefully approached and considered.

For instance, many attempts to overcome such tensions suggest the highly popular research stance of reflexivity in which researchers regularly write themselves—as I do here—into the research to demonstrate and make plain the researchers' position and intents. There is no escaping, for instance, my position as an academic in a relatively elite university, or my experiences as a queer white woman committed to projects of solidarity and justice. I have not been homeless, but I care deeply about the lives of those who are. I cannot help but bring layers of interpretation to this research, the questions that I ask, the things that I see and the way that I write it. I am, in other words, very much within the research. Within in the sense that it is born out of my interests and also within in the sense that it arises from my interactions with sellers, from the act of sitting on upturned milk crates on sidewalks and plastic shopping centre chairs, standing on street corners, and 'bearing witness' to the experience of 'others'.

This research experience is sensory and affective; as much as something a seller might say to me might spark a jolt of understanding, so too might the smells, sights, touches, and sounds of 'the field'; tears, laughter, looks, awkward silences and body–body interrelationships are central to the research (see also Robinson 2011). It is impossible, also, to feign the look of an impartial, but interested, researcher when sellers are speaking about the feeling of the cold that pushes up through the soles of their shoes and up their bodies into their bones when working through winter, or when they share memories of a previous time of professional work and home ownership that seems so out of reach to them now. There is a corporeal dimension to the research, and the knowledge it creates (Robinson 2011).

Yet, in writing in my relationship to the research I am not attempting to assert absolute authorial legitimacy over 'the field' and the research knowledge. To understand 'other' experience does not always require corporeal comprehension, and nor is it always unproblematic (Robinson 2011). Rather, by recognising the embodied and invested nature of this research, I am acknowledging that what follows here is just one representation of a possible many. Thus, whilst my biography and experience are obviously deeply interwoven into the research, the lives of those who I met in Melbourne, San Francisco and London are not mere muses for a projection of my interests: their lives, their experiences, their understandings and their stories count. There is a serious ethical question surrounding the responsibility of bearing witness to 'others'. To write on the experience of sellers is also about being respectful and responsible with regards to the time and effort sellers took to spend time and talk with me. Thus, whilst there are clear dangers of reifying 'voice' as the 'authentic truth' in qualitative research, there are also dangers of moving too far away from the people who spent time and energy talking to me (see Gerrard et al. 2017).

Moreover, the writing and authorising of what counts in this reflexivity still remains in the hands of the researcher. As Skeggs suggests, "The ability to be reflexive via the experience of Others is a privilege, a position of mobility and power, a mobilization of cultural resources" (2004: 129). Similarly, it is vogue for research to establish research partnerships and collaborations, and to claim that in and through such partnerships comes empowerment.

However, in reality there are no clear or universal ways in which to address research power, and in fact no way to completely overcome it. As Back writes, "Claiming that research participants are empowered through the research process conceals some of the inevitable unevenness of agreement, consent and participation" (2007: 18).

The politics of representation is exacerbated within research that takes as its focus marginalised people and, more specifically, those that are readily identified—physically and bodily—as 'other'. The academic reliance on 'visible evidence' can reify and assert the authority research knowledge rendered through the detailed observation and confessional testimony of those deemed 'other', marginal, different (Skeggs 2004). Research, therefore, is invested in a process whereby "some people are made visible and public, whilst Others [such as researchers] are allowed to occupy and have access to the private" (Skeggs 2005: 156).

It is important also to consider the ways in which such knowledge becomes academic capital and currency. The work of making some lives visible, and in particular those who are marginalised and different, is a work practice connected to the territorialisation of knowledge. Academics, for instance, often create expert and authorial positions based on 'ownership' of their research data (and research participants) to become 'claimstakers' on and off the lives of Others (Tuck and Yang 2014). Here 'other' people's testimony can be rendered as property within the academic sphere, a sphere in which the researcher retains the rights to represent, to interpret, to analyse and ultimately to know (Skeggs 2004).

The confessional cultures of academia are mimicked and amplified in a social welfare field, in which charities, services and government agencies also demand the confessional testimonies of clients. People who are homeless and poor often have to tell their personal story over and over to multiple services and workers in order to access assistance and their basic rights, including housing and unemployment benefits. Trevor Gale (2005), for instance, notes the ways in which the personal stories of poverty and difficulty are often treated as unreliable anecdotes, and must be told multiple times.

Researchers of marginality have highlighted many of the complexities that arise in this research relationship. In recent years, there have been a number of papers that describe, for instance, the trauma, the comfortableness, the awkwardness and the danger to personal safety that many researchers feel when talking to people about their life experience (e.g. Sherry 2013; Cloke et al. 2000; Johnsen et al. 2008). Whilst such reflections provide important insight into the research process, I suggest that we need to go further, and reflect upon the ways in which research practices mirror problematic confessional cultures, in which people are asked to narrate a story of deprivation and disadvantage in order to access social services and welfare.

The Everyday and the Research

For this project, methodologically, the focus on the everyday provided a means to engage in these tensions of research and representation. First and foremost, this book is concerned to understand the everyday experiences and understandings of working and learning for homeless street press sellers. Practically, this means that this book is not searching for the secret inner meaning of the 'homeless self'. Nor were the interviews and conversations I had with sellers attempting to surface tales of, trauma, failure, defeat, pain or loss.

This was a purposeful decision. In part, this is a question of research practicability. This research was carried out in public spaces—on street corners, cafes, curbs, parks, shopping malls and food halls. These are not the appropriate spaces in which to probe about experiences of trauma. The decision is also about retaining focus on the everyday work and learning experiences: this is a book concerned with the work practices of homeless street sellers. All research has its limits, and this is one that I decided early on. In practice, this meant conversations with sellers focused on their work practices, and that I did not ask sellers questions that I also would not be prepared to answer had they asked me. And indeed, on more than one occasion, sellers did 'turn the tables' and ask to know more about my background and me.

Moreover, I wanted to go to particular effort not to replicate the sorts of dynamics that regularly arise in the sorts of interviews required to access services and assistance. This meant that I did not want sellers to think that they had to reveal their scars of the past and wounds of the present in order to participate in the research. I did not, for instance, start interviews with a barrage of questions surrounding age, marital status, drug use or current housing status. Such standard 'demographic' or 'risk factor' knowledge—the bread and butter of more quantitative sociologies and service-based interviews for housing and welfare—has less significance for a study concerned with understanding the everyday lived experience, or, at least their significance is contextual. Of course, most of the time answers to these sorts of questions eventually emerged later in the interviews. Though, as a result, for instance, when the conversation would eventually turn to their age, some sellers chose to speak in general terms—not telling me their specific age.

Thus, conversations and interviews focused on the everyday practice and experience of work: routines of the workday; feelings and understandings about work; the balancing of work and leisure and personal time; the perceptions and experiences of learning and self-development through work; hopes and desires for future work and education; experiences of previous work and education. In other words, the focus on the everyday meant that this research was primarily concerned with understanding the routines, rituals, habits and taken-for-granted activities, understandings, practices and learnings that underpinned the experience of working as a homeless street press seller.

It probably comes as no surprise, however, that despite a focus on the everyday routines of work, sellers invariably discussed their past and present experiences of poverty and trauma. To state the obvious, to be homeless and to be poor is traumatic, stressful, painful and in most cases all-consuming. Moreover, sellers are well experienced at confessional forms of interviews—conducted by social workers, researchers and government workers—and volunteered much of the information that I did not ask about. These conversations, led by the sellers themselves, uncovered the wounds of the systemic failures of our current social and governmental arrangements to provide for those who are at the pointiest end of social inequities. Seller conversations were almost always framed by the everyday stress experienced: the stress of managing the realities of having no money and in some cases precarious shelter; of serious and ongoing health concerns, disabilities and chronic pain; of caring for children or ill loved ones; of grieving children taken into care; of difficult personal intimate relationships including past and present experiences of domestic violence; of countless forms and appointments required with job agencies which displayed little interest in assisting them; and of managing addictions.

These are visceral and ever-present concerns. Vendors cried and wept talking of their experiences of trauma, including the stress of having to stretch out their meager income to support themselves and their families. Many of the male sellers would jump out of their chairs lifting their shirts or trousers up to reveal old and new wounds and scars, or present their hands to reveal missing fingers, from injuries gained at factory machines and other manual labouring work. Others—both women and men—would want to talk at length about the constant round of appointments and medical care required for ongoing and profound health concerns, including cancer treatment, psychological care in the aftermath of domestic violence and long-standing disabilities and additions. Many would press photos of their children, sometimes living in care or with a family member, into my hands and talk eagerly of upcoming visits and the frustration of being apart. Often, the stress of these concerns centred on the time that it took out from work as sellers and on the potential loss to income. Without a salary or sick pay, sellers managed incredibly precarious income streams alongside pressing health issues, which required both time and money.

In addition to the tape-recorded interviews with sellers in Melbourne, San Francisco and London, I also spent tim—often days at a time—with sellers in all three cities whilst they worked, chatting in between magazine sales and on their breaks. Whilst I can never claim to know how it 'feels' to be a homeless street press seller, this part of the research was concerned with coming to a closer understanding of the lived reality, and everyday routines, of the work involved with selling homeless street press. Interviews can provide some level of insight, but in this research I wanted to go further than an analysis of what people talk about. This time occurred in all three cities of the study, but by far the most time I spent hanging out with sellers was in Melbourne, where I spent approximately 18 months visiting, revisiting and spending time with sellers—some regularly, some one-off.

These times were always negotiated on an ongoing basis with sellers, in order to ensure that I was not interrupting their sales, or overstaying my welcome. The levels of involvement in the research varied significantly, and were constantly negotiated. In order to be able to get a sense of a 'typical working day', many times instead of sitting with sellers, with their permission I sat slightly away from them and observed their work and the interactions created in the selling of homeless street press. These observations were invaluable for me in generating a more tacit understanding of the sorts of work practices carried out by sellers, and the ways in which this work is positioned within the wider context of the city.

Lastly, some of the sellers in Melbourne also documented their working day using photography. Here, I gave sellers a disposable camera and asked if they could document a typical day's work with the camera. I met with sellers once I had processed the camera film, and we discussed the photos. These photos provided an insight into sellers' work and daily routines that would have otherwise remained out of reach of the research. Sellers, for instance, took photos of their commute, at key moments in the day, including 'selfies' of themselves with regular customers, and the moments in which they 'clocked' on and off to work. The photos also revealed the mundane moments in the everyday—photos of crowds walking by, empty streets and the traffic revealed the aesthetic texture and temporal logics of the everyday. These photos are discussed predominantly in Chap. 4.

The Sellers

The research was undertaken across three cities. Melbourne, the primary base of the research, involved ongoing and sustained research over approximately 18 months. Over this time, I talked with 40 sellers of *The Big Issue*, as well as one ex-seller. As noted above, each seller had different levels of involvement in the research. Some I interviewed just once, others I met with weekly or fortnightly over the course of a few months, others I met with every couple of months over a year. Some consented for me to come and spend time with them at their pitch whilst they worked; others preferred to only have recorded interviews or informal chats on their breaks or at the end of the day. In San Francisco and London, I interviewed 12 sellers in each city, and met with a handful of them to spend time with them whilst they worked.

In all of the cities, I spent time in, and interviewed the staff of, the different homeless street press—*The Big Issue* in Melbourne and London, and *Street Sheet* in San Francisco. This included interviews with current staff responsible for seller support and administration across all three cities, and also those who were involved in establishing the street presses, but who were no longer formally working within the organisations. These interviews, which I draw from significantly in Chap. 3, as well as in Chap. 5, were invaluable in developing an understanding of the emergence of homeless street press as an activist initiative in San Francisco, and as a social enterprise in London and Melbourne. They also provided insight into the contemporary practices and aspirations of these organisations as both substantial interventions into politics of homelessness and the production of informal work for the homeless.

In what follows, all the names have been changed in order to protect the anonymity of those interviewed. Yet, in writing a book on marginality I also want to ensure that the sellers do not become written out of the text. So often the lives of those who are marginalised—their experiences and opinions—are smudged from view in the representation of floating interview quotations far from the context of the person speaking. Commonly, in the tradition of ethnography, research will attempt to avoid this by providing in-depth biographical narrative and context (see e.g. Gowan 2010). The difficulty for this project in providing biographical narrative and context is the question of anonymity. One of the key aspects of the research was that I was an independent researcher, not formally connected to *The Big Issue* in London or Melbourne and the *Street Sheet* in San Francisco, or any government agency. A significant part of this was assuring sellers that I would maintain their confidentiality, and would not pass on anything they told me to other sellers or any organisation. For most sellers, this was of paramount importance. There were some who wanted their names, and where they worked, to be published (largely in the hope of boosting their public profile and therefore their sales). However, for the most part, anonymity was contingent for sellers' involvement in the research.

Moreover, the question of anonymity is more than (the not so simple) matter of confidentiality and privacy. At the heart of this are ethical and political questions about the responsibility of research to those who have taken the time and effort to be involved. This responsibility is undeniably risky business. To research and write on the experiences of 'others' is always enmeshed with the possibility of misrepresentation, as explored above. Part of this is recognising that what I write here is just one interpretation of experience, made possible only by my own involvement in, and personal relationship to, the research. Sellers were given the opportunity to read through transcripts of their interviews, and many did do this, but ultimately this book is written by me, and represents my interpretations.

In what follows, therefore, names have been changed and I attempt a respectful representation of the experiences, practices and perspectives I witnessed. Focus is maintained on the everyday experiences of work, and care has been taken not to construct representations of sellers' personal histories and present experiences as a list of 'risk factors': drug and alcohol abuse, family breakdown, school failure and so on. Hidden behind, or rather, screaming out from such risk factors are much more complicated and messy life histories and, most importantly, much more complicated and messy social relations that create the conditions for structural poverty and homelessness. Ultimately, it is these relations that this book aims to problematise and investigate, in and through a careful examination of the practices of work and learning in one of the most important—and marginalised—emerging 'informal economies' in advanced capitalist nations.

References

Australian Human Rights Commission. (n.d.). *Violence, Harassment and Bullying and Homelessness.* https://bullying.humanrights.gov.au/violence-harassment-and-bullying-and-homelessness

Back, L. (2007). *The Art of Listening.* Oxford/New York: Berg.

Back, L. (2015). Why Everyday Life Matters: Class, Community and Making Life Liveable. *Sociology, 49*(5), 820–836.

Baldry, E., Green, S., & Thorpe, K. (2006). Urban Australian Aboriginal Peoples' Experience of Human Services. *International Social Work, 49*(3), 364–375.

Bhambra, G. (2009). *Rethinking Modernity: Postcolonialism and the Sociological Imagination*. London: Palgrave Macmillan.
Boltanski, L. (2003). *Distant Suffering*. Cambridge: Cambridge University Press.
Bourdieu, P. (1977). *Outline of a Theory of Practice*. Cambridge: Cambridge University Press.
Breman, J. (2013). A Bogus Concept? *New Left Review, 84,* 130–138.
Cloke, P., Cooke, P., Cursons, J., Milbourne, P., & Widdowfield, R. (2000). Ethics, Reflexivity and Reserach: Encounters with Homeless People. *Ethics, Place & Environment, 3*(2), 133–154.
Connell, R. W. (2008). *Southern Theory: The Global Dynamics of Knowledge in Social Science*. Sydney: Allen and Unwin.
Constable, N. (2012, February 4). One-third of Big Issue Sellers Now Romanian. *The Daily Mail*. http://www.dailymail.co.uk/news/article-2090012/One-Big-Issue-Sellers-Romanian-homes-AND-claim-benefits.html#ixzz41LfwIVl6
De Certeau, M. (1988). *The Practice of Everyday Life*. California: University of California Press.
Ecker, J. (2016). Queer, Young and Homeless: A Review of the Literature. *Child and Youth Services, 37,* 325–361, ifirst.
Erikson, K. (2008a). On Sociological Writing. *Sociological Inquiry, 78*(3), 399–411.
Erikson, K. (2008b). Kai's Response to Howard, Hana, Ben and Dorothy. *Sociological Inquiry, 78*(3), 437–442.
Fanon, F. (2008 [1952]). Black Skin White Masks. London: Pluto Press.
Farrugia, D., & Gerrard, J. (2016). Academic Knowledge and Contemporary Poverty: The Politics of Homelessness Research. *Sociology, 50*(2), 267–284.
Felski, R. (1999). The Invention of Everyday Life. *New Formations, 39,* 15–31.
Gale, T. (2005). *Rough Justice: Young People in the Shadows*. New York: Peter Lang.
Gerrard, J. (2013). Class Analysis and the Emancipatory Potential of Education. *Educational Theory, 63*(2), 185–202.
Gerrard, J. (2017). The Interconnected Histories of Homelessness and Labour, *Labour History* (awaiting print publication). Accepted 27 Oct 2016.
Gerrard, J., & Ball, J. (2013). From *"Fuck, Marry Kill* to *Snog, Marry, Avoid?"* Feminisms and the Excesses of Femininity. *Feminist Review, 105,* 122–129.
Gerrard, J., & Farrugia, D. (2015). The 'Lamentable Sight' of Homelessness and the Society of the Spectacle. *Urban Studies, 52*(12), 2219–2233.
Gerrard, J., Rudolph, S., & Sriprakash, A. (2017). The Politics of Post-Qualitative Inquiry: History and Power. *Qualitative Inquiry, 23*(5), 384–395.
Gowan, T. (2010). *Hobos, Hustlers and Backsliders: Homeless in San Francisco*. Minneapolis: University of Minnesota Press.
Havemann, P. (2005). Denial, Modernity and Exclusion: Indigenous Placelessness in Australia. *Macquarie Law Journal, 5,* 57–58.
Highmore, B. (2002). *Everyday Life and Cultural Theory: An Introduction*. London/New York: Routledge.

Johnsen, S., May, J., & Cloke, P. (2008). Imag(in)ing 'Homeless Places': Using Auto-Ethnography to (Re)examine the Geographies of Homelessness. *Area*, *40*(2), 194–207.

Jones, M. M. (2016). Does Race Matter in Addressing Homelessness? A Review of the Literature. *World Medical and Health Policy*, Published online first on 20 June 2016, doi:10.1002/wmh3.189.

Lefebvre, H. (2004). *Rhythmanalysis: Space, Time and Everyday Life*. London: Bloomsbury Publishing.

Marx, K. (1972). *The Marx-Engels Reader*, R. C. Tucker (Ed.). New York: W. W. Norton & Company.

McLoughlin, P. J. (2013). Couch Surfing on the Margins: The Reliance of Temporary Living Arrangements as a Form of Homelessness Amongst School-Age Home Leavers. *Journal of Youth Studies*, *16*(4), 521–545.

Miller, K., & Du Mont, J. (2000). Countless Abused Women: Homeless and Inadequately Housed. *Canadian Women Studies*, *20*(3), 115–122.

Morris, S. (2012, January 18). Big Issue Seller Wins Right to Claim Housing Benefit. *The Guardian*. http://www.theguardian.com/media/2012/jan/17/big-issue-seller-wins-right-housing-benefit

Neilson, B., & Rossiter, N. (2008). Precarity as a Political Concept, or, Fordism as Exception. *Theory, Culture & Society*, *25*(7–8), 51–72.

O'Donoghue, L. (1998). *Can We Call Australia Home: An Indigenous Perspectives of Housing*, Fifth F. Oswald Barnet Oration. Melbourne: Ecumenical Housing Inc & Copelen Child and Family Services.

Paradies, Y., & Cunningham, J. (2009). Experiences of Racism Among Urban Indigenous Australians: Finding from the DRUID Study. *Ethnic and Racial Studies*, *32*(3), 548–573.

Peel, M. (2003). *The Lowest Rung: Voices of Australian Poverty*. Cambridge: University of Cambridge Press.

Reay, D. (2007). 'Unruly Places': Inner-City Comprehensives, Middle-Class Imaginaries, and Working-Class Children. *Urban Studies*, *44*(7), 1199.

Robinson, C. (2011). *Beside One's Self: Homelessness Felt and Lived*. Syracuse: Syracuse University Press.

Sassen, S. (2014). *Expulsions: Brutality and Complexity in the Global Economy*. Harvard: Havard University Press.

Sherry, E. (2013). The Vulnerable Researcher: Facing the Challenges of Sensitive Research. *Qualitative Research Journal*, *13*(3), 278–288.

Skeggs, B. (2004). Context and Background: Pierre Bourdieu's Analysis of Class, Gender and Sexuality. In L. Adkins & B. Skeggs (Eds.), *Feminism After Bourdieu*. Oxford: Blackwell Publishing.

Skeggs, B. (2005). The Making of Class and Gender Through Visualising Moral Subject Formation. *Sociology*, *39*(5), 965–982.

Skeggs, B. (2011). Imagining Personhood Differently: Person Value and Autonomist Working-Class Value Practices. *The Sociological Review*, *59*(3), 496–513.

Smith, D. E. (2005). *Institutional Ethnography: A Sociology for People.* Oxford: Alta Mira Press.
Smith, D. (2008). From the 14th Floor to the Sidewalk: Writing Sociology at the Ground Level. *Sociological Inquiry, 78*(3), 417–422.
Spivak, G. C. (1988). Can the Subaltern Speak? In C. Nelson & L. Grossberg (Eds.), *Marxism and the Interpretation of Culture* (pp. 271–313). Bassingstoke: Macmillan Education.
Standing, G. (2011). *The Precariat: The New Dangerous Class.* London: Bloomsbury.
Strangleman, T. (2017). Deindustrialisation and the Historical Sociological Imagination: Making Sense of Work and Industrial Change. *Sociology, 51*(2), 466–485.
Sudbury, J. (Ed.). (2005). *Global Lockdown: Race, Gender, and the Prison-Industrial Complex.* New York/London: Routledge.
Suleri, S. (1992). Woman Skin Deep: Feminism and the Postcolonial Condition. *Critical Inquiry, 18*(4), 756–769.
Te Riele, K. (2006). Youth 'at Risk': Further Marginalizing the Marginalized? *Journal of Education Policy, 21*(2), 129–145.
Tuck, E., & Yang, K. W. (2014). Unbecoming Claims: Pedagogies of Refusal in Qualitative Research. *Qualitative Inquiry, 20*(6), 811–818.
Wacquant, L. (1996). The Rise of Advanced Marginaliy: Notes on Its Nature and Implications. *Acta Sociologica, 39,* 121–139.
Wacquant, L. (2008). *Urban Outcasts: A Comparative Sociology of Advanced Marginality.* Cambridge: Polity.
Wagner, D., & White, P. (2015). Breaking the Silence: Homelessness and Race. In S. Haymes, M. Vidal de Haymes, & R. Miller (Eds.), *The Routledge Handbook of Poverty in the United States* (pp. 456–462). London/New York: Routledge.
Warren, T. (2015). Work-Time Underemployment and Financial Hardship: Class Inequalities and Recession in the UK. *Work, Employment & Society, 29*(2), 191–121.
Watson, J. (2016). Gender-Based Violence and Young Homeless Women: Femininity, Embodiment and Vicarious Physical Capital. *The Sociological Review, 64*(2), 256–273.
Wilson, L. (2003). This Land Was Forcefully Taken. *Labour History, 85,* 200–201.

CHAPTER 3

Homeless Street Press: Historical and Contemporary Connections

In this chapter, I explore the emergence of homeless street press as an activist, social enterprise and work-based initiative. The chapter starts first with a reflection on the historical and social conditions from which the homeless street press arose. Here, building upon my previous work on the interconnecting histories of homelessness and labour (see Gerrard 2017b), I consider the ways in which homeless street press connects with the broader experiences of unemployment, itinerant work, poverty and the struggle for social change. This is not to say that homelessness can be simply framed solely in terms of (un)employment. However, it is to say that homelessness cannot be understood apart from the social relations of work.

Second, this chapter examines the emergence of *Street Sheet* and *The Big Issue* more specifically, drawing on interviews with past and present staff at *The Big Issue* in London and Melbourne and *Street Sheet* in San Francisco. Here, I chart the multiple pronouncements made about the organisational purpose of homeless street press: self-help, activism and entrepreneurial work. Following from this, third, the discussion positions homeless street press within the wider literature and context of informal economies and moral exchange markets. Finally, I turn more specifically to the contexts of the research upon which this book is based. Drawing on my fieldwork, I briefly reflect on the organisational spaces of the three different homeless street presses as a means to further explicate the commonalities and differences across them.

© The Author(s) 2017
J. Gerrard, *Precarious Enterprise on the Margins*,
DOI 10.1057/978-1-137-59483-9_3

HOMELESS STREET PRESS: HISTORIES OF HOMELESSNESS AND WORK

He built the road,
With others of his class he built the road.
Now o'er it, many weary mile, he packs his load,
Chasing a job, spurred on by hunger's goad.
He walks and walks and walks and walks
And wonders why in hell he built the road. (Anonymous 192?)

'Hobo', 'bum', 'panhandler', 'beggar', 'tramp', 'vagrant', 'destitute', 'vagabond', 'drifter', 'swagman', 'bag lady', 'sundowner': all these terms in different times and places have been ascribed to those who are visibly homeless. Often, these terms are understood and used as synonyms. They reflect, however, subtle and important notes of distinction. In the first instance, they are historically and geographically contingent. In the nineteenth century, for example, it was common to speak of hobos in America, swagmen and sundowners in Australia, and tramps in America and England. Second, they also mark crucial differences in experience and identity, which in turn reflect moral judgements steeped in notions of undeserving/deserving, lazy/productive. There are delineations in meanings and experience when it comes to homelessness: to be a tramp, swagman or drifter, for instance, is different to being a hobo, bum, beggar or panhandler. Fox writes on the importance of these distinctions in *Tales of an American Hobo*: "In the argot of the road 'a hobo was someone who travelled and worked, a tramp was someone who travelled but didn't work, and a bum was someone who didn't travel and didn't work'" (1989: xvi). It is here that the interconnection of the past and present experience of homelessness so clearly relates to the social relations of work and what is means to be a 'good' and 'productive' citizen (see Gerrard 2017b).

The figure of the homeless itinerant (mostly male and 'white') worker is significant in the histories of the US, England and Australia. Indeed, despite national differences in the experience and understanding of homelessness and itinerant work, the transience of work and workers is a common characteristic of capitalist economies. Both maligned and romanticised, homeless itinerant workers were in different ways essential for the economic growth of England, the US and Australia (see Gerrard 2017b; Higbie 2003; Cresswell 2013; Fumerton 2006; Beier and Ocobock 2008). They provided (and continue to provide) a cheap and transitional workforce across rural and urban areas, and were and are central to the development of labour relations. Thus, itinerant work, and the creation of homeless itinerant workers, is connected to the expansion of capital and commodity markets growing too quickly for the creation of housing, communities, services and facilities. It is also created by precarious employment markets and the tendency for capitalism to cultivate highly insecure work that forces workers to travel (see Beier and Ocobock 2008). The 'right' to housing or employment in one particular place, in other words, is not a given (see e.g. Troy 1992).

Of course, race, gender and colonial relations mediate the experiences of labour, home and homelessness and the right to housing (see Gerrard 2017b). Writing on the history of US 'hobo workers', Higbie, for instance, writes, "divisions of ethnicity and race were key to where, when, and how often seasonal labourers found work and what kind of work they performed" (2003: 12). As I have written elsewhere, a narrow focus on the white male itinerant worker eclipses the narratives of homelessness for women, Indigenous people and people of colour (see Gerrard 2017b). In Australia, for example, Indigenous and women itinerant workers—'swagwomen'—are far less often evoked in the public memory of 'the swagman', despite their presence (see Beckett 1978; Gerrard 2017b).

Moreover, as noted earlier, the displacement of Australia's traditional owners of the land, and use of housing as a means to 'civilise' (Attwood 2000), highlights the significance of race, racism and colonialism in the rights and social norms surrounding housing and work. In addition, the significance of the home in cultivating gender relations, traditional 'women's work' and distinctions between the private and public domains has clear ramifications for a consideration of homelessness (see Lake 1991; Gerrard 2017b). Here, moral judgements surrounding what is 'right' and 'moral' within the home intersect with the experience of homelessness and the provision (or lack of provision) for housing elsewhere: in this way, out-of-wedlock pregnancy, diverse sexuality or other perceived deviancies not tolerated 'within the home' become a provocation homelessness. From vagrancy, to destitution, itinerant work, workhouses, boarding houses and 'lying in homes' for 'wayward' women, what we now refer to as homelessness has had a multitude of expressions.

The long diverse history of homelessness and work provides the backdrop for the emergence of homeless street press. Whilst the contemporary emergence of homeless street press is connected to what Eric Hobsbawm describes as the 'rediscovery of poverty' in the midst of the post–Second World War 'Golden Age' (1994), the history of homeless street press stretches much further back—most particularly in the US context. In the early twentieth century, the paper *"Hobo" News* connected itinerant workers across the US. Established by the 'International Brotherhood Welfare Association' (IBWA) in a similar vein to the contemporary forms of homeless street press, *"Hobo" News* was sold by itinerant workers as a means to supplement their income (Adrian 1992).

"Hobo" News, like some (though not all) of the contemporary versions, also straddled an itinerant worker/homeless readership along with a 'settled' or housed readership (Adrian 1992). Addressing its readership in 1915 *"Hobo" News* urges:

> Now, there are, in this country, over two millions, as a vast army of men who live the life of the casual, migratory and most of the time, unemployed men, whom you call the HOBOES. They are doing the work of the World, and you have never been given a chance to understand them until you bought this paper.

Also similar to the contemporary iterations (as I explore below), *"Hobo" News* served as an alternative news outlet, connected to movements for the self-organisation and education of workers. Nels Anderson makes note of the political purposes of *"Hobo" News* in one of the first sociological investigations of homelessness, *The Hobo: The Sociology of the Homeless Man* (1923). Anderson suggests many 'hobos' "look with disapproval upon the so-called 'capitalist' press", turning to radical press as an alternative, such as *"Hobo" News* (1923: 186).

With a readership of up to 20,000 *"Hobo" News"* signals the cultural and social import of itinerant workers and homelessness in early-twentieth-century US (DePastino 2003: 103). It also points to political distinctions in class politics. The IBWA took a different approach in comparison to the International Workers of the World (IWW), which also proclaimed support for, and membership of, itinerant workers. "*The Hobo in Song and Poetry*" (n.d.) states IBWA's object as uniting "the migratory workers, the disemployed, and the organized of both sexes for mutual betterment and development, with the final object of abolishing poverty and introducing a classless society." However, in distinction from the more assertive class politics of IWW, the IBWA understood its primary political task to be one of "education, cooperation and uplift" (DePastino 2003: 103). *"Hobo" News* was its main organ for this purpose, publishing articles that linked itinerant workers to union campaigns, political issues and the culture of itinerant work including poems and songs (Adrian 1992).

Political divisions, the emergence of rival *Hobo World* and the death of *"Hobo" News*' founder meant that the paper appeared to dwindle by the end of the 1920s. It was, however, revived in the 1930s and 1940s and gained cultural and political fashion, appearing, for instance, in a 1940 publicity photo shoot of folk musicians Woody Guthrie and Burl Ives in New York (Petrus and Cohen 2015: 18–20). Guthrie's music was inspired by his frustration at the social and material dissonances between skid row's poverty and the wealth of New York City (*ibid*).

In the post-war period, it was the economic downturns in the 1970s that brought heightened attention to social inequality, including what was popularly described as a 'war on poverty' in the US. Across cities and nations, by the 1980s the visible spectre of poverty was unavoidable. Hobsbawm (1994: 406) writes:

> *As for poverty and squalor, in the 1980s even many of the richest and most developed countries found themselves, once again, getting used to the everyday sight of beggars on the streets, and even the more shocking spectacle of the homeless sheltering in doorways in cardboard boxes, insofar as they were not removed from visibility by the police.*

In response, throughout the 1960s, 1970s and into the 1980s an increasing collection of survey and research literature attempted to describe, count, understand and intervene into 'the poor' (see Gerrard 2017a).

In this context, homeless street press emerged not as an intervention into the lives of the homeless, but as something initiated by the homeless. Contemporary homeless street presses arose from the radical activist cultures in the US. In 1960s and 1970s San Francisco, community street press proliferated as radical student and community groups attempted to further their cause (see Ashbolt 2013). For example, in Berkeley the Telegraph Avenue Liberation Front sporadically published its paper *Spare Change* throughout the 1970s. Filled with activist news and events, including legal challenges to police violence and the defence of the famous Berkeley People's Park, *Spare Change* explicitly engaged in the politics of poverty, begging and homelessness. On the front page of the first edition they declare,

> *We are the Telegraph Avenue Liberation Front. We rapped on the ave about a street paper. This is it. We call it Spare Change because it is illegal to say Spare Change on the ave or anywhere in Berkley. It is not illegal to sell newspapers.*

Now Spare Change is a street newspaper. Pick up some Spare Change and shout "Spare Change". You might sell a few and pick up some spare change at the same time, but for sure you won't be busted for saying "Spare Change". (Anonymous 1970?)

As this quote references, the emergence of this press must be understood in connection to the criminalisation of begging (or panhandling), and correspondingly the affordances under the US First Amendment which allows the distribution and selling of street newspapers as an expression of free speech.

Alternative street press were not only confined to Berkley's radical circles. Across the bay, alternative and activist street presses also flourished—most particularly in the Tenderloin, the small central San Francisco neighbourhood home to significant numbers of homeless people, shelters, homeless organisations and the infamous San Francisco 'skid row' (and one of the core sites of the research for this book). As put by ethnographer Teresa Gowan in her study of San Francisco homelessness, the Tenderloin represents "a world of poverty, a layering of multiple and diverging forms ranging from the utter abjection of the most far-gone street alcoholics to the much more ambiguous situation of the long-term apartment and hotel residents" (2010: 66). Nestled in the centre of the city, Tenderloin "intimately rubs against the hotels and upscale stores of Union Square, forcing tourists and downtown workers to recognize the city's chasm between rich and poor" (*ibid*: 65).

Here, in the 1970s activist and community-based street press culture thrived. For instance, in 1977 the homeless shelter Central City Hospitality House established *The Tenderloin Times*, bringing together activism with local news. Its impetus emerged from informal conversations at Hospitality House's drop-in centre, where it was agreed that there was a need for a paper to distribute the news and events of the Tenderloin (McCarthy 1977: 2). Writing on its foundation, Peter McCarthy (*ibid*) suggests that for the homeless people who put the paper together, it "will be their weapon against odds that overwhelm them, their tool to cut through the red tape of bureaucracy and finally bring attention to our environment, the area the city overlooks and takes for granted so often". Its intention therefore was to serve the interests of the Tenderloin community by providing news of social and recreational value and by "making known the medical, financial, housing and job-seeking services available" (*ibid*). It also regularly reported on protests against evictions and for the rights of the city's homeless and poor. In the mid 1980s, reflecting the changing refugee populations of San Francisco, *The Tenderloin Times* started to publish articles in English, Vietnamese, Cambodian and Lao (Waters and Hudson 1998: 311).

It is hard to establish just how much these street presses were conscious of their historical antecedents. At least one offered an explicit referent: *Boxcar: A Journal of the Women's Itinerant Hobo's Union* (WIHU), publishing its first issue in 1977. In its introductory article, *Boxcar* states explicitly that it is named after the infamous Bertha Thompson (a.k.a "Boxcar Bertha"). Boxcar Bertha, a founding member of the WIHU in the early twentieth century, was popularised by the book *Sister of the Road*, first published in 1937 (Reitman 1982). In *Sister of the Road*, Bertha recounts the lively 'hobo' culture, including many women 'hoboes', and anarchist and socialist women involved in hobo politics and who offered food and shelter (*ibid*: 42-3). This autobiography helped to give prominence to women's experiences in what was often a male representation of itinerant work and homelessness (see also Cresswell 1999; Hall 2010; Gerrard 2017b).

Throughout the 1970s and 1980s, a range of community street press connected to homeless organisations proliferated. This included *Golden Gate* founded by San Francisco's The United States Mission, a Shelter for the Homeless. Its first edition published in September 1986 features an article on the life of homeless man Ken Crabtree, who last worked three years prior and who "spends his days wandering around in rags, bumming cigarettes, and standing in lines for free meals". "Somehow," the article laments, "the glad tidings of the economic recovery never quite trickled down to the likes of Crabtree" (Misaloswki 1986). *Golden Gate* was not intended to be sold by homeless sellers, but aimed to provide a supplementary income for the shelter whilst reporting "on the issues that touch the lives of both gays and straights—in short, issues affecting everyone. These include the plight of the homeless, AIDS, rents, small business, restaurants, entertainment and the fine arts", as put by the publisher and editor Pat Rocco (1986: 2).

A year later, after finding herself homeless in San Francisco, Myrnalene Nabih founded *The Homeless Times* in 1987. Nabih intended the paper to be written for and by homeless people and hoped it would fight stereotypes, connect San Francisco homeless to refugees all over the world, and provide a stream of income: homeless people could buy the magazine for 20 cents, and then resell copies for 50 cents (Nix 1990). The year 1988 saw the founding of another homeless street press, the monthly *By No Means*, which included poetry and writing from San Francisco Bay Area homeless women and men as well as articles on local and poverty issues. "*By No Means*", declares the editorial, "publishes news of conditions among homeless and refugee groups in this country and elsewhere through a mixture of direct first-person accounts and interviews with human rights and legal advocates" (Carson and Garcia 1991). Unsurprisingly, this diverse culture of street press reflected a range of—often contested—views and approaches. For instance, the editor of *The Homeless Times* found herself heavily criticised after publishing a purportedly homophobic article. The local gay and lesbian community—including many of San Francisco's homeless—responded fiercely, defending their rights (see letters page, *The Homeless Times*, July 1991, no. 6).

Street Sheet and *The Big Issue*: Activism, Self-Help and Social Enterprise

The long interweaving history of homelessness and work, and more specifically of homeless street press, gives the context for the contemporary versions. In the US, homeless street press was (and is) a national movement. For instance, 1989 saw the arrival of both *Street Sheet* (which now lays claim to being the longest running homeless street press), published by San Francisco's Coalition on Homelessness and *Street News* in New York City. Both were imbued with campaign and activist intent, whilst offering "sellers a modest but nonetheless viable alternative to panhandling" (Howley 2003). In 1992, Chicago's *StreetWise* similarly aimed to provide an alternate income stream whilst engaging the public with issues surrounding poverty and homelessness—literally recruiting its first sellers by setting up a stall outside of their donated office space (Green 1998). These city-by-city initiatives eventually led to national coordination, with the first North American Street News Summit held in Chicago in 1996. A second summit in 1997 led to the establishment of the North American Street News Association (NASNA).

It didn't take long for this American venture to have international reach. Indeed, it was New York's *Street News* that inspired the founder of *The Big Issue* to establish an English counterpart to this flourishing US based initiative in 1991 in London. The story of the London establishment of *The Big Issue* is largely told in *Coming up from the Streets* (2002) authored by journalist and writer Tessa Swithinbank, who had worked for *The Big Issue* in various roles in the eight years prior. She recounts how *The Big Issue* was inspired when Gordon Roddick, established businessperson and husband to the skin care company The Body Shop founder, Anita Roddick, came across *Street News* when visiting New York.

Returning to England, Gordon Roddick went about setting up an English version of the paper with financial backing from The Body Shop. He approached John Bird, an old friend from the late 1960s with a personal history of homelessness and experience in the publishing industry to help set the magazine up (Greenstreet 1995). John Bird remains editor-in-chief of *The Big Issue* in England to this day. After the relative success of *The Big Issue* in London, Roddick and Bird began to seek avenues for international expansion. As early as 1993 there was interest in establishing *The Big Issue* in Australia, though it was not until 1996 that the magazine first arrived in Melbourne. This expansion has been undeniably successful. As stated on their UK website, "Created as a business solution to a social problem, *The Big Issue* has inspired other street papers in more than 120 countries, leading a global self-help revolution" (*The Big Issue* n.d.).

The partnership between Bird and Roddick has been integral to the development of *The Big Issue* in both form and content. Most significantly, it is through this partnership that the magazine ethos of social enterprise developed. As I have outlined elsewhere (Gerrard 2017a), *The Big Issue* differs significantly from the North American papers that first inspired it. John Bird, for instance, is a vocal champion of social enterprise. He connects social enterprise to a market-based participatory democracy, in which individual citizens can engage in, and benefit from, empowering self-help. Thus, the emergence of *The Big Issue* was intertwined with the knitting together of business models and interests with social causes in the emergence of social enterprise (*ibid.*).

Street Sheet

Principal differences lie in the intent of the street presses. In similar fashion to the many of the prior initiatives, *Street Sheet* has radical activist roots. The Coalition on Homelessness publishes the *Street Sheet* to distribute activist news and analysis. The Coalition, founded in 1987, arose from the housing crises of the 1980s in San Francisco. It is a grass roots organisation that campaigns for the rights of homeless people in San Francisco, in which many former and still homeless people participate. Its purpose, unchanged from when it was founded, is to "give poor and homeless people a voice in the shaping of public policy and the development and operation of programs that directly affect them. The mission of the Coalition is to address the systemic causes of poverty and homelessness" (Dotson 2012: 1).

Reflecting on the establishment of *Street Sheet*, Lydia Ely recollects that it started in December 1989 with a modest newsletter with a print run of 500 as a means to publicise the work, politics and activities of the Coalition (Ely 1997). Ely states it was not until an invitation from famous musician Phil Collins to distribute their newsletter at a concert that the thought—and opportunity—to extend their circulation occurred. With thousands of leftover papers after the concert, they decided to give the paper to "Coalition volunteers and panhandlers who could use the cash" to sell (ask for donations) on San Francisco streets for $1 (*ibid*). It was so popular that from then on the Coalition began to view the *Street Sheet* as an important means to engage the San Francisco public with issues of poverty and homelessness, as well as their own volunteers and panhandlers. Ely writes (*ibid*: 3):

> *The Street Sheet is the same as it was in 1989: the voice of the Coalition on Homelessness and its advocacy; a source of information not presented by the dailies and weeklies; an outlet for expression by homeless people; and a place where not only the problems but the solutions are discussed in depth, in a manner that can be understood by the layperson and yet does not insult the reader's intelligence.*

The editorial policy of the *Street Sheet* demonstrates the paramount connections of the street press to the activist work of the Coalition. Consistently appearing on the back page of the newspapers, the editorial states:

> *The Coalition on Homelessness, San Francisco, is made up of homeless and formerly homeless people, representatives of the over 50 service, shelter and housing providers, advocacy groups, and neighbourhood and religious organizations.*
>
> *The Coalition's staff, more than three-quarters of whom have been homeless, write most of the articles in the Street Sheet. ... The Street Sheet welcomes your written contributions and artwork but cannot guarantee that they will be printed. Enclose a self-addressed stamped envelope to have your work returned to you.*

This connection to political grassroots activism is also central for the past and present staff and organisers of the Coalition and *Street Sheet*. Jim, one of the founders of the Coalition and *Street Sheet*, who I spoke with while in San Francisco, is adamant that the *Street Sheet* is an activist tool, not alternative employment, or a tool of self-help or business.

First and foremost, Jim views the *Street Sheet* as being centrally concerned with generating news and analysis from the perspective of the homeless and poor of San Francisco. *Street Sheet* is a mouthpiece for the Coalition on Homelessness, or, as Jim puts it, "It's an empowerment tool for an organisation." The content and editorial independence of the newspaper, therefore, is foundational. Jim says, "It's a vehicle for us to be able to say every month or now every two weeks—'here's what we're about, here's what we see, here's what we think'—and not have the editors at the *San Francisco Chronicle* or somebody else edit our shit or force us in to responding to their questions. We get to write exactly what we want."

Thus, the transformative potential of *Street Sheet*, in Jim's view, lies in its role as a communication and campaign device. Consequently, Jim places limits on its transformative potential for sellers. He says, "I get a little like pissy when people start talking about it as this benevolent empowerment tool: what's so empowering about selling a god damn newspaper!?" Jim is clear in his view of homeless street press, "It's not a job—they can call it whatever they want—but it's not a job." He continues, "You know, it's just a paper, there's so many other ways of engaging people for economic benefit in the poverty world that the street newspaper shouldn't be the employment sector. ... When you look at the whole apparatus around poverty and homeless, the street newspaper should be the lowest run of the corporate ladder."

Natalie, a current worker at *Street Sheet*, also stresses its purpose as a campaign device with a commitment to the voices and views of homeless people when I spoke to her at the Coalition offices. When I asked her what she thought of *The Big Issue*, she responded:

> I think it's just a very different model from ours. I mean ours serves a purpose for us and it comes from a political place and supports the organisation and the work of the organisation. So I would say that that's our primary, and then the secondary is having this opportunity for people to be able to make money. And we see it as sellers doing us a favour to get it out there. We really wanted it advertising free. ... We want be able to get the voices of homeless people out there without any kind of compromising situations. ... We're hoping people are getting the Street Sheet to read the Street Sheet, to learn about the issues and hopefully get inspired to become involved.

Nevertheless, Natalie still emphasises the import of the *Street Sheet* as an income avenue for the city's poor and homeless. She explains, "The idea is basically for homeless people themselves to have a venue for their voice to be heard—a creative outlet, writing, journalism, poetry, artwork—and have an alternative media publication where we can put our issues out there unfiltered, ... and at the same time creating an alternative income for folks." Importantly, this informal income is just that: there is no formal structure to selling the *Street Sheet*: sellers receive the *Street Sheet* for free, and then 'sell' it on by walking the streets of San Francisco and asking people for donations for the paper.

The Big Issue

While *Street Sheet* and *Street News*—and their predecessors such as *Spare Change*—see their purpose in part as forming a 'legitimate' means for the homeless to panhandle whilst spreading political and activist news, *The Big Issue* understands its purpose differently: as forming a legitimate alternative form of work. With the underpinning motto of 'a hand up, not a hand out', *The Big Issue* is premised on the possibility of producing opportunities for work for those who are otherwise excluded from the mainstream labour market. Correspondingly, *The Big Issue* believes in the possibility for personal and social change through the creation of this work practice.

As I have also explored elsewhere (see Gerrard 2017a), at the time of its establishment, teaming with John Bird, *The Big Issue* founder Gordon Roddick "insisted that it operate as a business" (Swithinbank 2001: 26). It is one of the first 'social enterprises'—a business with a social cause (Gerrard 2017a). This business approach, combined with the financial support from The Body Shop, means that *The Big Issue* was and is enmeshed in business culture from its inception. By selling the magazine to sellers (who then sell on the paper for double their purchase price thereby making half profit for each sale)—rather than giving it away as many of the US papers do (such as *Street Sheet*)—"The paper would re-energize the work ethic in people's lives: it would be a method of motivating them and help to create choice" (Swithinbank 2001: 26). Thus, at the core of *The Big Issue* is the notion of entrepreneurial self-help: the capacity for individuals to engage in activities that might assist them in their own individual struggle against poverty.

Yet, in many ways, *The Big Issue* retained much of the activist and community-based ethos of its US counterparts. At its inception in England, *The Big Issue* was filled with London-based politics, news, events and reviews, and significant amounts of the magazine were dedicated to homeless issues and experiences. In 1992, for example, *The Big Issue* was the face to a campaign initiative launched by the homeless organisation Shelter and The Body Shop. 'The Key Issue' aimed to raise awareness of significant housing budget cuts in London in the lead up to the national 1992 election. The campaign, advertised in *The Big Issue* April 1992 issue, entitled 'Election Reflections: Your Election Guide' urged The Body Shop customers "to help them collect at least 100,000 keys—one for each extra home which must be provided annual over the next five years to avoid a housing disaster". The keys, to be given to The Body Shop shops around London, were to be turned into a giant sculpture and presented to the new "Prime Minister after the election as a permanent reminder of a problem that will not just go away". At the time, Anita Roddick called the campaign the "most political" of The Body Shop's to date (*ibid*).

Nevertheless, unlike the US papers *The Big Issue* is not run out of—or formally connected to—a homeless organisation, campaign group or service. This creates subtle—and less subtle—differences. For example, the magazine does not place at the centre of its practice the need for the magazine to be written and run by homeless people, nor does it foreground the necessity for grass-roots collective campaigns as the basis for social change. Whilst it does have a focus on reporting on issues to do with poverty, and sets aside one page within the magazine for content from sellers, it is not principally an organ for homelessness activism and voices (see Howley 2003).

Celebrating *The Big Issue's* one-year anniversary in London, the editorial explains the three primary reasons for the paper (Editorial 1992: 1): first, "because we wanted to offer homeless people a chance of making a legal living" thereby offering the means to "earn their own wages entirely free from the change of receiving handouts"; second, to provide a means to generate and enhance the social esteem of homeless people so that they "could gradually gain the necessary confidence with which to move off the streets"; third, to offer a chance for the homeless to learn "basic skills that disappear on the streets", such as managing money and "handling all the things that come up when you are helping yourself". Here, it is individual dispositions and capabilities—confidence, skills, esteem and self-help—that are placed at the centre of *The Big Issue's* business model and represented as core issues to be addressed to solve homelessness, along with the need to move people away from living on so-called 'hand outs'.

Thus, the notion of sellers engaging in individual self-help is central to *The Big Issue* business model. Combining advocacy, self-help and enterprise, Paul Please (1996: 12), then managing editor of *The Big Issue* Australia, put its goals in its very first Melbourne issue this way:

Firstly, THE BIG ISSUE aims to provide an opportunity for homeless and disadvantaged people to have a self-earned income while interacting positively with the community. Secondly THE BIG ISSUE is a project which will raise community awareness of the issues faced by people who face homelessness or other disadvantage.

Here, *The Big Issue* combines self-help and empowerment messages with a desire to create more 'positive' interactions and community awareness. As Teasdale (2010: 28) suggests, "Using homeless people to sell a product can be seen as bridging a divide between philanthropists and self-help."

Thus, *The Big Issue* took its business and employment aspirations to a new level. It is one of the first examples of 'social enterprise': the business and market-based response to social problems (see Gerrard 2017a; see also Teasdale 2010). To be sure, the paper retains much of its focus on raising public awareness of homelessness. Nevertheless, founder Gordon Roddick's insistence that it was a viable—and profitable—business shifted the paper's focus. The magazine had to be seen as a desirable commodity not just a voice for the homeless: the connection to the social issue of homelessness and poverty occurs for *The Big Issue* though the lens of business and enterprise. As I have discussed elsewhere (Gerrard, 2017a), this blending of social and business concerns is emblematic of a wider concern with individual agency in the 1980s and 1990s, which—in the context of emerging neoliberalism—connected citizen action and social responses to poverty with market- and corporate-based practices.

Over the past few decades, the differences between the North American homeless street press papers and *The Big Issue* have perhaps become more pronounced. As *The Big Issue* has gained prominent public and political support, the magazine has increasingly styled itself like other general interest magazines. Whilst *Street Sheet* remains a basic news print paper, *The Big Issue* is a glossy magazine; and whilst the *Street Sheet* features news about police violence and poverty on its front covers, *The Big Issue* is proud to have celebrity covers—perceived to be key for its saleability. In other words, the focus of *The Big Issue* as a commodity embedded in a business—albeit with a 'social conscience'—means that the paper has developed with different intents, and to different ends—despite the many correspondences across the different homeless street press. As Howley (2003: 283), notes, there are clear divergences: "On one side of the debate are activists who use the paper to address issues related to social and economic injustice; on the other are business oriented publishers providing entrepreneurial opportunities to the homeless" (see also Torck 2001).

Indeed, there are—and were—clear tensions between the US activist-based papers and the UK-entrepreneurial papers. For instance, *The Big Issue* attempted to expand into the US market in the mid-1990s, targeting in particular Los Angeles, which at the time did not have a homeless street press (Swithinbank 2001). According to Jim, this put many of the US papers on the defensive: they did not want a strong business-model street press to encroach on the US activist street press market and culture. This attempted expansion also highlighted tensions surrounding the precarious form of income and labour offered by *The Big Issue*. US sellers complained that selling the magazine was far from alternative labour. It looked and felt too much like an alternative to panhandling: for it to be labour it needed to be waged and secure (Swithinbank 2001). Eventually, John Bird, who was in Los Angeles to help establish the North American arm of *The Big Issue*, trialed full-time waged workers selling the magazine on a 9–5 basis. Yet, in the end, the attempt of *The Big Issue* to break into the US market was unsuccessful and was ultimately abandoned.

The Informal (Moral and Entrepreneurial) Economies of Homeless Street Press

Despite their differences, these various iterations of homeless street press all represent important sites of informal labour and of the informal economy. As I explore below, these magazines both provide a form of work for sellers and have created a highly moralised exchange market in which the magazine commodity is bought and sold for consumption. Whether the focus is on activism or on the provision of alternative work, the selling of these magazines and newspapers on street corners constitutes a significant form of income accrual for the marginalised and disenfranchised. Of course, as explored above there are undoubted differences in how this is understood across the two papers. These differences mean, for instance, that unlike *The Big Issue* many within the *Street Sheet* do not frame sellers' activities as 'work' in the formal sense, and talk rather of a 'dignified' income stream. Nevertheless, despite differences in purpose, like *The Big Issue*, the *Street Sheet* effectively creates a means for people to earn money who would otherwise be begging.

Homeless street presses have created a commodity, a (decidedly morally charged) exchange market and an income stream. Whilst this may not be work in the formal sense, it is a form of work. In the case of *The Big Issue*, this is perhaps a little more clear, particularly as the organisation's proud motto in London is 'working, not begging'. In this case, sellers have responsibilities to declare their earnings to the state, and must buy the magazine (at half price) before being able to sell it on. Sellers effectively make $3.50 in Australia ($3 at the time when I was conducting this research) or £1.25 in England per sale, having bought the magazine for that price and selling it on for double ($7 or £2.50). There is a formality in this system, which is reflected in the ways in which workers can conduct themselves. *The Big Issue* has a code of conduct that sellers must sign, which makes clear that sellers cannot engage in any activities that look like, or may be associated with begging as well as outlining appropriate public behaviour (e.g. not being intoxicated whilst selling, not aggressively selling). Sellers are also restricted in their movements. They are assigned 'pitches'—particular corners or street locations—where they must stand and are not allowed to walk around the city and sell at the same time. Whilst the *Street Sheet* also has a code-of-conduct sellers sign, it is less concerned with distinguishing itself as a form of work, and more concerned with establishing stipulations surrounding appropriate public behaviour, such as, for instance, sellers not engaging in violent aggression or making sexual or bigoted remarks.

Many within *The Big Issue* organisation consider the creation of work for those who are excluded from the mainstream employment market, as a radically important act. For instance, talking with me about the establishment of *The Big Issue* in Melbourne, Peter outlines the fundamental premise of the organisation: the need for practices of empowerment that are not beholden to welfare organisations, and which provide genuine pathways for work that do not expect homeless people to compete in the highly unequal mainstream labour market. Peter says,

> *[Do you know that saying] 'Give a man a fish he eats for a day, teach a man to fish he eats for a lifetime'?. ... Well that's the biggest load of crap that was ever said by man. ... What we do is we teach people to fish and then say, but I own the river. And then we charge people to come down to the riverbank and we don't empower people. And what The Big Issue did was create a river only homeless people could fish in. For once they didn't have to fight people who were more educated, didn't have their substance issues etc. ... So by creating this—you could almost literally draw it on a footpath—this is your river to fish in and, you know what? Nobody else can fish here. This finally gave them a space where they had opportunity.*

In the case of *Street Sheet*, the work created is more ambiguous. As with many of the other North American homeless street presses, sellers are given the paper, and do not officially sell it, but ask for a donation. It is therefore not considered, officially, a work practice. This is important: as noted above, what legally protects US sellers in their request for donations is the First Amendment, which constitutionally prohibits laws that impede the freedom of speech, press and the right to peaceful assembly. For sellers, this effectively protects them against potential city laws that might suggest that they are panhandling, begging or loitering (which are often criminalised).

In selling the *Street Sheet*, therefore, sellers are exercising their rights in relation to the freedom of the press, and are officially not considered to be selling goods and services. At times, this First Amendment protection has some ambiguity and has been contested. In some cities, for instance, city officials have attempted to contest the legality of homeless street press (e.g. Garrison 2011). In the case of San Francisco, it does provide some protection in the context of a growing list of other infringements and codes that directly impact the homeless, such as laws against: loitering in the vicinity of ATMs; fighting in public; trespassing, aggressive pan handling; urinating and defecating in public; consuming alcoholic beverages in public; camping and or sleeping on a public street or park; and sitting or lying on a public sidewalk between the hours of 7am and 11pm (see http://sanfranciscopolice.org/public-interaction-homeless).

Despite these differences, homeless street press in all its varieties can be understood as a work practice. It is productive in the sense that it creates a goal-oriented activity that is personally—and increasingly socially and culturally valued. It is also productive in the sense that it produces an income stream from the sale of a commodity, albeit highly precarious and informal. In recent decades, a growing collection of research literature on informal economies in both the 'North' and 'South' highlights the complex practices of work and labour that are not captured by narrow definitions (see Sassen 1994; Gaber 1994; Turner and Schoenberger 2012). This scholarship points to the diversity of labouring practices that exist outside, or on the margins, of the regulatory framework of the state. The importance of the informal economy has particular significance from a global perspective, given that in some nations the vast majority of workers earn their livelihoods from within the informal economy (see Breman 2013).

Saskia Sassen's work on informal economies in the mid-1990s highlighted the presence and function of informal economies within advanced capitalist countries, such as England, Australia and the US. Challenging the perception of informality as an anomaly, she suggests that informal economic practices are not regulatory 'violations', but 'fractures', a "necessary outgrowth of advanced capitalism" (Sassen 1994: 2291). In other words, informality is a recurrent pattern *within* the regulated economy. This points to the incapability of formal regulations or narrow definitions to capture the full breadth of economic activity, particularly when so many are structurally excluded from participation.

Homeless people, for instance, have long been engaging in 'entrepreneurial' activities in the attempt to get by (e.g. Balkin 1992). More recently, a range of research has pointed to the complex intersections between informal and formal economic activity, as the excluded and poor struggle to make a living (e.g. Williams and Nadin 2010; Gowan 2010). In this understanding, economic activity—and associated work practices—are far more than simple market exchanges: they signify important social relations.

Homeless street presses are one form of work activity that sits on the 'margins of economic legitimacy' (Cockburn 2014). The magazines and papers are commodities, bought and sold on the market of the street. However, the work and exchange practices of the homeless street press indicate that this market is steeped in moral presumptions surrounding deservingness, worthiness and charity. The magazines and paper are never disentangled from the social goals of the organisation, and this is carried into the exchange moment between seller and buyer (Cockburn 2014). In other words, the value of the magazine is connected to sellers' experience of homelessness, and their demonstration (or performance) of helping themselves through being 'sellers', rather than perhaps beggars—a theme taken up in greater depth in Chap. 5.

Homeless street press is an economic practice involving both production and consumption. Homeless street press has created an exchange market that brings homeless street press sellers in contact with buyers through the purchase of the magazine or paper. Foundational to this, is the contemporary growth of ethical consumption as a form of social and/or political action. Contemporary homeless street press exist within a growing field of practice characterised by morally charged purchasing, in which individual buyers demonstrate their care for others or social causes through their purchase power (see Cabera and Williams 2014). Here, commodities are infused with worth beyond their utility, and are charged with meaning and purpose related to social good. Ethical consumption has become a kind of 'rationality' through which consumers make choices about commodity purchases. The contemporary market place is filled with ethical decision making: from fair trade, to free range eggs, sweatshop free clothes, organic produce and recycled paper. Such decisions are, as Barnett et al. (2005) note, imbued with complex judgements and practices of ethics, morality and the politics of responsibility.

Writing on an ad campaign run by transnational café company Starbucks called, 'It's not just what you're buying. It's what your buying into', Zizek (2009) describes this as a part of 'cultural capitalism'. Here, the company describes the value of its commodities in terms of fair trade ("good coffee karma") and the creation of the right atmosphere and comfortable space within Starbucks cafés. Zizek (2009: 53–54) contends:

> *The "cultural" surplus is here spelled out: the price is higher than elsewhere since what you are really buying is the "coffee ethic" which includes care for the environment, social responsibility towards the producers, plus a place where you yourself can participate in communal life...*

In other words, ethical consumption is as much to do with 'buying in' to a particular ideal as it is with the affective and moral dimensions of consumption. To participate in ethical consumption 'feels good': it is a purchase that validates a particular ethical stance and a way of living and, correspondingly, assists to produce the 'ethical' self. In this way the act of ethical commodity consumption is strongly framed by contemporary practices of self, in which citizen-consumers are positioned as individual social actors through their consumption choices (Barnett et al. 2005).

Importantly, ethical consumption relies upon a perceived social worth and need in the purchasing of products. This is particularly the case when ethical consumption is linked to entrepreneurial endeavours. Pictures of smiling coffee farmers, for instance, lend force to the overall 'message' and purpose of fair trade coffee. Similarly, the popular crowd-sourced microfinance website Kiva.org provides a platform for people from the 'South' to pitch their entrepreneurial ideas to potential lenders. As Roy (2010: 33) states, through these platforms, "The Third World poor woman is no longer a figure at a distance. She is now both visible and accessible." This is the contemporary deserving poor, brought to the ethical consumer, and available for judgement via their computers, tablets and phones. Roy suggests Kiva allows users to integrate their "conscientious practices with the techno-social rhythms of their daily lives." In such a market place of entrepreneurial philanthropy, the 'deserving' and 'working' poor must compete to demonstrate their worthiness for the adjudication of 'everyday' venture philanthropists (see Bajde 2013). This creates a particular consumer relationship, in which ethical decision-making occurs around the worth of a project *and* the worth of the person who is selling it.

Research on the motivations of buyers of *The Big Issue* indicates that purchase choice is largely tied to a desire to make a responsible and ethical consumption. Well above the perceived use-value of the magazine as something to read, buyers purchase *The Big Issue* first and foremost to help the homeless (Hibbert et al. 2005). Hibbert and colleagues found that the appearance and manner of sellers impact the choice whether or not to buy the magazine (ibid). This is a complicated and morally charged terrain. In Hibbert's study, buyers are more likely to buy magazines from sellers who look needy. Because the purchase was linked to helping the homeless, buyers want to feel that their purchase is validated in this pursuit and a key way for them to do this is to make judgements about sellers, either based on appearance or their manner. As is explored in this book this also has implications for the ways in which the work is lived and felt by the sellers. As Lindemann (2007: 42) suggests, "In selling the *Street Sheet*, sellers likely must perform homelessness in a way that is nonthreatening yet sufficiently 'homeless-looking' to elicit sympathy and donations." Work involves the careful management of appearances in order to cultivate the 'right' conditions for an exchange encounter (see Goffman 1959).

Ultimately, sellers are engaged in highly productive, yet precarious and relatively informal, forms of work connected to ethical consumption. Importantly, despite being formally 'unemployed' sellers are engaged in productive labour. Researching these forms of labour, therefore, sheds light on the multitude forms of work that occur within and on the margins of waged employment, as I consider in more detail in the Chap. 5.

Researching *The Big Issue* and *Street Sheet*

To end this chapter I draw on my research fieldwork to reflect on the organisational sites of this research: *The Big Issue* in Melbourne and London, and *Street Sheet* in San Francisco. In doing so, my aim is to tease open some of the complexities and diversity of homeless street press highlighted in this chapter.

Tucked behind a 158-year-old majestic gothic church in the city's north lies the unassuming Melbourne office of *The Big Issue*. This was the first street press office I visited. The space, demarcated by different rooms, is the base for the seller support and editorial offices. Sellers arrive to pick up magazines, or to chat with seller support staff in the front office, whilst editorial staff work in the next room, its walls pasted with posters of the magazine's front pages. It is a relatively rundown space, with creaky floorboards, and which has provided a rent-free basis for *The Big Issue*, thanks to the Wesley Church next door. Whilst I was there interviewing *The Big Issue* staff about their understanding of the purposes and practices of the magazine, it was clear that the space was used somewhat fluidly, as sellers came in and out—chatting with staff and collecting magazines (one seller, for instance, was also using the car park to park his car—which was also his home). Yet, at the same time, the different rooms clearly demarcated the spaces: seller support occurs over a counter whilst staff offices are in a different room.

The casual tenor of the Melbourne seller support office is fundamentally distinct from *The Big Issue* main office. Also based in Melbourne, the main office is located within a slick office building in the centre of the city decked out in white and glossy finish. As far as I could tell, the only sellers who regularly visit these offices are those who are part of the Women's Enterprise (a scheme to support women sellers with non-street-based work whereby they pack subscription postage) and those sellers who are selected to conduct school talks (a scheme designed for school classes to come and visit the offices and to learn about homelessness by hearing from a seller about their life experiences). The presence of this separate, and more corporate-style, main office reflects the positioning of *The Big Issue* as a social enterprise; as, in other words, a socially conscious business.

The politics and meaning of space were perhaps heightened for me when I travelled to San Francisco shortly after visiting the Melbourne offices. In San Francisco, the Coalition on Homelessness office is situated amidst the skid row of Tenderloin. On my many walks from the subway to the office, I passed through the fast-gentrifying Market Street into the Tenderloin, a small district packed with single occupancy housing and homeless services. The streets are lined with homeless and poor women and men passing the time walking through the streets, standing and chatting on street corners, sleeping and resting on old mattresses and on the curb. The office itself is marked by a fairly non-descript doorway with the Coalition's sign atop. It has a buzzer to be called up, but generally a "hello" gets you in.

The office is mostly open plan, with a couple of campaign and meeting rooms attached to the large shared office space. Workers and volunteers greet whoever comes up the stairs, and ask what they can help with. Whilst

I was there, most people appeared to either want assistance in dealing with state bureaucracies or the police or collect their free copies of the *Street Sheet*. On my first visit, I waited in a small waiting area in front of the shared desks—a few chairs against the wall. The office was buzzing: people on the phones, others chatting across the office, sellers coming in to collect their *Street Sheets*, people moving through. And whilst the waiting area was clearly distinct from the rest of the office, there was a fluidity in the space as people moved in and through as they pleased—regulars and friends clearly meeting up. The office itself is plastered with activist posters and stickers with political art and slogans: "people over profits", "fight the war at home: end homelessness", "no more homeless deaths", "house keys not handcuffs", "we are all San Franciscans", "how many people do you need to start a revolution? There are 15,000 homeless people in San Francisco: Is that enough?"

The difference between the London and San Francisco *Street Sheet* office is stark. The *Big Issue* London office in Vauxhall provides the primary point of distribution for sellers to buy magazines in London. The Vauxhall office consists of a large space painted white and empty apart from a small collection of functional chairs and tables. Seller support and distribution workers of *The Big Issue* are set back in a separate room and separated by a large counter. The walls are bare apart from a couple of *Big Issue* posters. One day, in London, I spent the day at the office seeing if there might be any sellers interested in being interviewed for the project. Throughout the day sellers came through the space, rarely stopping to sit down, using it simply to buy magazines.

These differences in space and place mark differences in practices and approaches of these homeless street presses. The physical space of the Coalition reflects the commitment to being an organisation of homeless people, with a focus on activism and campaign work. Many of the volunteers and workers at the Coalition on Homelessness were and are homeless. Indeed, at the time I was there, all of the staff involved in seller support and *Street Sheet* editorship and distribution were homeless and had sold the *Street Sheet* at one point or another. Distinctions, therefore, between staff and sellers were blurred. In contrast, *The Big Issue's* focus on creating a commodity with general interest—albeit embedded within a political concern for homelessness and a desire to highlight the voices of the homeless—makes for a more business-oriented space and approach to sellers. Sellers, in *The Big Issue* sense, are homeless people seeking employment. Subsequently, their offices have a more official feel and are separated out depending on function, such as in Melbourne where the main office reflects its organisational orientation towards the business model of social enterprise and in London where there are clear demarcations between sellers and *Big Issue* staff.

These differences of course count: these street presses have different ethos, city contexts and associated practices, all of which impact the experience of sellers. Yet, despite variances in activist, self-help and social enterprise approaches, homeless street press marks an important and growing informal economy, reflecting the diverse contemporary social and cultural understandings of the cause of, and solutions to, poverty, homelessness and unemployment. These street presses are common in their creation of an informal economy and work—a 'legitimate' income generation—for those marginalised from formal employment. As this book now turns to, the lives that this impacts most are the women and men across cities transnationally who wear their poverty and homelessness on their sleeve to try and generate income and sell homeless street press.

REFERENCES

Adrian, L. (1992). The World We Shall Win for Labor: Early Twentieth-Century Hobo Self-Publication. In J. P. Danky & W. A. Wiegand (Eds.), *Print Culture in a Diverse America*. Urbana/Chicago: University of Illinois Press.

Anderson, N. (1923). *The Hobo: The Sociology of the Homeless Man*. Chicago/Illinois: The University of Chicago Press.

Anonymous. (1970?). Untitled Editorial, *Spare Change*, Berkley: Telegraph Avenue Liberation Front, p. 1.

Anonymous. (192?). The Blanket Stiff. In The Hobo in Song and Poetry: The Most Complete Hobo Song Book Ever Issues, Containing All the Old Favourites, Cincinnati: The International Brotherhood Welfare Association (3).

Asbolt, A. (2013). *A Cultural History of the Radical Sixties in the San Francisco Bay Area*. New York: Taylor & Francis.

Attwood, B. (2000). Space and Time at Ramahyuck, Victoria, 1863–85. In P. Read (Ed.), *Settlement* (pp. 41–54). Cambridge: Cambridge University Press.

Bajde, D. (2013). Marketized Philanthropy: Kiva's Utopian Ideology of Entrepreneurial Philanthropy. *Marketing Theory, 13*(1), 3–18.

Balkin, S. (1992). Entrepreneurial Activities of Homeless Men. *Journal of Sociology and Social Welfare, 19*, 129–150.

Barnett, C., Cloke, P., Clarke, N., & Malpass, A. (2005). Consuming Ethics: Articulating the Subjects and Spaces of Ethical Consumption. *Antipode, 37*(1), 23–45.

Beckett, J. (1978). George Dutton's Country: Portrait of an Aboriginal Drover. *Aboriginal History, 2*(1), 2–31.
Beier, A. L., & Ocobock, P. (Eds.). (2008). *Cast Out: Vagrancy and Homelessness in Global and Historical Perspective*. Athens: Ohio University Press.
Breman, J. (2013). A Bogus Concept? *New Left Review, 84,* 130–138.
Cabera, S. A., & Williams, C. L. (2014). Consuming for the Social Good: Marketing, Consumer Capitalism, and the Possibilities of Ethical Consumption. *Critical Sociology, 40*(3), 349–367.
Carson, J. W., & Garcia, J. M. (1991, November). Editorial. *By No Means: Homeless View Points, A Monthly News and Opinion Magazine,* Fall No. 33, 4(3).
Cockburn, P. J. L. (2014). Street Papers, Work and Begging: 'Experimenting' at the Margins of Economic Legitimacy. *Journal of Cultural Economy, 7*(2), 145–160.
Cresswell, T. (1999). Embodiment, Power and the Politics of Mobility: The Case of Female Tramps and Hobos. *Transactions of the Institute of British Geographers, 24*(2), 175–192.
Cresswell, T. (2013). *The Tramp in America*. London: Reaktion Books.
DePastino, T. (2003). *Citizen Hobo: How a Century of Homelessness Shaped America*. Chicago/London: The University of Chicago Press.
Dotson, K. (2012). Triumphs of an Underdog. *Street Sheet,* p. 1.
Editorial. (1992, September 18–October 1). *The Big Issue.* No. 14, p. 1.
Ely, L. (1997). The Street Sheet. *The Street Sheet,* p. 3.
Fox, C. E. (1989). *Tales of an American Hobo*. Iowa: University of Iowa Press.
Fumerton, P. (2006). *Unsettled: The Culture of Mobility and the Working Poor in Early Modern England*. Chicago/London: The University of Chicago Press.
Gaber, J. (1994). Manhattan's 14th Street Sellers' Market: Informal Street Peddlers' Complementary Relationship with New York City's Economy. *Urban Anthropology and Studies of Cultural Systems and World Economic Development, 23*(4), 373–408.
Garrison, J. (2011, April 21). Nasville's Homeless Issues Paper Director Says Freedom of Press at Stake in Brentwood Battle. *The City Paper.* http://nashvillecitypaper.com/content/city-news/nashvilles-homeless-issues-paper-director-says-freedom-press-stake-brentwood-battl
Gerrard, J. (2017a). Welfare Rights, Self Help and Social Enterprise. *Journal of Sociology, 53*(1), 47–62.
Gerrard, J. (2017b). Interconnected Histories of Labour and Homelessness. *Labour History, 112,* 155–174.
Goffman, E. (1959). *The Presentation of Self in Everyday Life*. New York: Anchor Books.
Gowan, T. (2010). *Hobos, Hustlers and Backsliders: Homeless in San Francisco*. Minneapolis: University of Minnesota Press.

Green, N. F. (1998). Chicago's *Street Wise* at the Crossroads: A Case Study of a Newspaper to Empower the Homeless in the 1990s. In J. P. Danky & W. A. Wiagand (Eds.), *Print Culture in a Diverse America* (pp. 34–55). Urbana/Chicago. University of Illinois Press.
Greenstreet, R. (1995, August 27). How We Met; John Bird and Gordon Roddick. *The Independent.* http://www.independent.co.uk/arts-entertainment/how-we-met-john-bird-and-gordon-roddick-1598309.html. Accessed 5 Feb 2016.
Hall, J. (2010). Sisters of the Road? The Construction of Female Hobo Identity in the Autobiography of Ethel Lynn, Barbara Stark and "Box-Car" Bertha Thompson. *Women's Studies, 39*(3), 215–237.
Hibbert, S. A., Hogg, G., & Quinn, T. (2005). Social Entrepreneurship: Understanding Consumer Motives for Buying the Big Issue. *Journal of Consumer Behaviour, 4*(3), 159–172.
Higbie, F. (2003). *Indispensable Outcasts: Hobo Workers and Community in the American Midwest, 1880–1930.* Urbana: University of Illinois Press.
Hobsbawm, E. (1994). *Age of Extremes.* London: Abacus.
Howley, K. (2003). A Poverty of Voices: Street Papers as Communicative Democracy. *Journalism, 4*(3), 273–292.
IBWA. (n.d.). *The Hobo in Song and Poetry.* Cincinnati: International Brotherhood Welfare Association.
Lake, M. (1991). Historical Homes. *Australian Historical Studies, 24*(96), 46–54.
Lindemann, K. (2007). A Tough Sell: Stigma as Souvenir in the Contested Performances of San Francisco's Homeless *Street Sheet* Sellers. *Text and Performance Quarterly, 27*(1), 41–57.
McCarthy, P. (1977). Communication at Last. *The Tenderloin Times, 1*(1), 2.
Misalowski, D. (1986). On the Street. *Golden Gate: A Publication of the United States Mission, a Shelter for the Homeless, 1*(1), 1.
Nix, S. (1990). Newspaper Offers Itself as Tool Against Poverty, Homelessness. Reprinted from the San Francisco Chronicle in *The Milwaukee Journal,* March 4, 1990, p. 6.
Petrus, S., & Cohen, R. D. (2015). *New York and the American Folk Music Revival.* Oxford: Oxford University Press.
Please, P. (1996). Editorial. *The Big Issue, 1,* 12.
Reitman, B. (1982). *Sister of the Road: The Autobiography of Box Car Bertha, As Told to Dr. Ben L. Reitman.* Edinburgh/London/Oakland: AK Press/Nabat.
Rocco, P. (1986). Letter From the Editor, *Golden Gate: A Publication of the United States Mission, a Shelter for the Homeless, 1*(1), 2.
Roy, A. (2010). *Poverty Capital: Microfinance and the Making of Development.* London/New York: Routledge.
Sassen, S. (1994). The Informal Economy: Between New Developments and Old Regulations. *The Yale Law Journal, 103*(8), 2289–2304.

Swithinbank, T. (2001). *Coming Up From the Streets: The Story of The Big Issue*. London: Earthscan.
Teasdale, S. (2010). Models of Social Enterprise in the Homelessness Field. *Social Enterprise Journal, 6*(1), 23–34.
The Big Issue. (n.d.). About Us, http://www.bigissue.com/about-us. Accessed 16 Nov 2016.
Torck, D. (2001). Voices of Homeless People in Street Newspaper: A Cross-Cultural Exploration. *Discourse and Society, 12*(3), 371–392.
Troy, P. N. (1992). The Evolution of Government Housing Policy: The Case of NSW 1901-41. *Housing Studies, 7*(3), 216–233.
Turner, S., & Schoenberger, L. (2012). Street Seller Livelihoods and Everyday Politics in Hanoi, Vietnam: The Seeds of a Diverse Economy? *Urban Studies, 49*(5), 1027–1044.
Waters, R., & Hudson, W. (1998). The Tenderloin: What Makes a Neighbourhood. In J. Brookes, C. Carlsson, & N. J. Peters (Eds.), *Reclaiming San Francisco: History, Politics, Culture*. San Francisco: City Lights Books.
Williams, C. C., & Nadin, S. (2010). Rethinking the Commercialization of Everyday Life: A "Whole Economy" Perspective. *Foresight, 12*(6), 55–68.
Zizek, S. (2009). *First as Tragedy, Then as Farce*. London/New York: Verso.

CHAPTER 4

Time Is Money

Quoting Benjamin Franklin at length, Max Weber introduces *The Protestant Ethic and the Spirit of Capitalism*, with the reminder that "time is money" (1984: 48). Capitalism is temporal: it cultivates an orientation towards, and an understanding of, time framed by capital accrual. Time that is not fruitfully utilised for the purposes of accruing capital—idle time—is time wasted (*ibid.*). Homeless people have long been considered to be idle par excellence: figures of unproductivity and laziness evoking a sense of crisis and disquiet in a society in which to work is a symbol of moral worthiness and good citizenship (see Gerrard and Farrugia 2015). In his exploration of the figure of the US homeless, Todd DePastino notes that in each generation the appearance of the homeless—from the tramp to the hobo, the transient and migrant, and the more modern-day 'skid row bum'—"signalled a crisis of home that was always also one of nationhood and citizenship, race and gender" (2003: xix). The paradox of these evoked crises is (as noted in Chap. 3) that past and present the homeless are far from unproductive, and often engage in work that represent significant expansions in capital and industry (such as in railways and rural itinerant work), or in work on the edges of formal employment (e.g. Gerrard 2016; Gowan 2010; Higbie 1997).

Nevertheless, the fear of idleness—as a social phenomenon, and as represented specifically in homelessness—is intricately sutured to the modern practices of work and citizenship. Idleness appears to offer the dark mirror reflection of consumption and production, indicating that time is 'wasted'

© The Author(s) 2017
J. Gerrard, *Precarious Enterprise on the Margins*,
DOI 10.1057/978-1-137-59483-9_4

when not working, not producing, not consuming. E. P. Thompson's historical account of the relationship between industrial labour and the importance of clocks, watches and time highlights the ways in which 'work-discipline' under capitalism is based on social practices of time. He writes, echoing Franklin, "Time is now currency: it is not passed, but spent" (1967: 61). Within the current context of advanced capitalism characterised by intensive consumption and precarity, time is captured by contemporary iterations of entrepreneurialism. All time is "economically relevant time", as Kathi Weeks puts it, through the consumption of commodities (Weeks 2011). Work in other words, shapes our lives inside and outside of work, a fact that is more pronounced as distinctions blur between work and non-work time.

Time is also, as I have written about elsewhere and explore further in Chap. 6, made productive through the need to be constantly cultivating and learning the skills, dispositions, culture and character that relate to the potentiality and maintenance of employment (Gerrard 2014). This, I suggest, is the spilling out of work prerogatives through and in learning and educational imperatives, through continuous informal and formal work on the self (*ibid.*). In other words the moral taken-for-granted embrace of work intersects with a concurrent moral taken-for-granted embrace of education and learning: the 'learning ethic' (*ibid.*).

In this chapter, I start with an account of homeless street press work through exploring the everyday working conditions, routines and rituals: how time is spent when working as a seller—drawn significantly from sellers' own photography of a typical day's work. By starting with everyday routines, as documented by sellers themselves, this chapter aims to attend to the "inherent liveliness of social life and its time signatures", as Les Back puts it (2015: 821). The everyday exists in the here and now, and thus turns research focus towards the seemingly mundane, the rituals, the movement of people and things, space and place, moments of interaction, feelings, meanings and practices (Pink 2012). It is also, of course, fundamentally underpinned by material realities, and in the context of homeless street press this is the profound poverty that sellers live in the day-to-day; lived in and through modalities of gender, race, class, sexuality and disability.

Thus, this discussion touches on the material conditions of this work, including the money earned and time spent trying to sell homeless street press. The themes and experiences touched on in this chapter—the importance of being productive, of learning to work, of working in—and for—the public, and of aspirations for the future—are taken up in more details in the chapters that follow. Here in this chapter, however, I focus on examining the everyday temporal contours of working as a homeless street press seller, providing an introduction to these themes through an account of a typical day's work.

First, drawing on the interviews with sellers from all three cities, I explore the fundamental importance of engaging in work for sellers, including the everyday routines it creates. Work routines create a welcome relief from the boredom of unemployment by providing a means to keep busy and occupied. Yet, they also come with their challenges, with many sellers earning little returns for the hours spent on the street, as sellers also struggle to get by. Second, I turn to an exploration of a typical day's work, based on Melbourne sellers' photographs. In Melbourne, where I had more time and opportunity to build relationships with sellers, I invited sellers I had regular contact with to take photos of a 'typical day's work'. I gave sellers disposable cameras, and after processing the film we met and talked about the photos. Drawing on the photography and the discussion with sellers about these photos, this chapter sketches the routines of a typical days work, exploring the ways sellers pass, and organise, time in their attempts to make money and get by.

KEEPING BUSY, GETTING BY

It's a sunny day in Melbourne. It's 11 am and I am sitting with Jon on the steps outside a café in one of the city's main shopping malls. We sit huddled so that we can hear each other over the sound of the passing trams and the busker crooning on the other side of the road. Around us shoppers and city workers bustle past. This is the first time I formally interview Jon, having chatted with him a few times on my walks around the city. When I asked him if he wanted to be formally interviewed, he was quick to say yes, but wanted to make a time when he wasn't working. At this stage, I had had a few experiences of sellers doing this and then not turning up, so I wasn't sure if Jon would come. He had arrived early, with his dog in tow. I start, where I usually start in these first interviews, by asking Jon how long he has been selling *The Big Issue*. He answers,

> *Yeah—it's going onto 6 years that I've been selling The Big Issue for. I found it to be alright: it keeps my mind off other things, which I don't need my mind to be at. Yeah, I like The Big Issue. It gets me out of the house and it gets me to do something constructively, instead of just sitting around at home moping and thinking of what to do. Whereas working with The Big Issue I just get up in the morning, shower, get dressed, and I sort of look forward to going to work. Because I am my own boss—so to speak.*

And I get to meet different people, which is good also, because at home I wouldn't do that. And I haven't got many friends anyway, but friends that I do have are mainly Big Issue sellers and people who buy The Big Issue. I've got a couple of regulars, and I talk to them quite a lot.

It's kept me out of a lot of trouble over the years, since I've been working with The Big Issue. If another job came along I'd certainly take it. I'm not going to do The Big Issue for the rest of my life.

Jon's reference to *The Big Issue* work as keeping his mind off other things, and as providing a useful means to creating routines and social relationships, is a regular account I heard from sellers in Melbourne, London and San Francisco. For many, the opportunity to work, no matter how precarious, is a welcome relief from the monotony and boredom of unemployment and homelessness. This is, perhaps, unsurprising: in a society coiled so tightly around the cultural, social and economic importance of work, participation in work practices for those who have been previously been so profoundly excluded can signify important feelings of worthiness and value. Importantly, for Jon and other sellers, this is both about the feelings and the conditions it created—the affective and material dimensions of work—and the creation of everyday work routines, habits and relationships. For most, the opportunity to be a worker provides a powerful sense of self worth that is deeply interconnected with the opportunity to identify with work culture and carry out work routines.

Across diverse seller experiences there is a desire to do something, anything—to fill their days, with something that feels productive. When I ask Troy, seller of *Street Sheet* for ten years in San Francisco, why he first decided to become a seller, he replies:

Well I actually didn't know it [Street Sheet], you know. I just I came in [to the Coalition on Homelessness] one time because I needed some money, some bus fare and somebody told me that I could come up here to get some Street Sheets and sell them right away. And it worked out for me that day so I was just like, Okay, I'm a retired vet and I ain't got nothing to do during the day and I want to do something positive and stay out of trouble and keep busy during the day. So I decided that I wanted to come here and do this. Why do I do it daily on a daily basis is because I stay out of trouble. It keeps me positive. Plus I make money and I got all the things I need for my little house.

Like Jon, Troy found the routines of work helpful to 'stay out of trouble', 'keep busy' and stay 'positive'. Troy is fastidious about his work as a seller: five days a week he spends the good part of the day "walking for miles" around San Francisco. The trip into the city itself takes him an hour, as he rents a small room outside the city where the rents are more affordable.

Across the three cities, when sellers talk about the significance of their work, most often this is made in reference to past feelings of stultifying unproductivity. Being a seller is a means to carve out a productive life, and to move beyond and away from the uncomfortable feelings—and judgements—of being unproductive. When I ask Tonya, a 43-year-old seller in Melbourne, what she was doing before she started to be a seller she explains:

> *I was just bumming around with my boyfriend, just at home sitting around doing nothing. And then we saw other vendors, and they said, 'Why don't you come and do The Big Issue again, Neil?'. Coz he [my boyfriend] used to do it years ago. And he said, 'Yeah, Okay. I'll get my girlfriend to do it'. So then we got the number off them and we just rang them up.*

As I explore further in Chap. 5, becoming a seller is interlaced with an experience of unemployment, begging, for some homelessness, unemployability and a desire to do something—to cultivate the routines, feelings, and identity of being a worker. As Ben (Melbourne, 47 years old) says, "Well, I couldn't get a job anywhere else. And, I was homeless at the time. And, I thought I'd make money. Instead of bludging." Bludging—an Australian colloquialism for not doing anything, most often associated with judgements of laziness—is a word that comes up again and again in the Melbourne interviews.

The idea of doing nothing and being useless before being a seller emerged in the interviews across the three cities. When I ask Margo (37 years old) in London why she first started to be a seller, she answers:

> *We were outside on the streets and it's a bit of money isn't it. You're not signing on, you're not doing anything yeah.*
>
> Jessica: *And so were you begging before you were doing The Big Issue?*
> Margo: *What was I doing, what was I doing before? I was just getting by here and there.*

For sellers, work routines are incredibly important. Whilst the ability to be flexible in the hours that they work is important for many, the temporal practice of routine work is foundational. Stacey, a 33-year-old seller in Melbourne, put it this way: "Well because of my post-traumatic stress disorder, I've got to keep myself busy and keep active 'cause if I slow down and stop then it all builds up on me. But if I keep myself active and keep my mind concentrating on other things then it doesn't affect me.... Hence the seven days' work."

Sellers have incredibly varied work schedules. Some, like Stacey, work seven days a week, and many work 8- to 12-hour days. Others work more sporadically—when they feel like it, and only ever three to four hours at a time in order to manage their exhaustion. These diverse experiences all speak to the ways in which sellers engage in highly precarious entrepreneurial work. It is a work practice that relies upon sellers' entrepreneurialism: their individual dedication, self-management, aspiration to sell and perseverance.

Sellers' experiences of this vary also due to the different organisational approaches. As noted above, sellers of *The Big Issue* in both Melbourne and London are allocated pitches and cannot walk around to sell the magazines, or sell on unallocated pitches. Many are on a waiting list to be allocated a 'permanent pitch', which would give some structure and continuity to their work conditions. Until they have a permanent pitch, sellers have to ring up the office and find out which pitches are available for the day. Sellers of *Street Sheet* have far more relaxed conditions and can sell whichever way they want—walking, standing, sitting—as long as it is not aggressive and that it is not too close to banks.

On the one hand the flexibility of the street press model offers some important—and prized—affordances. It is a work practice open to anyone who wants to do it and requires no test or measure of ability. It also creates work in which sellers do not feel as if they are being closely monitored by an employer, and in which they can choose their hours. Yet, on the other hand, when combined with precarity and poverty this flexibility comes with financial insecurity, and highly individualised pressures of potential failure: failure to sell, and ultimately, failure to generate income. The notion of 'choice' and 'choosing' to work seems particularly thin when sellers' choices are driven by poverty and a material struggle to get by day-to-day.

Indeed, it is important to recognise the many sellers who work because the welfare they receive—across San Francisco, London and Melbourne— is simply not enough to get by. Overwhelmingly, sellers recount incredibly tight budgets, in which welfare payments have to be supplemented with other income. Conversations about money arise again and again: it is—along with physical safety—the most pressing concern on sellers' minds. This is perhaps unsurprising, given the significant existing international research that documents how unemployment benefits do not buttress against poverty and material deprivation (see Rodgers 2015; Morris and Wilson 2014; Murphy et al. 2011; Shildrick and Macdonald 2011). Many sellers in Melbourne, for instance, either receive job seeker allowance (unemployment benefits) and are actively looking for work or receive disability welfare payments which do not require them to work, but yet need further income in order to make ends meet. In almost every interview, sellers lament with urgency the pressing requirement to generate income and to manage their finances down to the last dollar: being poor is exhausting and consuming.

Another recurrent concern for sellers is the need for them to cultivate the disposition of perseverance, and patience, particularly in the face of precarious—and often bad—sales. When Melbourne seller Gabby (33 years old) tells me about having bad days when she does not want to work, I ask her what she does:

> *I think of not having any money, smokes, or food and I think, you know, I hate it, I don't want to do it. But then I think Okay, I can do this, I will do this. And I just try my best to get the negative energy away from me. And I just force myself to actually get up and go right—I gotta do it. I gotta do it, because no one else is going to do it for me.*
>
> *Jessica: And then once you are there at your pitch?*
> *Gabby: Once I am there it takes about half an hour to go 'Aghhhh! I wish I wasn't here!' But then once an hour kicks in and I make the money, then I'm like—see it's not too bad, it's better, its better, its better. And then I start getting positive and positive and positive. And then there are other days when it's so bad, but I am doing it and I hate it, and I am so depressed. And I am like—I wish I wasn't here! But its just perseverance! That's what it is. Perseverance.*

Gabby, whose experiences are explored further in Chap. 5, often struggles with low sales and some days only makes $20. As an entrepreneurial form of labour, which is also dependent on the judgement by the buyer that the seller is deserving (see Hibbert et al. 2005), many sellers struggle to translate hours on the street into much-needed income. Many have days where they only sell four magazines in six hours, whilst others boast that they sell ten in an hour. In my experience of being with sellers whilst they worked, I observed some sellers in which hour after hour are spent without sales, and others who are far more successful. The financially successful sellers appear to be those who are able to 'perform' for the public in ways that are welcoming and entertaining. Thus, the potential for sales is highly dependent on how sellers can perform themselves, and how the public (and potential buyers) receives them, as further explored in Chap. 7.

Sellers' experiences of the city space more broadly are mediated in and through their work practices. Gender, race and disability invariably count in the ways in which sellers navigate the city space and cultivate their work practices. For instance, by far the majority of sellers are men: this is a work practice that attracts men more than women. And for the women who do work, they are more (though not always) likely to sell in 'quiet' ways. Many of the women press their backs against shop walls, trying to take up the least amount of space possible, and sell by just holding out the magazine in front of them, not calling out. The contrast of this approach to the vivacious and commanding sales techniques of many of the men, who engage people passing by making jokes and offering compliments, is stark. When I ask Jan, a 48-year-old Melbourne seller, what her first day was like, she answers:

> *I don't know about the first day. I remember it wasn't easy—you know, you are standing out there and you are trying to sell a product. You have to be very patient. Look, sometimes you get new sellers and a couple of hours pass by and they don't sell anything and they get very frustrated, but you have to be patient. Having the patience is hard. Just getting used to that. Because I've had some sellers come up to me and say, 'Oh, you should approach people and ask if they want to buy the magazine.' But I am not comfortable doing that, and I think, I hope they [The Big Issue office] don't ask me to do that, because it's not something I'm comfortable with. But I have the freedom to do it whatever way I want to do.*

Disability also counts. One seller in Melbourne who is in a wheel chair talks to me about his frustration of being literally overlooked on busy street corners, being bumped and jostled as people walk hurriedly past. Both Matt and Adrian, Indigenous Australians, tell me about their fears that they might experience racism. Both have intense relief that they have not experienced overt racism, and now Adrian in particular takes pride in talking to buyers about his Aboriginal heritage and culture. To put it simply, the histories, material conditions, identities and experiences people carry with them mediate their expectations, aspirations and experiences of working as a seller.

These everyday work experiences are also framed by the individual histories and/or present experiences of homelessness. For some this involves rough sleeping—thinking of a plan throughout the day as to where they might sleep; or it may involve calling round to see if there's a couch or spare room available at friends and family; or it involves handling life at a boarding house or refuge—which often have stipulated hours of waking up, curfews and rules regarding drug and alcohol use; or it might involve managing the money for private rental rooms or their public housing flat. Across these experiences the ever-present potential of becoming homeless, or the traumatic past experience of being homeless, are never far from sellers'[4] thoughts. Homelessness is not just about living rough or houseless. It is also about the material and affective conditions of poverty, and the profound powerlessness over the conditions in which you live.

When I meet with Ben, for instance, on a Friday afternoon in Melbourne, the first thing he talks to me about is how his earnings are good, as it will mean he will be able to buy dinner in the evening. As I sit with him he pulls out the earnings that he has made so far, and counts it out with me. He had started the day with $30 in his pocket, and is now up to just under $90 following some good sales and a generous tip of $50 from a passer-by. These tips are by far the most coveted aspect of working as a seller, often making the difference between a bad day and a good day. After an hour of working at his pitch whilst I sit with him, he heads to buy some more magazines to get him through the last couple hours of work for the day. He gets me to look after his things as he walks up, but is nervous to do so as today he has all of his worldly possessions with him: a large canvas bag three quarters full, which, he tells me, contains a sleeping bag, blankets and his clothes. His TV, Ben explains, is in the car park at *The Big Issue* office.

I ask him why he is now sleeping rough, as he had been staying in a boarding house. He explains that the boarding house, which cost most of his pension money, had promised big breakfasts and dinners within the cost of the weekly rent. Having moved in he discovered that there was a cap of just one small bowl of cereal for breakfast. "Look at me!" he exclaims, "I'm a big guy! I need more than that, and besides, I don't eat lunch, so I need enough to get me through till dinner." After asking the boarding house staff if he could have two or three bowls to get him through the day, but being refused, he decided that it was better to sleep rough than spend his money on rent at a place that doesn't give him enough breakfast.

When I ask him how he feels about sleeping rough again, he replies, "It's fine, I've been doing it on and off since I was 10. I know lots of places. I've got my spots—I'll be fine. It's fine—you just roll out your sleeping bag and go to sleep!" He is, however, also in and out of hospital at the moment for asthma and I wonder and worry what sleeping rough will do for his health. When he comes back from getting more magazines, the sales are slow. He's so keen to sell that he accepts a sale from someone who doesn't have the full amount of money. Eventually, at around 8 pm, he calls it a day and treats himself to a dinner at a fast-food chain across the street.

As with Ben, across seller experiences is the overarching precarity of, and necessity for, income, which is tied to the potential to have agency and power with regards to housing, livelihood and health. Adrian, for instance, recounts how he overcame his fear of selling through the act of making sales and generating income. He says, "Yeah, three bucks, four, and five, and six. So—yeah ... I overcame that fear, which it was always hidden I suppose, it had been put there, and I just saw my life—but, then it became regular customers, starting talking, word got out, and a lot of people were coming." Even those who are confident of their sales always add a caveat acknowledging the insecurity of their income.

When I ask Al (41 years old), one of the more financially successful sellers, if he finds the insecurity of his income difficult, for instance, he replies:

I think it's very good, I've always done better than an hourly rate of pay, I believe. Cause what I do at the end of the day, I add up all my purchases plus the money I've got in my pocket, minus any money I might have had to start with and get cash out later and figure out how much that is per hour. And it's usually over twenty an hour, sometimes thirty an hour. But on a day like this it could drop to ten an hour. You never know... You never know.

Al is right that the minimum wage is just under $20 an hour in Australia. But his caveat, thrown in at the end, that it could get down to $10 an hour indicates that his potential earnings are often times aspirational rather than actual. Indeed, many times I see Al working he stresses about not making enough and hypothesises endlessly about the possible reasons for a lack of sales: weather, time of the year, time of the day, events in the city, economic downturns, the particular magazine cover of *The Big Issue*....

For some income insecurity means that they take a pragmatic day-to-day approach: working out how much they need for the day and working until they get that amount. For others, it is necessary not to think about aims. San Francisco seller Ray (in his 50s) explains to me,

You can't do it like, 'Oh I am going to get $40 a day because I have been here for eight hours and I get five dollars an hour.' You've got a take that all the way out of your mind. If you have that on your mind you are going to be very disappointed. ... You just don't worry about the money and you just approach it diligently. You'll make $20 or $40 if you know what you are doing.

Most sellers talk about the possibility that each day brings considerably different income. When I ask Margo in London if she gets a similar income from day to day, she replies:

> Oh no, no, no. Before, when I did it before it was kind of regular but now in the last few years you never know. One day it could be up, the next day it could be shit, the weekend could be brilliant and the next one's rubbish. It's totally different, no rhythm at all anymore.
>
> Jessica: What would be a bad day? How much would you sell in that day?
> Margo: Make a tenner the whole day.
> Jessica: That's not much.
> Margo: Over six hours. That's a six-hour day.
> Jessica: And a good day?
> Margo: Fifty.

However, £50 (or its currency equivalent) is a rare experience for most sellers. Like Margo, sellers live in perpetual hope of the possibility of and hope for these 'big' earnings, but live in reality on much less day-to-day.

A Day's Work

Sellers' photographs of a typical day's work are an incredibly useful and powerful means for sellers to visually document, and talk about, the everyday lived experiences of their work and the routines—and feelings—that characterised their working day. Thirteen Melbourne sellers took a disposable camera and agreed to document a 'typical day's work', which we then discussed at an interview once I processed the photos. The approach sellers took to documenting a day's work varied considerably. Some sellers took a photo of what they saw every hour or so from the pitch. Fran (49 years old), for instance, who is resolute about her work routines: working six days a week from 7 am, and often for 12 hours, documented the view from her pitch throughout the day. Her photos reveal a constant stream of people and Melbourne trams passing by as she sits at her pitch on an upturned crate waiting for sales. Other sellers took photos of their regular customers who they saw in the day, or over a few days. Smiling back in the photos that Al (41 years old) and Rachel (in her 50s) took, for instance, are the faces of people who bought the magazine—holding it proudly up for the camera—or workers who regularly pass their pitch beaming with a thumbs up.

Image 1 Rachel's photo

Many sellers venture into the city early in an attempt to capture the rush hour market. Standing at the entries to train stations, and outside towering office blocks, sellers are witnesses to the start of the city day. For some, such as 63-year-old Patricia, getting to the city before 7 am is partly about working the rush hour, and also about saving money as she can make use of the 'early bird' commuter discount on the train. Like all sellers Patricia counts every dollar and makes constant negotiations surrounding the use of her time and her work hours in order to maximise her small earnings. Andrew (47 years old) is also one of these early-rise sellers. For Andrew, a workday involves an early commute from his housing commission flat, as he is keen to try and make as much as he can in the morning.

Like Al, Andrew is one of the most financially successful sellers I meet in Melbourne: his sales technique is like a performance, calling out compliments to people as they pass and rhyming about topical city events or current affairs. From outward appearances, he seems by all accounts a vivacious and confident salesman. This is a brief account of Andrew's sales techniques one overcast and windy day in Melbourne from my field notes:

Andrew has positioned himself directly outside a major shop in Melbourne's main outdoor mall, and is calling out loudly. Somehow, amidst the loud city noises including the trams screeching past Andrew manages to command the space with his loud voice. His style reminds me of a fish or vegetable market: 'GET YOUR BIG ISSUE!', he calls out, "This magazine is really great; you can read it in your smoko break! GET YOUR BIG ISSUE!"

He doesn't stand still. He's bobbing from foot to foot, and is actively engaging everyone who walks past. He gets a lot of smiles and nods from people as they walk past.

An older woman comes to buy a magazine. It's a brief but seemingly pleasant exchange. I can't hear what they are saying, but they are both smiling and nodding at each other. As soon as she leaves he is back calling out, searching the faces of the people passing by for possible signs of a sale.

The mall brings a slow but steady stream of people past Andrew. He seems to target particular people walking down, and rhymes to them—often catching their look and exchanging smiles as they walk past.

A man sitting behind me tuts and turns to stare at Andrew. Andrew doesn't notice.

Another man stops to buy a magazine. Again, it's a quick exchange and Andrew gets back to calling out as soon as he is putting the money away in his pocket.

Talking about the photos he took, however, prompted Andrew to talk about a different dimension of his work. Yes—he likes being a 'larger than life' seller personality, but this is something that he has to manage. He describes to me the relatively quiet life he leads as he talks about the first few photos: photos of a coffee cup where he has breakfast and of the tram stop on his commute into work.

The photo that we rest on is one of a dark doorway in Melbourne. I return to this photo and Andrew's account of it in Chap. 7. This photo opens up an exchange between Andrew and I that may have otherwise been left aside: something that he sees as mundane, but necessary, in managing his working self. Andrew explains to me that it is in this doorway that he changes from himself and into his *Big Issue* self. Keen for his neighbours not to know that he is a *Big Issue* seller, Andrew waits until he gets

92　4　TIME IS MONEY

Image 2　Andrew—Superman doorway

to the city to transform into 'Big Issue man', as he describes it, putting on his *Big Issue*-branded vest and hat in the same dingy doorway in the city every morning. For Andrew, the movement (temporal, physical and affective) into work is one that involves a very distinct change: from Andrew to '*Big Issue* man'. These sorts of translations and transitions done in the movement in time and space from home to work, and in the workspace that is also the city-space are a part of the cultivation of everyday work routines and rituals.

Like Andrew, Stacey starts her day early. She lives in the outer suburbs of Melbourne where she can afford the rent. She had been living with her mum until that fell through, and then she was homeless—sleeping on the couches of friends and family day-to-day, whilst still working most days as a seller. Just now she's managed to find a place she can afford to rent with her boyfriend, and it takes her around an hour and a half to commute into the city. Her photos start also with her journeying into the city: with her on the train, passing time as the train makes its way into Melbourne's centre.

Talking to me about the photos, Stacey talks about the nervousness and excitement of coming into work. Stacey is new to being a seller—around three months in—and it is the first job she has really ever had, having tried and failed to get a job at a supermarket and the fast-food chain McDonalds. Stacey is also ever concerned about her own personal safety when working in the city. Both women and men talked to me often about this, but of course their experiences are undeniably shaped by gender and gender-based violence. Stacey, for instance, is concerned that her public work makes her more exposed to being tracked down by her ex-partner. Her concern is not naïve: this has already happened once leading to an assault in public.

At 33 she is one of the younger sellers that I meet. On this day she is on her way to *The Big Issue* seller meeting: a fortnightly morning tea in which sellers can receive the new edition hot off the press and find out the magazine's content and helpful selling tips. Once she's at her pitch, the first photo she takes is of her first $20—placing it next to her own $20 she had in her pocket when she started work that day. She grins at me when we pick out the photo, proud of her earnings.

As we go through the rest of her photos, documenting different times at her pitch and her breaks when she goes to grab a coffee from McDonalds, she reflects on the ups and downs of her work. She tells me that she recently had a day when she sold 50 magazines. This would be a total of around $150 for the day, which is just over a day's work on minimum wage in Australia. That day is by far her best day, it was a "happy day at work" she tells me. The day that we are talking about in her photos,

Image 3 Stacey—First $20 for the day

though, she only sells around 11 issues, which would have amounted to around $33. There is, literally, no way of knowing the earnings day-to-day, and like most other sellers, Stacey spends a lot of time thinking and talking about what she would like to earn, how much she has earned so far in the day, and what sorts of days make her happy or sad.

Stacey and I look at the photo where she has decided to knock off for the day. It's a 'selfie' picturing her sitting and smiling on the train back home. She explains that at three o'clock, having sold 11, she was too tired to keep working. She's concerned though that 11 simply is not enough, and so discusses how one of her plans to make more money is to refer people on to working as a seller. She gets ten free magazines for every person she refers to *The Big Issue*. I ask her how this strategy is going, and she admits that no one has taken up her referral so far, but she's hopeful.

The rhythm of everyday work circulates around the moment of sales. When working, sellers are constantly searching and hoping for sales, even those who are not actively calling out. Jan, for instance, is quiet seller. I first met her in Melbourne, but over the course of the year she moved to a regional town, taking her work as a *Big Issue* seller with her. We meet to talk about her photos, which show a sleepy town with a very slow stream of people passing by. She has tried to make herself as visible as possible making a big sign that says, '*Big Issue, Helping the Unemployed and Homeless*', and attaching it to the fence behind her. When I ask her how her sales are going, given how quiet the streets seem to be she replies, "Yeah a lot of people do just pass by and barely even notice me. Like I get the occasional person that will but it's just not busy. I don't know if it's because they go to Melbourne and they pick them up from Melbourne or somewhere else, because quite often I will get comments that they've been down to Melbourne and they've gotten *The Big Issue* in there." I ask Jan what she does when she has lots of people walking past and ignoring her, and she sighs,

> *Oh it can be a bit hard, like I don't like to annoy people by approaching them. I just pray and hope they notice me.*
>
> *Jessica: How does it make you feel?*
> *Jan: Oh I get disappointed. As a seller you want to be able to make good sales and people don't even notice you. It can get a bit frustrating, especially you get those days where it is busy: there's a lot of people around but it's like you're not standing out in the crowd.*

Matt's (38 years old) discussion of his photos also revolves around the bad-sales day that he was having. His photos show him in a series of positions at the four different pitches he had worked to over the course of his day. The photo series starts with a photo of the sun out, and him standing grinning holding the magazine up. Each photo is carefully choreographed. There's one of him peeking out from the bushes in the gardens behind his pitch, by the end of the day, there's a shot of him lying down with his hands in his head on a bench. Like Jan, Matt tries to make his pitch as visible as possible, displaying the magazine by propping copies up on the fence. He often brings a plastic chair to sit on, and a music player. He shows a photo of his pitch at an entry to a Melbourne train station and is clearly frustrated when he tells me that he only sold two magazines, whilst another seller around the corner sold 22. On this day, he works into the night. He tells me he doesn't remember when he finished, but that he wanted to make as much money as possible as he is trying to fix his car, which is also his home.

Sellers' routines are also framed by the different ways that they manage working in public on the city streets. This involves needing to know where the nearest toilets are and where the closest cheap coffee and food places

Image 4 Matt—Parliament Station pitch

are. For Jan, a photo of a park represented her lunchtime, where she sits and eats a sandwich she buys from the supermarket. However, for most of the sellers lunch is a luxury that they do not entertain; it is coffee that gets them through from breakfast to dinner. Tony (45 years old), for instance, tries to get through the day without having to buy lunch. He explains, as he shows me a picture of a pitch near a train station in Melbourne that this pitch is near a sandwich shop that gives away free sandwiches to the homeless at 4 pm. He tactically tries to get this pitch when he rings up *The Big Issue* offices in the morning to find out which spots are free for the day so that he can have some food in the afternoon.

Tony's first photo is a photo of the gambling venue 'TAB'—of which there are many in the city. As a recovering gambler, Tony struggles daily not to go in. He explains that on his walk into his pitch comes his first challenge of the day: not to gamble (which he described to me in an earlier interview as a good way to pass the time when there is nothing else to do). Like Matt, without a 'permanent' pitch Tony moves around throughout the day, depending on which pitches *The Big Issue* have available for him to work at.

As a *Big Issue* seller, Tony's navigation of the city requires, as I discuss further in Chap. 7, a constant awareness of how he is interpreted and understood. Now in a public housing flat, Tony is 45 years old and

Image 5 Tony—TAB

has worked as seller for nine years. Before that, when he was homeless and rough sleeping, then in transitional housing for three years, whilst he waited for a council flat for two years. He tells me he used to walk the streets picking up the butts of cigarettes so that he could roll a smoke. Now, he works when he needs to, managing his gambling habit, and holding aspirations of a better future. His last few photos of his typical day's work are of him arriving home to his flat: set in a towering concrete block of council flats. He shows me a photo of his dog, of him cleaning his flat, and of his desk with a pen and a book open. Tony had started university as a younger man to complete a law degree before getting sick in his third year. After that he worked as a ledger clerk, a community worker, in administration, at supermarkets and as a storeman (which he did alongside The *Big Issue* before he was let go just a few months before I met him).

Throughout all this time, Tony has harboured dreams of becoming a writer. In our first interview he talked about having not written for ages, and having writers block. Now, he explains he has started back at studying. I ask if this means he is thinking of going back to do a course, and he replies that he's just doing it himself—studying languages. He says, "I have always been okay at studying. I don't mean to brag, but I was always quite bright and able to cruise. But if you actually want to learn something you do have to self motivate yourself a little bit, even if you are at school." Tony's work as a seller, and self-education, highlights the profound problems of a welfare system that identifies particular forms of education and work as 'productive' and 'valuable', whilst others go unacknowledged and unvalued. Tony's labour and study, in other words, go unrecognised and are pushed to the periphery in a system that only recognises particular forms of work and education.

Tony and I go through the photos he has taken of the different pitches, of him buying more magazines from *The Big Issue* office once he has sold out of his stock, and we get to one of him on the tram home. He says:

> Here's my tram again on my way home.
>
> Jessica: I see you're wearing your [Big Issue] vest- Do you like wearing the uniform?
>
> Tony: I do like it sometimes. I used to take it off all the time when I wasn't at work. But now I wear it more even when I am just walking up the road—I used to take it off, but now I just leave it on.
>
> Jessica: Why has that changed?
>
> Tony: Because in the beginning I felt a bit snobby about it. Just the way people do seem to see people differently in uniform. It's just the little things. Like you go in to a café wearing a uniform and you say, 'Oh I'll have a long black', and they

always give it to you in a take away cup. Every time just about. If you take your uniform off you'll get it in a proper cup. I am not saying that for everyone, but with some people there is a little bit of a thing about it.
Jessica: How does that make you feel when it happens?
Tony: It doesn't make me angry now, I just roll my eyes and get used to it. Because it's just guaranteed: when I ask for a coffee they don't ask me if I want have here, or take away, it just always comes in a take away cup. [Laughs] It doesn't bother me. I am not afraid to go for a coffee in my uniform now. But I know it'll come in a take away cup! [Laughs].

Here, Tony's reflections indicate the sorts of navigations sellers must make in city space. Working as a homeless street press seller renders sellers recognisable as homeless and poor—particularly for *Big Issue* sellers, most of whom wear the brightly coloured vests. This is necessary for sales, but has the effect of cultivating particular judgements about them, which reinforces their feelings, and experiences of marginality and exclusion.

Like Tony, Oli (52 years old) doesn't have a permanent pitch, and moves around the city a lot. He prefers it this way. Unlike Andrew, he doesn't want to become a city 'character' or a big '*Big Issue* personality', and so prefers not to become too well known at a particular spot in the city. His photos start with a picture of a bank machine where he gets out money to buy his first magazines of the day. Like many other sellers I meet, Oli works on a very slim profit margin. Sellers often work in batches of magazines over the day in order to manage the risks of not selling all of them and being left with stock. Sellers have to buy the magazines out of their own pocket, and are not able to give back excess stock to the office. Working in batches involves sellers buying and selling what they can afford (sometimes this can be as low as one or two) and then racing back to *The Big Issue* office, or The Body Shop outlets where they can buy more. At times, when sellers are working from their financial bare bones, this involves racing from their pitch to buying magazines at least every hour, as they attempt to accrue earnings for the day.

Also like Tony, Oli has been to university—starting a degree in his younger years, which he had to abandon due to mental illness. He's worked doing administrative work in the public service, in factories, as a 'dish pig'—washing dishes in kitchens, and a bit of metalwork (his dad's trade), before becoming long-term unemployed and homeless. It's been at least 18 years since he's had a job as a factory hand, and at 52 he now describes himself as too "over the hill" to get employment. His background means that when he first started out as a seller, he was incredibly nervous and didn't think of it as a serious job. In our first interview, he tells me, "I was more or less sending it up. I thought this is not a serious job, you know, I was used to working in factories, and in the public service you know, working nine till five. ... but I just wanted to get paid, it was just to make money."

Now, a big part of the significance of *The Big Issue* work for Oli is a sense of identity and belonging. He explains:

> *The Big Issue gave me a sense of belonging into a company.... I knew that we were able to help the homeless, and I constantly am aware that I'm possibly potentially homeless myself. Like, the boarding house residence [where Oli lives] are classed as homeless by the government, even though we pay rent it's considered homeless—but, I was unemployed but not homeless. At one stage I was homeless, I got evicted from my house, I was unemployed but busking, and the landlord basically said I had to move out, so a friend put me up as an emergency, and I became aware that any moment in your life you can be—you can lose your home.*

The potentiality for homelessness, and the past experiences of homelessness, unsurprisingly pressed on sellers' minds. In many ways, this is exacerbated by the many hours spent on the city's streets, where they experience the everyday hustle and bustle of the city for hours on end and have contact with the city's many homeless.

Oli usually has enough money to buy two or three magazines each day, and that is all he is aiming to sell. This means that on an average day Oli makes around $9. When I ask him what time he usually starts, Oli replies that it could be anywhere between 8:30 am and 4 pm, depending on how he is feeling and what else he has on that day. Oli is a towering figure—a large, tall man—and has been a seller for around 13 years, and, unlike Tony, he still walks the streets of Melbourne 'rolling bumpers'—cigarettes from the butts of other cigarettes found on the street. He tells me that he knows that buyers "don't want us to smoke", they want us to be "all positive", but he is struggling to quit and that everyone has their vices.

When we meet to talk about the photos he has taken, he tells me that he has only worked one day so far in the week—Monday, and he sold one magazine in three hours before calling it a day. Showing me photo of another pitch, Oli reflects on the boredom of his work. He explains, "Yeah this is one of my regular pitches. It's often very boring, you know, looking at ... that's the sunshine; it's got the tree aspect to it. I hardly even notice the trees for the buildings. But that's an example of what I see. That's the ever-moving crowd walking around I am motionless, the street is moving around me." Here, the stretching out of time, as Oli wait for sales, collides with the sensation of immobility amidst movement. Patience and perseverance require time and they require commitment to standing or sitting at their pitches, whilst the rest of the city passes-by.

As we look through his photos, I note that there are a lot of photos of cafés. Oli laughs, "Yeah I do a lot of café hopping. Cafés are a big part of the job, I do lash out and buy the lattes because otherwise I feel that um—I need a break from being on the street and—that's the café where I'm off the street relaxing." He admits that this coffee habit, as he describes it, might not be so good for profits, as he often ends up spending all his earnings on coffees for the day. A big part of this for Oli is managing his discomfort of being in crowds in the city, something he loathes (and sometimes fears), but sees as a necessary evil of the job.

He shows me a photo of a women's dress store and explains that this is what he can see opposite his pitch, and that he's thinking "there's a person in there selling stuff inside, I'm selling stuff outside, everything's well and

Image 6 Oli—The view of trees from his pitch

good." Like Tony, however, Oli's movements around the city throughout the day are not trouble free. He shows me a photo of a major phone company store, just near his pitch. On a break he went inside to look at some phones as he is thinking of upgrading his phone and wanted to check out the computers. He quickly became aware, however, that his presence was not welcome:

> They said to me, "Excuse me would you like to buy something, are you buying something?" and I go, "Oh no, I'm just checking out the computer because I was interested in what the computer could do". And they sort of suggest to me that they didn't really want me to do that. This is the thing about vending and salesmen because we're all individuals and we all have certain judgements on people. I don't think you could just go up and say like "Can you not look at my magazines because they're not buying them!" I walked in off the street, the salesman's law was "No we don't want you in here" and so now I don't go in there to play with the computers.
>
> Jessica: What do you think about that?
> Oli: I think it's an outrage because sometimes I like to distract myself with what the street can offer. Well, maybe it's not an outrage, I agree with the guy, I was just more or less fiddling around with stuff. I think he thought I was a bit cheeky.

Oli's experiences reveal how sellers are both in the open, and open to, the city, whilst also facing moments and feelings of exclusion and denial. Connected to these exclusions is awareness that they are being judged for their apparent homelessness. Faced with cruel judgements and exclusions, Oli oscillates between outrage and acceptance, knowing that ultimately he is not welcome in shops if he cannot buy their products.

For Al, this doesn't bother him so much. He is an energetic salesman, who is happy to be associated with *The Big Issue*, and happy to be judged as homeless as long as it makes more sales. He also takes the entrepreneurial possibilities of *The Big Issue* work to its full extent. He has a permanent pitch, which means that he has to go there regularly in order to maintain it as his (if he misses too many days in a row, he might lose his permanency). He works voraciously. When talking with him about his photos he is less interested in the pictures he has taken and more absorbed about counting his earnings and projecting his potential earnings for the day. He tells me he is trying to work every day at the moment, as it's mid-November and the streets are filling with Christmas shoppers.

He tells me that he lives, sleeps and breathes selling *The Big Issue* and that often at home he writes notes to himself of good selling lines that he can use the next day, and makes them up in his head as he is travelling to work. His time is spent, in other words, productively in the service of his work. Al, like all good salespeople, has studied and understands his market. When I ask him if he finds it hard to get going in the mornings when he's working seven days a week, he replies that he doesn't, but he does find the early mornings difficult, so he only comes in at 7 am two times a week:

> *Only twice a week I offer that to the really early people, people who start at seven thirty or eight o'clock. And there are a few of those around. A lot of people come in their casual clothes, in their jeans and go for breakfast and then you see them about eight thirty and they walk past with their brief case and they've got the suit on. It's like a different person. But it's hard to catch them on their way to work, they're down to the last minute, they can't stop, especially if you haven't got change, they can't wait for you to get change. That's why it's good to catch them in their leisure time, even if that's early in the morning. I still believe there's more sales to be made later at night. So I believe I'm allowed to—I can let myself sleep in, start at ten or eleven like I did today and I will go through to seven, seven thirty, even eight o'clock tonight.*

For Al, his time on and off work rotates around the best selling time. The potential to be working anytime means that for Al he is constantly aware that he could be making more money; he could be working. This approach has meant that *The Big Issue* staff have insisted that he takes more breaks so that he does not burn out from the work.

Al attributes his current housing also to *The Big Issue*. It was the savings from his first two weeks of working as a seller ten years ago that meant he could move out of a family member's garage (who didn't know he was camping there because they were away) and into one of Melbourne's notorious boarding houses. He has now upgraded to a slightly better boarding house, which he describes as a kind of large motel room. He is proud of paying rent, and is keen to distinguish himself as someone who is acting responsibly, as opposed to the undeserving homeless. He says:

> *I know it sounds hypocritical because I am working for The Big Issue. But I am only in it for my own self interest, to be honest. I don't really care about those homeless people. I think that that's their problem, they want to look dirty, they*

want to look homeless because they get more donations. Not everyone, there are the exceptions, people who are genuine they've got nowhere to turn, no one who loves them, no family, no friends, and they don't know what to do. Them, I feel sorry for. But most of them have chosen a career out of being homeless. I am sorry to say it. And it sickens me. I actually think, what am I doing, why am I helping these fools!

Al is keen to distinguish himself as a responsible, entrepreneurial worker and the 'other' homeless, who let themselves be dirty, and make a 'career' out of being homeless. Here, homeless street press work sharpens lines of distinction between productive/unproductive, lazy/entrepreneurial, and deserving/undeserving—the long-held politics of poverty on the street.

Al's boarding house also drives him to work. He tells me that 3 out of the 60 residents work, and that he "goes mad" when spending a day staying home. *The Big Issue* therefore is both tied to his identity as an entrepreneurial worker who is not rough sleeping, and to the need to manage the conditions of living in a crowded boarding house. Al attributes his success to his hard work and perseverance: it is about all of the hours he has put into work over many years. In an earlier interview, Al describes his market as something that he has built himself, "Ten years of being in the same spot where you found me. People know where I am, and even if they are far away they know they can come down and buy a mag and say hello." Al projects an image of a self-made entrepreneurial worker. He has built up his business and customers, crafted his selling techniques, and the thought of work is never far from his mind. Watching him work, he is constantly moving. His gaze follows everyone who passes him, and he is enthusiastically friendly, saying hello to everyone. When sales are down, he is even more active and more earnest in his engagements with people passing by. On these days, he literally runs from his pitch to The Body Shop where he can buy magazines, not wanting to waste a single minute of possible earning time.

On one of these days when I am sitting by his pitch, he comes over to me every few minutes lamenting the lack of sales. "Only four in half an hour!" he exclaims. It's raining and it's cold, but Al is determined. He stands in his T-shirt, no umbrella, hair soaked with his *Big Issue* magazines in a plastic folder to stop them from getting wet. He calls out continuously, carefully surveying the space and watching for signs of possible buyers. I am struck by the way in which Al calculates and projects his work: tallying up the amount of magazines sold, working out the hourly rate of each day he works, constantly judging the success of his time working. This is, of course, what it is like to live in poverty—to continually fret about money. And Al's experience of this is now mediated by his identity and work as a *Big Issue* seller, an entrepreneur. He calls out into the rain, "Buy a magazine, I desperately need to sell it; I've sold nothing all hour; give me the power."

REFERENCES

Back, L. (2015). Why Everyday Life Matters: Class, Community and Making Life Liveable. *Sociology, 49*(5), 820–836.

DePastino, T. (2003). *Citizen Hobo: How a Century of Homelessness Shaped America*. Chicago/London: The University of Chicago Press.

Gerrard, J. (2014). All That is Solid Melts into Work: Self-Work, the 'Learning Ethic' and the Work Ethic. *The Sociological Review, 62*, 862–879.

Gerrard, J. (2016). The Interconnected Histories of Labour and Homelessness, *Labour History, 112*, 155–174.

Gerrard, J., & Farrugia, D. (2015). The 'Lamentable Sight' of Homelessness and the Society of the Spectacle. *Urban Studies, 52*(12), 2219–2233.

Gowan, T. (2010). *Hobos, Hustlers and Backslides: Homeless in San Francisco*. Minneapolis: University of Minnesota Press.

Hibbert, S. A., Hogg, G., & Quinn, T. (2005). Social Entrepreneurship: Understanding Consumer Motives for Buying The Big Issue. *Journal of Consumer Behaviour, 4*(3), 159–172.

Higbie, T. (1997). Indispensable Outcasts: Harvest Laborers in the Wheat Belt of the Middle West, 1890–1925. *Labor History, 38*(4), 393–412.

Morris, A., & Wilson, S. (2014). Struggling on the Newstart Unemployment Benefit in Australia: The Experience of a Neoliberal Form of Employment Assistance. *The Economic and Labour Relations Review, 25*(2), 202–221.

Murphy, J., Murphy, S., Chalmers, J., Martin, S., & Marston, G. (2011). *Half a Citizen: Life on Welfare in Australia*. Sydney: Allen & Unwin.

Pink, S. (2012). *Situating Everyday Life*. London: Sage Publications.

Rodgers, H. R., Jr. (2015). *American Poverty in a New Era of Reform* (2nd ed.). London/New York: Routledge.

Shildrick, T., & Macdonald, R. (2011). Biographies of Exclusion: Poor Work and Poor Transitions. *International Journal of Lifelong Education, 26*(5), 589–604.

Thompson, E. P. (1967). Time, Work-Discipline, and Industrial Capitalism. *Past & Present, 38*, 56–97.

Weber, M. (1984). *The Protestant Ethic and the Spirit of Capitalism*. London: Allen & Unwin.

Weeks, K. (2011). *The Problem with Work: Feminist, Marxist, Antiwork Politics, and Postwork Imaginaries*. Durham/London: Duke University Press.

CHAPTER 5

Being Productive: Working, Not Begging

This chapter explores the meanings, experiences, and identities that are cultivated in the work practices of selling homeless street press on the city streets of Melbourne, San Francisco and London. These experiences point to the many practices of productivity that occur on the margins, and the foundational importance of work for those who are excluded from formal or mainstream employment. This, I suggest, demonstrates the ways in which the contemporary dynamics of the work ethic operate, creating a sense of shame and frustration for those who cannot work, and thus the impetus to engage in productive work (see also Weeks 2011; Dunn 2010; Karabanow et al. 2010). A large part of this is the lived reality of unemployment, poverty and homelessness: the boredom, the feelings of shame for not working, and the constant worry about not having enough money.

Being 'productive'—albeit variously understood and enacted—underscored both the organisational purposes of the street press, and of the experiences and understandings of the sellers. This chapter outlines the varying ways in which sellers identified with being and feeling productive: doing something; doing anything. In these stories I trace the many experiences from begging into homeless street press work (and sometimes back to begging), and the lines of distinction sellers draw around themselves being deserving and undeserving, often supported by *The Big Issue* in Melbourne and London, though less so by the *Street Press* in San Francisco. Specifically, I address the differing practices and understandings of 'work' for the sellers, focusing on two core dimensions: first, the

© The Author(s) 2017
J. Gerrard, *Precarious Enterprise on the Margins*,
DOI 10.1057/978-1-137-59483-9_5

articulation of working in distinction from begging; second, the diverse identities and feelings of being a worker constructed by sellers in and through their engagement in the entrepreneurial work practices of selling homeless street press.

To do this, I start first with Gabby and Rob's experience of begging and homeless street press work. Reflecting on Rob and Gabby's accounts, I then consider the challenges posed by begging and homeless street press work to formalised and narrow understandings of work. Next, I explicate some of the tensions in distinguishing street press selling from begging, most particularly for *The Big Issue* organisation and its sellers. Finally, this chapter ends with an investigation into the experiences, meanings and feelings of entrepreneurial labour as a form of productivity for the sellers across the three cities.

Gabby and Rob

I first meet Rob and Gabby on a Melbourne street corner. Both in their mid-30s, Rob has the official bright red *Big Issue* vest on—provided for sellers to help make them visible and give them organisational legitimacy on busy city streets—and he and Gabby are crouched over a bag sorting through *Big Issue* magazines. I approach them and ask them if they want to talk to me about their experience as sellers, and they jump at the chance. As I listen back to the recording of this interview to write this, it pulls me back to this first interview: the three of us nestle together on a small ledge set just back from the busy and noisy street, the voice recorder balancing on top of my bag in-between us. Gabby and Rob start by leaning into the voice recorder, deliberately speaking to it in an attempt to make sure that what they say is recorded. As the interview progresses, they start to forget about it. Rob in particular jumps up from the ledge—standing, pacing and gesturing as he talks—more often than sitting.

Over the next year, I spend a lot of time with Rob and Gabby: if one of them is working, usually the other is also working somewhere else in the city, so after chatting with one, they would send me off to see the other. When I first met Rob and Gabby they had been selling *The Big Issue* for around two years and at the time they felt like this was their only option. Whilst by no means a universal experience, like many others their entry into selling homeless street press came from their experience of begging, or, to put it more specifically, their experience of the criminalisation of begging in Melbourne (as it is also in London and San Francisco).

I ask Rob and Gabby, "How did you first start selling *The Big Issue*?"; and Rob answers:

> Well I was begging for money, and I was just getting into trouble so many times with the police for begging, so it was either that, or keep begging and keep getting locked up...
>
> Jessica: And you had that happen to you?
> Rob: Yep—I got locked up for eight days. And then after that, I thought, 'Nup—I am not doing it.' So I went to The Big Issue and signed up.
> Jessica: Did you know anyone who was doing The Big Issue at that time?
> Rob: No, the police recommended it to me. They said, 'You know, you'd be better off going to The Big Issue, because that way it's legal and you're allowed to do it, and you won't get caught begging anymore.'
> Jessica: And how about you Gabby?
> Gabby: Yeah, basically I was begging as well, and the cops kept pulling me up, arresting me, telling me that if I don't stop begging it's going to be longer and longer. I was locked up for four days. And then I was locked up for eight days and then I said, 'Nup! Enough is enough'. And I did know people in The Big Issue, and they explained it to me: it's legal, it's less hassle, and the cops can't touch you. So even though the cops were saying it and I thought nup, but I had friend in there, so I thought, Okay I'll do it.

For Gabby and Rob, the tension between working as a seller and their life on the street as homeless beggars is constant. They have both received reprimands from *The Big Issue* for attempting to sell the magazine in ways that are too close to begging. Gabby, for instance, has a tendency to call out, "C'mon! I need the money!" in the attempt to drum up sales, rather than the more organisationally approved, "Get *The Big Issue*! Help the homeless and long term unemployed!" In both Melbourne and London, *The Big Issue* requires sellers to sign a seller code of conduct in which sellers agree (among other things) not to beg on their pitch, and this includes encouraging buyers to give money rather than buy the magazine.

Difficulties also arise for Rob and Gabby because their friendships with other beggars mediate their experiences as *Big Issue* sellers. In this first interview, Gabby and Rob talk a lot about their fellow 'street friends'—those who are begging around Melbourne—and how they see these friends as their community, more than other *Big issue* sellers. They keep to themselves and do not go to the fortnightly *Big Issue* meetings.

In my second interview with just Rob, he talks at length about how he and other 'street people' (homeless beggars) do not like another seller Fran because of the ways she treats beggars. He says:

> *The funny thing is that every street person in the city hates Fran.*
>
> *Jessica: Really!?*
> *Rob: They can't stand her!*
> *Jessica: How come?*
> *Rob: Oh—if I'm here, a bloke could be begging say right over there and if he was begging over there, she'd walk all the way over there and say—'Can you fuck off now!? Get out of there or I'll call the police'. [...] She won't have anyone on her entire block—she'll walk around and make sure. So people have been saying to me—'You go there, you go there, you're the only one that doesn't pick on beggars, we can get along with you'. Because I don't give a shit. If people want to give them money, give them money. It's up to them. And I have people coming up to me and say, 'Oh I've given him five bucks so I might as well buy a magazine off you'. So it doesn't bother me.*

Later, however, Rob's view of beggars changes. For a few months whenever I see Rob and Gabby, they seem to be more obviously struggling. They are often stressing about making enough money, and are keen to be working as much as possible to get sales. This is, however, something of an elusive goal. Gabby and Rob often talk about only making somewhere between four and ten sales a day each, which equates to $12–$30 for a day's work. In my third taped interview with Rob I ask him if he'd ever go back to begging. He answers:

> *No. I would if I had no choice and they kicked me out of The Big Issue—no I still couldn't do it, not any more.*
>
> *Jessica: How come?*
> *Rob: I don't know. I just have different values, beliefs and dignity now.*
> *Jessica: What do you think are the different values between the different types of work?*
> *Rob: Hmm, I mean I don't have anything against people that beg, that's their choice, that's their only means of work for them. The main difference is they don't want to. Plain and simple they don't want to, they don't want to work as a Big Issue person. I know them, a lot of beggars, I've spoken to them and told them to do The Big Issue, and they say, "Nah, I get more money" and*

I go "But you get into trouble," and they go "We don't care." I understand because I used to say "I don't care." It took me six months to be convinced to do The Big Issue.

One day, around the time of this third formal interview, I meet Rob on his pitch—one of the busiest in Melbourne. With the passing pedestrian traffic, Rob is forced to stand with his back flush up against the glass shop front. There is just enough room for him to carefully hold out a few copies of *The Big Issue* in front of him and not get jostled by the dozens of people who zip around him at any given moment. He tells me that he's tired. He tells me he almost fell asleep on his feet at his pitch the other day. With his eyes locked with mine, he tells me that he needs the money, he is worried that he is not going to make enough for the day as it's 2 pm and he has only sold four so far.

As I arrived, I noticed that a police officer was chatting to him. I ask him about it and he explains:

> *They said to me, since you've done The Big Issue you two [Gabby and himself] have been fine. And I said I know, because we don't need to do anything else, because we used to be begging everyday and fighting with them all the time. But ever since I've done The Big Issue I don't get bothered at all. They're happy that we're doing The Big Issue. They go—we don't have to worry about you anymore. Whereas dickheads who keep begging, keep screwing it up for everyone else!*

When I ask Rob if he thinks other beggars should be *Big Issue* sellers too, he quickly retorts,

> *Yeah. They should make it compulsory! If you're begging too many times, you get locked up in jail. When I was doing it they would give you 2 chances and then you got locked up for four days and then another four days and then two months in jail! So—why not go back to that? It'd force guys to do it.*
>
> *Jessica: You say that even though you used to do begging?*
> *Rob: Yeah.*

For Gabby, the distinctions between selling and begging also became more profound. One interview she and I sit in a busy food hall in the centre of the city. Her arms are outstretched over the plastic table and she leans in towards me, talking to me about the difficulty of working in public on the street as a homeless street press seller—something I explore further in Chap. 7, but also of her confidence building. I ask her if she also needed confidence to beg, she replies:

> Of course you need a lot of confidence and you need to be able to switch off. There's nothing different between the two, but you've just got to be, I don't know, you've just got to take the plunge and go, "No I don't want to beg, I don't want to get money for nothing". Everyone has a right to do what they want, but I'm telling you, I just think, I'm sorry, begging is wrong, totally wrong.
>
> Jessica: Even though you used to do it?
> Gabby: Even though I used to do it. Absolutely, it is not right. And looking back now, yes I did it and I'm not proud of it. But I got another chance to do something else. So why would you want to sit there and just, the people, just give you money, why? It's wrong. It's not right. I don't know, that's my opinion, I don't dis them, I respect and understand them but if I didn't do The Big Issue, I wouldn't do it. I would do nothing; I would rather do nothing. [...] I would figure out other things to do.

Working on the Margins

Across the two other cities sellers echo Gabby and Rob's shifting judgements surrounding the distinction between begging and working. In London and San Francisco, as in Melbourne, begging is illegal and strongly frames the experiences of working for sellers. In the context of the criminalisation of begging selling magazines and newspapers becomes a legitimate means to generate income. It also, as Rob and Gabby's experiences point to, cultivates very different understandings of self-as-worker as distinct from self-as-beggar. Working as a seller even for the more activist and less work-focused *Street Sheet* (as I explore below) still creates lines of distinction between begging in ways that demarcates homeless street press work as 'productive' and begging as 'unproductive' labour. This is exacerbated when sellers feel they must compete with beggars for income generation, seeing each other as contesting for the public's purse. Here, lines of distinction between deserving and underserving, productive and unproductive, become pronounced and encouraged by the overarching lack of income and the daily grind of poverty.

Rob and Gabby's experience of moving from begging and into work as a homeless street press seller, raise a range of questions surrounding the nature of work and the presumptions surrounding what is work in contemporary society. The question of what is work, and of distinguishing homeless street press work from begging or panhandling, arose in a variety of ways in the project. As I go on to explore below, sellers variously understood their work, ranging from 'legitimate' and 'dignified' begging to fully fledged entrepreneurial self-employment. The distinctions made between work and begging are supported to varying degrees by the homeless street press organisations, with *The Big Issue* declaring selling as work far more assuredly than the more activist approach of the *Street Sheet*. Indeed, in London sellers have the phrase "working, not begging" on their badges. Despite these organisational differences, across the three cities the legal legitimacy of selling homeless street press—as opposed to begging—does indicate differences in the practice of selling; differences lived and felt by sellers. Most particularly, the closer proximity of homeless street press selling to work meant that these practices are invariably framed by contemporary understandings of productivity, and worthiness.

Writing in post-depression London and Paris, George Orwell (1975: 153–54) prods and pokes at the distinctions between work and begging:

> *It is worth saying something about the social position of beggars, for when one has consorted with them, and found that they are ordinary human beings, one cannot help being struck by the curious attitude that society takes towards them. People seem to feel that there is some essential difference between beggars and ordinary 'working' men. They are a race apart—outcasts, like criminals and prostitutes. Working men 'work', beggars do not 'work'; they are parasites, worthless in their very nature. It is taken for granted that a beggar does not 'earn' his living, as a bricklayer or a literary critic 'earns' his. He is a mere social excrescence, tolerated because we live in a humane age, but essentially despicable.*
>
> *Yet if one looks closely one sees that there is no ESSENTIAL difference between a beggar's livelihood and that of numberless respectable people. Beggars do not work, it is said; but, then, what is WORK? A navvy works by swinging a pick. An accountant works by adding up figures. A beggar works by standing out of doors in all weathers and getting varicose veins, chronic bronchitis, etc. It is a trade like any other; quite useless, of course- but, then, many reputable trades are quite useless.*

Orwell's provocations raise the question, what are the *essential* differences between a beggar and a worker? A beggar, Orwell reflects, is considered a "social excrescence, tolerated because we live in a humane age, but essentially despicable", judged as such because they do not earn their living (1975: 154). Formal and strict sociological categorisations of 'work' and 'productivity' do little to capture the ways in which the unemployed, the poor and the homeless engage in a range of activities that are far from idle.

Orwell provokes a critique of the assumptions that underpin moral judgements of deservingness, productivity and value when begging is a form of income generation, Orwell suggests, just like any other (*ibid.*). Thus, there is a need to mobilise a wider understanding of work practices that recognises the informal economies created on the margins, such as the work of homeless street press sellers, and which accounts for the complex drive to employment and productive work on those margins. This requires, as Orwell suggests, a need to reconsider the everyday contours of seemingly 'unproductive' lives, and critically approach taken-for-granted distinctions between workers and non-workers. This also requires considering the significance of the work carried out on the seeming 'margins' of society and of mainstream employment markets.

Indeed, at a time of rising under-employment, and requirements to engage in work or to demonstrate activities undertaken in the search of work whilst unemployed, the lines between 'productive' and 'unproductive' work are blurred. There is a set of new social imperatives surrounding the relationship of work practices to learning and self-development, cultivated by notions of individual responsibility and governmental requirements for learning and earning activities for job seekers (see Adkins 2017; Gerrard 2014). As governments make dole payments conditional on participation in work, work-seeking and education programmes, work and education become tied together as performances and practices of a deserving and productive citizenship (Gerrard 2014). In other words, the presumption of 'unproductivity' in the lives of the unemployed is problematised by the new imperatives for job seekers to engage in work and educational schemes (Adkins 2017). Adkins writes that in the demands for the unemployed to engage in workfare, training, counselling, cv-building sessions and so on, unemployment has become "a highly eventful state" (2012: 635). In addition, as noted in Chap. 3, the existence of informal economies troubles the notion of the idle unemployed, or the idle homeless, many of whom are engaged in a range of activities necessary for getting by (e.g. Balkin 1992; Williams and Nadin 2010; Cockburn 2014; Gaber 1994).

Moreover, Kathi Weeks notes that formal waged work is not only central to the lives of those whose day-to-day existence is structured by its cultural, economic, and social demands. In our society, in which formal work forms the basis for so much of our taken-for-granted routines and expectations, work is also fundamental for those who do not work. Importantly, this is both about the intense feelings of failure and lack for those who do not engage in paid work, and about the many activities the unemployed do in an attempt to alleviate their unemployment.

Unemployment, therefore, is not 'bare space' characterised by emptiness. Rather, unemployment is a core site of productivity, of labour and of capital (see Adkins 2017). This insight is in part driven by a need to understand work and labour as multifarious under capitalism—including, for instance, the many forms of unpaid labour that are central to—rather than peripheral to—social and economic relations. Feminist contributions to labour studies are particularly helpful here in offering a more expansive approach to understanding the practices of work (see Glucksmann 1995). This involves recognising, on the one hand, that waged work creates inclusions and exclusions with profound impact and that, on the other hand, this waged work does not constitute the full extent of labour practices occurring within capitalism. As Hannah Arendt so lucidly observes (1998), reproductive and 'uncounted' or hidden labour is not only central to the relations of production; it also reflects and creates social and cultural norms, roles, presumptions and practices of power. In this expansive view, begging and selling homeless street press can be understood as a form of labour—that is not set apart from formal employment to wage relations, but entirely dependent on and related to it.

Thus, there are two core contemporary trends that are foundational to the ways in which work is practised and understood that underpin the experiences of homeless street press sellers. First, as mentioned, is the rise of workfare and the requirement that the unemployed to actively engage in work, or work-seeking activities. Here, individuals become responsible for demonstrating and performing their engagement with work-related 'self work', including education and training, in order to maintain welfare payments (see Gerrard 2015). This has created a kind of 'learning ethic', operating in conjunction with the 'work ethic', which I explore further in Chap. 6 (see also Gerrard 2014). In the contemporary context, the 'workfare' activities required of jobseekers, and more voluntary activities such as begging and homeless street press selling, muddy neat divisions between the employed and unemployed. This is not to say that there are no differences between the employed and unemployed. As Denning states, "Under capitalism, the only thing worse than being exploited is not being exploited", and 'wageless life' is a core dimension to this (2010: 76). Rather, it is to suggest that unemployment is not the useless off-cut of employment, and to recognise the overlapping practices of formal and informal economies. 'Wageless life' is not devoid of productive activity, and it is central to the broader organisation of economic and social relations (Denning 2010).

Second, and relatedly, is the ballooning of the 'shadow employment market' and the accompanying contemporary figure of the good worker as the entrepreneurial worker. Currently, labour markets are experiencing widespread transformations: from the growth of precarious 'zero-contract' hour work, to the emergence of what has been dubbed 'bogus self-employment': a field of work in which people are dubbed self-employed entrepreneurs, but for whom work is highly precarious and underpaid (see Williams and Nadin 2010: 202). Moreover, the rise of entrepreneurialism has reinforced the notion that work can and should be an authentic reflection of self, which involves fully giving over oneself, and which is connected to continuous striving and self-development (see du Gay 1996; Kelly 2013; Scharff 2016).

Both of these trends ultimately cultivate highly precarious work cultures, in which the employed and unemployed are encouraged to put their 'full selves' into obtaining and maintaining work, and in which they must constantly be engaging in self-development and education in order to ensure employability. As explored in Chap. 3, in different ways this was supported by the purposes and practices of the three different homeless street press organisations. Staff at these organisations spoke passionately about their commitment to street press as a means to bring productivity and activity to homeless people's lives, though their definitions and understandings of this were distinct. Most particularly for *The Big Issue*, there was a kind of 'recuperative' impulse in the organisational hopes: to at the very least provide a source of productivity that is denied to those who are excluded from work, and to encourage sellers to 'help themselves'.

Thus, there is a need to avoid narrow understandings of supposedly 'idle', 'unproductive' or 'wageless' lives. Of course, many of these trends are not categorically 'new'. Contemporary scholarship has a penchant for emphasising and demarcating the 'newness' of precarity, entrepreneurialism and insecurity, but these experiences are more usefully understood as a new iteration of a tendency within capitalism to cultivate highly precarious forms of work: in other words, as a 'new' particular historical iteration. Whilst contemporary 'workfare' policies and practices are linked to the political project and practice of neoliberalism (see Jessop 2013), the fear of idleness has long prompted government intervention into the lives of the homeless and unemployed (see Shildrick et al. 2012; Field 2013; Gerrard 2017). Moreover, there are complex interrelations between the concern of idleness and unemployment and the concern surrounding homelessness and destitution (see Gerrard 2017). Homelessness is often perceived as the representation par excellence of idleness, and thus has—and continues to—prompt work-based initiatives in response.

It is important to understand homeless street press in this context. Whilst it is clearly a specific response to homelessness (as discussed in Chap. 3), it is also shaping, and has been shaped by, broader trends in employment. When work is so central to the ways in which society is organised, and the sorts of relationships, identities and meanings, created about ourselves and others, the emergence of homeless street press as a form of marginalised work raises important questions surrounding the form and function of work in contemporary society. Whilst undeniably homeless street press has a range of purposes and intents (including for instance raising the public profile and understanding of homelessness), through the literal creation of a commodity, and with this a legitimate (and legal) exchange market—it effectively creates a new form of work and productivity for those otherwise excluded from employment.

DISTINGUISHING (MARGINALISED) WORK: NOT BEGGING

Most particularly for *The Big Issue*, the distinction of selling as work is a paramount organisational focus. The organisational motto 'a hand up, not a hand out' is strongly framed by a notion of helping sellers to help themselves and offering pathways into employment—an intention examined further in the final chapter of this book. As a transnational organisation *The Big Issue* places strong emphasis on selling as work: it is, as noted above, considered working, not begging. For Rob and Gabby in Melbourne, the distinctions are drawn by *The Big Issue* around the ways in which they try to sell the magazines, as they were chastised for overly aggressive sales techniques that emphasised their need for the money, rather than the value of the commodity that they are attempting to sell: the magazine.

In the case of London, this means that in addition to being banned from begging on their pitch, sellers must also refrain from sitting or lying down, as these behaviours may be "associated with begging". As well as stating that sellers will not consume alcohol or drugs, be aggressive, look after children under the age of 16, or "behave in any manner likely to bring *The Big Issue* into disrepute", the London *The Big Issue* code of conduct states that sellers will not:

> *Beg or busk whilst wearing The Big Issue badge/uniform or holding a copy of The Big Issue magazine.*
>
> *Sell in any way associated with begging, including sitting or lying down, or using a cup or bowl to collect money*

Whilst in London a number of sellers I spoke with mentioned a new rule that had been recently been put in place, stipulating that sellers must sell 35 magazines a week in order to maintain a 'permanent pitch'. Permanent pitches, as already noted, are much sought-after by sellers, as it means that they have some security over where they work, and some opportunity to establish regular customers and social relationships, in an otherwise volatile and precarious employment context and space.

In London, when I interview Anna, one of the key seller support staff members within *The Big Issue*, it emerges that this ruling is about securing the financial viability of *The Big Issue* and ensuring that sellers are working, not begging:

> Jessica: *The sellers mentioned something about a thirty-five minimum sale, is that right?*
>
> Anna: *That's correct. You need to sell thirty-five magazines a week now to get a pitch. And recently we've said you need to sell thirty-five magazines to get a permanent batch a week. Which is seven magazines if you work a five-day week: seven magazines a day. So that's one an hour if you work a seven hour working day.*
>
> Jessica: *And what's the purpose of that?*
>
> Anna: *... Really it's for the vendors themselves. Because we don't feel that somebody having a good pitch and selling twenty magazines a week is good enough. For the vendor or ourselves. And what I mean by good enough is the fact that we're a company that relies on sales. So if we don't sell magazines, we have stopped trading, or the price of the magazine gets very, very expensive. So we need to sell a certain amount of magazines to operate.*
>
> *We are an alternative to begging. Lots of vendors will—the magazine is two pound fifty to the public. I've lost count the amount of times that a vendor will come in and say—'Yeah I sold five magazines today and made a hundred pounds.' Well that's great for the vendor but it's actually useless for us. So we have to force somebody to help themselves. They need to sell a certain amount of magazines otherwise it's holding a label—'Poor me, give me some money'.*

That's not the idea. The idea is to sell a product and to have some sort of pride in what you're doing. Because otherwise it's just a form of begging. And I don't think we should exist if we are going to do that. I think we should just let people beg if you're going to do that. So it's really about making people do it properly And it's for the interest of the company because we need to sell the magazines.

Anna expresses concern that sellers are effectively begging on their pitches by encouraging customers to 'give tips' rather than buy the magazine: to give sellers money without actually taking a copy of *The Big Issue*. When talking with Anna, I was struck by the tensions surrounding the business model of *The Big Issue*. Sellers making money without actually selling the magazines poses a challenge to the need for *The Big Issue* to be a self-sustaining business, reliant on its sales. The organisational model relies upon sellers diligently and devotedly selling the magazines—and putting this before the potential to 'beg' or get extra 'tips' from customers. They can 'use' their homelessness as a means to promote the commodity, but not as a means to overly-promote their need for money in ways that could be interpreted as begging. When they do the organisation feels that they have to, in Anna's words, "force somebody to help themselves" .

Many London sellers mention the difficulty of not being able to sit down whilst on shift, and many felt that the new 35-magazine-sale rule exacerbated their working conditions. Sellers openly rely on 'tips' from their customers to get by. When I ask Dale, a 46-year-old seller of three years, how many sales he is aiming for in a day, he answers:

Well at the moment I could be selling five in an evening rush hour. The amount of cash that I get on top in tips makes it worth it, but if I didn't get any tips I wouldn't even bother. I would probably go and beg or look for some other type of work. At the moment we've got this minimum quota where we have to sell thirty-five a week otherwise we're going to lose our badge. Well to me that's just slave labour because, you know, we're self-employed right? And if I go out and tried to sell more than thirty-five Big Issues a week, it means I've got to stand around for six hours. And I will probably get a pound an hour, sometimes even less.

For 40-year-old Will, the new rule also raises questions surrounding the productivity of sellers, and the difficulty getting sales. He tells me:

You have to sell thirty-five. What happens if you don't, what happens if you're not very outgoing? ... It's not fair. Potentially people are going to have to buy thirty five magazines and what happens if you only sell twenty!? You've wasted fifteen and that's what, potentially about thirty, thirty-seven pound fifty wasted? I don't think it's very fair.

This rule therefore draws a line around what is understood to be 'working' and to be 'productive' in an otherwise incredibly open and accessible form of work.

Distinctions between begging and working are not just important for the organisation *The Big Issue*. Across the three cities, for many sellers the move into selling homeless street press did not come from an experience of begging. For some, an experience of long-term unemployment, often exacerbated by ongoing disability or illness, is accompanied by stultifying boredom and a desire to do something, anything—to be productive in some way. As with those who had an experience of begging, working as a seller is often one of their only options to engage in some form of employment and income generation. For these sellers, begging was and is not an option that they would ever consider. James (58 years old) in London, for instance, explains when I ask him if he had ever begged:

No, no. I just don't feel I could. No matter how desperate times have been in the past, I just couldn't see myself doing it. [...] [Working as a seller] gives you back self-belief and—there's a word I'm trying to find... It gives you back yourself, self-discipline and just gives you a lot back, you know, the stuff that you've forgot about. Really you're thinking 'I'm not going to do that in a month of Sundays,' but you're not begging. You're actually doing a service. I was surprised the amount of nice people that I've met and they've actually stood there and spoke to me. And they say, 'Hello I'm Maxine and I just want you to know that I work here so I will buying off you every week' and I say, 'That's very kind of you, thank you very much.' It's a buzz, honestly it really is.

Here, for James and others, selling provides an important avenue to work, and its distance from begging is important for many sellers. The power of working, and of having customers stop and buy the magazine, for James gave 'him back to himself'. Here, selling work cultivates feelings of dignity, as it offers a means for people like James to engage in socially and culturally valuable work: a 'service' as James puts it.

Sometime after I spoke to Rob in Melbourne, I meet Fran—the seller mentioned by Rob as loathed by many of the homeless beggars. Fran (50 years old) is one of the longest-serving sellers in Melbourne and works long days—10 to 12 hours, starting early to try and makes sales in the work rush hour. Like Rob, she doesn't have a moral objection to begging, but rather views it as bad for her sales, and as something that is not worth the risk of possibly being picked up by the police. Likes James, Fran views her work as an important and dignified means of accruing income. Over the years, she tells me, she has built up a strong positive attitude and excellent customer service skills, which means she has a number of regular buyers. When I ask her if she had ever begged, she offers a resolute no, but then describes the experiences of people leaving her money when she was rough sleeping on the streets of the city a few years ago. For her there is a clear line of distinction between that (and her current work as a seller) and the act of begging.

The distinction between selling and begging is also important for the sellers of San Francisco's *Street Sheet*, where the lines between begging and working are far more ambiguous than *The Big Issue* in London and Melbourne. Indeed, unlike *The Big Issue* code of conduct, the *Street Sheet* seller contract states clearly in its first paragraph: "This is not a job. You neither work for, not represent the Coalition, yet your conduct and professionalism is a direct reflection on this organization." Yet, as with the Melbourne and London sellers the capacity to have an alternative to illegal begging or panhandling, to be engaging in an activity with more positive social connotations and within the law, is of profound importance.

The significance of selling work rests as much on the sorts of responses people get from the public, as it does on the feelings and identifications of the sellers themselves. For Ray, in his 50s, selling *Street Sheets* rather than panhandling is a means to have different interactions with the people who buy off him.

Some people say you do better financially panhandling than selling the Street Sheet. But if you panhandle you've got to be ready for the fact that most people are going to say get a job, or nothing at all.

Here, distinctions between begging and selling were most strongly drawn around the identity and meaning of work, and the sorts of interactions it provides for. The importance of being a worker cannot be overstated. Across the three cities, despite differences in understandings of what constituted work, and how closely homeless street press selling approximated working, being a seller was an important identification as doing something worthwhile, something productive.

Yet, because the *Street Sheet* is an activist paper, an organ of the Coalition on Homelessness, many sellers understood what they did as a form of 'dignified' or 'legal' panhandling or begging. For some San Francisco sellers, selling homeless street press was far from what could be understood as work. Here the closeness of the selling papers to panhandling, and the activist intents of the paper, means that Ray doesn't understand it as work—but more like 'volunteering' or 'panhandling with a gimmick'. This is also emphasised by the fact that San Francisco sellers get the paper for free (unlike with *The Big Issue*), and 'sell' it for a donation on the street. Ray says,

> *I don't think of it as work. I guess I think of work in the five hours sense. I do approach it somewhat like work but it's more free than that because you can stop whenever you want and do whatever you want. You can take it with you, you can give it away if you just wanna spread the word in case someone doesn't have the money. So that's not exactly like what work is. It's more like volunteering.*
>
> *The other thing is that it is yours. Work is something that you do for somebody else. With the Street Sheet you get all of the money from when you sell it, so it is not that you were doing something for somebody else. It's that you're getting the word out, so I assume that that's kind of like work but that you are making money for yourself. So it's kind of like panhandling with a gimmick. So I don't see it as the same thing is work. It is more like experimenting to see how you can do it.*

Some sellers actively blur the boundaries between begging and selling. For Kyle (48 years old), for instance, it depends on how he feels, or whether or not people seem particularly interested in the *Street Sheet* when they pass by, as to if he will try and sell them the paper or just ask them for money for a meal. When talking about this, I ask him if he thinks there is a difference in how people respond to him depending on whether he is selling the *Street* Sheet or asking for a meal. He says:

> *Well—it's a good thing—you do both at the same time. I would say it's important to do that, because you are giving them options. If you have sign, then you have the Street Sheet next to the sign, and the sign states what you are trying to raise money for—whether it's a hot meal or a guitar or a hot bath. [...] You've got to look at individuals, as they are approaching you. You look at their face: if you smile and they smile, you have a chance. There is no point in hounding someone. I have seen some people try and do the whole spiel—and you can see the person is really not interested. I just say—'Okay thank you, have a nice day.' Sometimes you got it, sometime you don't. God—we are in a recession—a lot of people are broke!*

This kind of hazy distinction between selling and begging is far more common in San Francisco, and emerges from the dynamics of the organisation as discussed in Chap. 3. When I ask Curtis (59 years old), for instance, whether or not he had ever panhandled he answers:

Yeah I panhandled! Yeah, of course. This is panhandling, but it's just legal panhandling! You don't think this is panhandling? I'm selling pieces of paper for money. I'm asking people to buy the paper for a donation. It's not legal to ask for money. It's a donation. The paper says it's a donation. When somebody asked me how much do you want, I say to them whatever you can give me!

ENTREPRENEURIAL IDENTITIES AT WORK

Joel (53 years old, San Francisco): I've had people say to me, 'Why don't you get a real job!?'
Jessica: What do you say to that?
Joel: 'Excuse me—I have a job!' 'Doing what?' 'This is what I do! I sell newspapers!' This is my job. I am my own boss, I set my own hours, I work when I want, you know, however many papers I want to sell for that day. This is my job.

For the sellers who strongly frame their activity as work, the flexibility of employment, and their status as being self-employed—as being their own boss, are of fundamental importance. Here, the significance of agency—of doing something meaningful—collides with the emerging dominant global ethos of entrepreneurialism, embraced in particular by the London and Melbourne *The Big Issue*, but still present in San Francisco sellers' accounts. Sellers across the three cities echo Joel's proclamation, 'I have a job!' 'I am my own boss!' 'This is my job'.

Sellers engage in highly precarious entrepreneurial work, which relies on high levels of self-agency, motivation and reliance. For many, the ability to control their workdays is a powerful and positive experience. When I ask Dom, a 26-year-old seller in Melbourne who used to work as an apprentice chef in kitchens what he likes about working with *The Big Issue*, he is quick to point to the fact that now he doesn't have a boss looking over his shoulder. Many sellers speak of experiences in previous employment in which they felt watched and scrutinised, and in which they ultimately felt that they failed because the work dried up, they were fired, or did not have their contracts renewed. In contrast, selling homeless street press is a form of work that is always there and open to anyone. There are no tests required to start selling homeless street press, and whilst there is some induction and training required as discussed in Chap. 6, it is one of the most accessible forms of work. In general, Dom did not like working as a seller. He didn't like having what he described as "frustrating" conversations with members of the public, having to "educate" them about the magazine and homelessness, and he didn't like competing for custom with beggars and charity workers, experiences that I explore further in the final chapter. Yet, for Dom, in his words, "The only thing that is working for me at the moment is that I choose when I want to work. I can go 'see ya!' whenever. I can walk away from a pitch and just go home."

Undeniably, the work of a seller is an enterprising practice: it is based not only on the need for sellers to manage their own time in an open and flexible plane of work practices; it also cultivates a sense of individual responsibility and a striving for personal fulfilment and autonomy (Rose 1992). More than two decades ago, Nikolas Rose suggested the 'enterprising self' is the 'calculating self', "a self that calculates *about* itself and that works *upon* itself in order to better itself" (1992: 146). For sellers, such a calculation is driven, and underpinned, by the material conditions of poverty and unemployment. Here, the open and accessible entrepreneurial work practices of homeless street press form the basis for the cultivating of work identities. Thus, notes of distinction between begging and unemployment and the entrepreneurial work of selling homeless street press form the basis of understanding of being a worker.

This distinction is powerfully significant to Emma. I meet Emma, a 33-year-old seller in Melbourne in a quiet pitch in the city. It is lunch hour, and a slow stream of mostly office workers passes her pitch. She stands in the centre of the slim pavement, moving quickly around to allow people to pass her as she tries to engage them to get sales. She and the people passing by do not seem particularly bothered by this. Later, she describes this to me as a 'dance' in which she tries to get out of the way of people whilst at the same time put herself 'out there' to drum up business.

We chat for a while, and she explains that her selling approach rests on being as friendly as she can to people as they pass by, in the hope that on their way back from lunch they will buy a magazine. She is one of the few women sellers that I meet whilst doing this research, and unlike many of the other women she is very commanding of the space. She stands confidently, moving to and fro, pointing her body to follow people as they walk past as she greets and compliments them on their hats, coats, bags, shoes, sunglasses... anything she lays her eyes on in order to open the opportunity for conversation and hopefully a sale. Many other women I meet are far more discrete and quiet in their selling, preferring to sit down, or stand up against the shops behind them leaving more room on the footpath for people to walk past, and choosing not to call out to sell.

As for all sellers, the gender dynamics of Emma's work are undeniable. Not only is the way sellers take up space in the city, feel safe, engage with buyers and project images of themselves is not just shaped by gender, race, class, sexuality and disability; gender, race, class, sexuality and disability are also shaped in and by these practices and encounters. Other researchers have also documented the gendered dynamics of informal economy, such as in Teresa Gowan's ethnography of the homeless men who did the vast majority of informal recycling work on the streets of San Francisco (2010). Although it is important to acknowledge the many 'visibly' homeless women (see May et al. 2007), narrow attention on (mostly male) rough sleepers creates vast gaps in understanding of homelessness. Such a focus can miss a wider experience of the so-called 'hidden homelessness' characterised by overcrowded housing, squatting, 'couch-surfing', boarding houses, car-sleeping, and so on. These wider experiences point to the ways in which homelessness and life on the streets is differently lived and felt, and to the racial and gendered dynamics of housing and homelessness.

In Australia, for instance, the inclusion of overcrowding is an important indicator of homelessness in order to recognise the experiences of Indigenous homelessness, whilst couch-surfing and car-sleeping recognises many young people, gay, lesbian, transgender, intersex and queer people, and women and children who might not be so visible as 'rough sleepers' (see Memmott et al. 2003; Fitzpatrick 2000). Homeless women are far more likely to be part of the 'hidden' homeless, due to the prevailing dynamics of gender-based violence, the associated tacit and nuanced ways in which women feel less safe in public space, and the social conditions of gender more broadly that ascribe women more strongly to the realm of the home (see Darab and Hartman 2012; Mallett 2004). Juliet Watson's research, for instance, highlights the ways in which homeless women often use intimate relationships with men in an attempt to be safe: an attempt that is highly precarious, not least because these relationships are not always safe themselves (see Watson 2016).

For Emma, safety is a consideration that is never far from her mind. As I discuss further in Chap. 7, the fact that this work is in public and on city streets means that sellers have to negotiate being in public, and on public show, as a basic condition of their work. Yet, for Emma, being seen and being recognised as an enterprising worker, as someone who is attempting to better herself, is a core part of her sense of belonging and safety in the city. In contrast to her experience of begging, her last 18 months of working as a seller has meant that buyers take more of an interest in her day-to-day health, ask after her, and sometimes even suggest she takes a break if she is looking a bit tired. She tells me, "I found with begging, people just automatically assume you're out for drugs because you're not going to work. But when you're with *The Big Issue*, it's more like this is someone who's put their own time and dedicated to try and sell the magazine."

The movement into becoming a seller, however, was difficult for Emma. She waited two years in profound poverty, squatting and begging, before deciding to try it. Like Dom she has also worked as a chef, but had to give up because of ongoing medical issues from which she is still recovering, and was profoundly embarrassed at the prospect of becoming a seller. She says, "I didn't want people to see me on the corner going from a chef uniform to selling *The Big Issue*—that's my biggest thing, what I think other people assume because I'm assuming someone else is assuming. I've learned to just fight it and actually feel good about it now. I love being out there." The most important part of this change in her is being recognised as a worker, and as someone who is working for herself and attempting to better herself.

The realities of poverty mean that this is an enterprising work that has to occur seven days a week, at least for a few hours, so that she makes enough money for "food and smokes". The apparent flexibility that homeless street press work provides is a double bind. On the one hand, it offers legitimate income generation without the surveillance and stipulations of waged work for those who are otherwise unemployed. On the other hand, it is highly precarious and involves the difficult management and negotiation of money, time, image and relationships. Most importantly, this entrepreneurial work is not necessarily a preferred option for sellers, but their only option. When sellers feel a deep sense of shame and boredom for being unemployed and/or begging and when they are struggling to make ends meet, the opportunity to work is profound. This is not only because it generates some income, but also because it enables them to cultivate the practices and identity of a self-employed worker. This occurs within a field of formal employment opportunities that is often empty or filled with badly paid, poor conditioned work: casual, insecure and without entitlements.

Patrick, a Melbourne seller, for instance, works two jobs – as a seller for *The Big Issue* and as a cook and kitchen hand in a busy inner-city restaurant. His employment as a cook and kitchen hand is just as precarious as his *Big Issue* work, with his employers often letting him know in the hour before his shift whether or not they need him. At least on one occasion he did not get paid for months, with his employers citing their own financial difficulties as their reason. During this time, he continued to work for them on the 'good word' from his employer that he would eventually get paid. In his previous job—also as a cook—he had saved up holiday pay over three years as a means to try and save whilst earning poor wages. However, after three years the employer took his holiday pay off him, refusing to pay him out. Talking to me while we drink a cup of coffee at a café a few doors down from his current job, Patrick is incensed at the injustice of this, particularly when his former employer was sending their children to an expensive private school and going on their own international holidays. He tells me:

> *I thought, 'Dude I did all this work for you, fifty hours a week for three years straight, I can't even have a holiday!' That really ticked me off. That's really not right. So it woke me as well to people who might be doing the right thing up to a point, but not all the way. Because these guys are taking their holidays to Malaysia every year, driving their four wheel drives, kids at Xavier College and that sort of thing, but you pay for that. It's just coming off your wages! So it's not really cool that way.*

For Patrick, therefore, *The Big Issue* offers a means to income generation that gave him some independence from dishonest employers and from being exploited in low-paid jobs with insecure conditions. "This is why I'm happier with The Big Issue," he says, "because everything's very fair dinkum, you know, what you see is what you get, there's no hidden catches or anything like that. You don't continually have a drama with getting your wage every week or getting ripped off after three years of hard work. So yeah it's a whole lot more straight down the line." Yet, *The Big Issue* work does not offer a true reprieve from the dynamics of exploitation and inequality that incenses Patrick: it still does not give him sick or holiday pay, and it certainly does not give him minimum or even a stable wage.

Enterprising work, therefore, emerges from the complex navigation of unemployment and poor employment opportunities. It is a claim to productivity, and a claim that comes with social recognition. Whilst sellers did experience derogatory abuse whilst working, in comparison to begging the ability to call back—'this is work!' is powerful. Nevertheless, this work, as explored in the following chapters, is still characterised by a permanent state of precariousness and insecurity.

REFERENCES

Adkins, L. (2012). Out of Work or Out of Time? Rethinking Labor After the Financial Crisis. *South Atlantic Quarterly, 111*(4), 621–641.

Adkins, L. (2017). Disobedient Workers, the Law and the Making of Unemployment Markets. *Sociology, 51*(2), 290–305.

Arendt, H. (1998). *The Human Condition*. Chicago: University of Chicago Press.

Balkin, S. (1992). Entrepreneurial Activities of Homeless Men. *Journal of Sociology and Social Welfare, 19*, 129–150.

Cockburn, P. J. L. (2014). Street Papers, Work and Begging: 'Experimenting' at the Margins of Economic Legitimacy. *Journal of Cultural Economy, 7*(2), 145–160.

Darab, S., & Hartman, Y. (2012). Understanding Single Older Women's Invisibility in Housing Issues in Australia. *Housing, Theory and Society, 30*, 1–20.

Denning, M. (2010). Wageless Life. *New Left Review, 66*, 79–97.

Du Gay, P. (1996). *Consumption and Identity at Work*. London: Sage.

Dunn, A. (2010). The 'Dole or Drudgery' Dilemma: Education, the Work Ethic and Unemployment. *Social Policy & Administration, 44*(1), 1–19.

Field, J. (2013). *Working Men's Bodies: Work Camps in Britain, 1880–1940*. Manchester: Manchester University Press.

Fitzpatrick, S. (2000). *Young Homeless People*. London/New York: Palgrave Macmillan.

Gaber, J. (1994). Manhattan's 14th Street Sellers' Market: Informal Street Peddlers' Complementary Relationship with New York City's Economy. *Urban Anthropology and Studies of Cultural Systems and World Economic Development, 23*(4), 373–408.

Gerrard, J. (2014). All that is Solid Melts into Work: Self-Work, the 'Learning Ethic' and the Work Ethic. *The Sociological Review, 62*, 862–879.

Gerrard, J. (2015). The Limits of Learning: Homelessness and Educating the Employable Self. *Discourse, 36*(1), 69–80.

Gerrard, J. (2017). The Interconnected Histories of Homelessness and Labour. *Labour History, 112*, 155–174.

Glucksmann, M. A. (1995). Why 'Work'? Gender and the 'Total Social Organization of Labour'. *Gender, Work and Organization, 2*(2), 63–75.

Gowan, T. (2010). *Hobos, Hustlers and Backsliders: Homeless in San Francisco*. Minneapolis: University of Minnesota Press.
Jessop, B. (2013). Putting Neoliberalism in Its Time and Place: A Response to the Debate. *Social Anthropology, 21*(1), 65–74.
Karabanow, J., Hughes, J., Ticknor, J., Kidd, S., & Patterson, D. (2010). The Economics of Being Young and Poor: How Homeless Youth Survive in Neoliberal Times. *Journal of Sociology & Social Welfare, 37*(4), 39–63.
Kelly, P. (2013). *The Self as Enterprise*. Farnham: Gower Publishing.
Mallett, S. (2004). Understanding Home: A Critical Review of the Literature. *The Sociological Review, 52*(1), 62–89.
May, J., Cloke, P., & Johnse, S. (2007). Alternative Cartographies of Homelessness: Rendering Visible British Women's Experiences of 'Visible' Homelessness. *Gender, Place & Culture, 14*(2), 121–140.
Memmot, P., Long, S., & Chambers, C. (2003). *Categories of Indigenous 'Homeless' People and Good Practice Responses to Their Needs* (Australian Housing and Urban Research Institute Positioning Paper No. 53). Brisbane: AHURI.
Orwell, G. (1975). *Down and Out in Paris and London*. London: Penguin Books.
Rose, N. (1992). Governing the Enterprising Self. In P. Heelas & P. Morris (Eds.), *The Values of the Enterprise Culture: The Moral Debate* (pp. 141–164). London/New York: Routledge.
Scharff, C. (2016). The Psychic Life of Neoliberalism: Mapping the Contours of Entrepreneurial Subjectivity. *Theory, Culture & Society, 33*(6), 107–122.
Shildrick, T., MacDonald, R., Webster, C., & Garthwaite, K. (2012). *Poverty and Insecurity: Live in Low-Pay, No-Pay Britain*. Bristol: The Policy Press.
Watson, J. (2016). Gender-Based Violence and Young Homeless Women: Femininity, Embodiment and Vicarious Physical Capital. *The Sociological Review, 64*(2), 256–273.
Weeks, K. (2011). *The Problem with Work: Feminism, Marxism, Antiwork Politics and Postwork Imaginaries*. Durham/London: Duke University Press.
Western Regional Advocacy Project. (n.d.). *California Homeless Bill of Rights*. http://wraphome.org/what/homeless-bill-of-rights/california-right-to-rest-act/
Williams, C. C., & Nadin, S. (2010). Work Beyond Employment: Representations of Informal Economic Activities. *Work, Employment & Society, 26*(2), 1–10.

CHAPTER 6

Learning to Entrepreneurially Labour

Most particularly for *The Big Issue* there is an underpinning assumption and hope that working as a homeless press street seller is educative. This is, in many ways, a form of informal work-based learning. It is a kind of subtle and delicate learning, in that it occurs through everyday practices: the kind of learning Biesta and colleagues describe as learning "by doing something in a new way, by speaking to others, by reading something, or by watching people" (2011: 1). This learning is strongly framed and determined by the field of practice in which it exists: entrepreneurial informal work on the margins. This is a field that is defined by a constitutive need for flexibility, adaptability and continuous self-work. Here, as with other forms of contemporary work, the homeless street press seller is both a worker and a learner (see Solomon 2005; Seddon 2004). In other words, the work of being a seller is complexly interconnected with the self-work of developing and learning the skills, dispositions, routines and character for work.

In this chapter, I explore the intersections of learning and labouring for sellers of homeless street press. I start by outlining of the intersecting demands of working and learning in contemporary work cultures in nations such as England, the US and Australia, drawing on my previous conceptual development of the 'learning ethic' (see Gerrard 2014). I then examine the different ways in which the organisations at the centre of this book approach the educative or learning bases of their work practices, teasing out differences in particular between *The Big Issue* and *Street Sheet*. The discussion then turns to 'lessons of the trade' as accounted by the sellers across the three cities. Here, I explore the complex ways in which sellers approach learning their trade as street press sellers whilst living in poverty, and how this intersects with the demands of being a worker in public space, attempting to attract morally charged sales.

FROM THE WORK ETHIC TO THE LEARNING ETHIC

Just as suffering has been medicalized, existence has been scholarized, and even becomes the subject of an apprenticeship. ... Now professional educators, through the institution of permanent education, succeed in convincing [women and men] of their permanent incompetence. The ultimate success of the schooling instrument is the extension of its monopoly, first to all youth, then to every age and, finally, to all areas. (Illich and Verne 1976: 14)

I start here with a provocative quote as a means to look underneath the ubiquitous taken-for-granted contemporary embrace of learning and education, most recently tied to the imperative to ensure oneself is improving for work. It was penned somewhat prophetically by infamous 'de-schooling' philosopher and critic Ivan Illich and Ettienne Verne in their 1976 treatise on education, *Imprisoned Global Classroom*. Illich and Verne's problematisation of the spread and predominance of education and learning offers a useful means to question the logics of, and attachments to, the social, moral, political and institutional heralding of education and learning.

Now, 40 years later, learning is routinely tied to the possibility of social mobility. Across national contexts, it is used as a core policy and practice response to homelessness, unemployment and poverty (Gerrard 2015; Rambla and Verger 2009; Robertson 2016). Over the past few decades, significant transformations in the labour market bolster the notion—and perceived criticality—for educational responses to unemployment (Livingstone and Guile 2012; Eichhorst et al. 2015). The hope placed on education has led to intensive reform surrounding both the provision of formal education, and the linking of welfare payments—and in some cases housing—to participation in education (see Gerrard 2015; Hutchinson et al. 2015; Williams 2011).

In the various attempts to maintain economic competitiveness, nation states are in different ways clamouring to ensure citizens engage in skill- and knowledge-development and cultivate the 'right' sets of work habits and dispositions for the modern labour market (Seddon 2004; Solomon 2005;

Milana 2012). Whilst this has obvious repercussions for formal educational institutions—from schools to universities and vocational colleges—it also suggests a far-deeper and engrained experience of learning and education as tied to self: self-development, self-actualisation and self management. It is in these ways that contemporary work intersects with education and learning, in such sites as homeless street press.

Importantly, this "so-called 'pedagogical turn' or learning turn", Alison Lee argues, "involves rapidly shifting boundaries for conceptions of education, pedagogy and learning, requiring in general a re-framing of social activity as learning" (2010: 70). This involves, I suggest, recognising the import of both informal and work-based learning. Paul Willis's *Learning to Labour* (1977) demonstrates the complex interconnections between the cultures and institutions of schools and workplaces. Yet, formal educational institutions can never fully encapsulate the diversity and breadth of learning experiences and practices. Learning occurs in the everyday and "is inextricably related to doing and being" (Biesta et al. 2011). It is, as Ferguson and Seddon note (2007), 'decentred', not defined by any one institutional practice, pedagogic relation or educational aim or system. Behind the systems, institutions, sectors and everyday practices of both formal education and work are diverse underbelly practices of learning and labouring.

Moreover, education and learning seeps into work practices. As Devos et al. (2010: 74) suggest:

Workplaces are one of the oldest learning spaces we have, and work-related learning, of both the formally accredited and the on-the-job, 'sitting next to Nellie' kinds, has been a powerful means of regulating the way work is done, relationships between people and between how people are institutions are managed, and working identities are developed and produced.

Informal and work-based learning across the life-course is far from marginal to the production and utilisation of knowledge and understanding (e.g. Biesta et al. 2011; Livingstone 2005). Everyday learning through, for instance, working as a homeless street press seller is in many ways just as important as formal education in the creation of identity, notions and practices of citizenship, and the exercise of social and cultural capital (Tuschling and Engemann 2006).

Thus, there is a profound link between education and work, and learning and labouring. Education, for instance, has proliferated through the self-development and learning required for the changing demands of work in a globalising and constantly changing economy (see Milana 2012; Gewirtz 2008). The intersection of learning and working, has given rise to what Solomon (2005) refers to as 'worker-learners' and 'learner-workers' (see also Seddon et al. 2010). The contemporary hope placed on education as an act of social mobility, self-transformation, and constant skills renewal connects everyday life with an educational ethos. Elsewhere, I develop the notion of the 'learning ethic' to recognise the ways in which learning and education are central to modern citizenship, woven into the moral fabric of what it is presumed to be a 'good citizen' (Gerrard 2014). This has clear relevance to homeless street press, in which sellers 'learn' or 're-learn' the habits and routines of (precarious, informal) work. Building upon Kathi Weeks' elaboration of the contemporary form and function of the work ethic (2011), I suggest there are distinct moral, cultural, governmental and material imperatives that encircle education and learning.

Developing Weber's initial thesis with a consideration of the contemporary dynamics of advanced capitalism and the insights afforded by feminist critics of labour, Weeks (2011) posits that in post-Fordist economies, the work ethic operates along a number of dynamic, shifting (and ultimately never complete) practice. Weeks suggests that the work ethic operates in and through: the taken-for-granted rationality associated with working; productivist and now consumerist values and practices on which our culture and society centres; a sense of moral responsibility tied to individual agency acted through wage dependency; the diverse take-up of 'labour' and 'work' as the solution to numerous inequalities; and, finally, the foundational importance of work for social and material inclusion and/or exclusion (Weeks 2011).

It is clear that these dynamic practices also operate when it comes to education and learning in modern citizenship. Education, like work, is a key social institution and practice that cultivates economic capacity, shapes identities, feeds the routines of everyday life, and which contributes to, and reflects, major trends in citizenship ideals and practices. Not only are education and learning social and institutional practices: they are also moral. Education and learning are central to the organisation of society, and to our sense of worth and value. These moral attachments give rise to a 'learning ethic'. Most recently, education is deployed as a vehicle to push forward with neoliberal trends in advanced capitalism in ways that reinforce the moral worth of participation in education (see Gerrard 2014). This includes, for instance, the transformation of education into a 'consumption' and debt-accruing practice; the presumption that education and learning can offer solutions to deep structural inequalities and hierarchies within the labour market and society more broadly; and the place of education in providing opportunities for inclusion and/or exclusion (*ibid.*).

Of course, the work and learning ethics operate very differently across contexts. There are no universal ways in which they are understood, lived and felt. Nevertheless, underpinning these diverse practices across local and global contexts is an increasingly assured moralised presumption that participation in education and learning is better than not: it is, in other words, a marker of being a 'good citizen' (*ibid.*). These sorts of dynamics are present in, for instance, the presumption that homeless street press marks a willingness to work *and* self-develop and learn to work, as opposed to, for instance, begging. From the cradle to the grave, to be learning is generally considered to be morally superior; and those who do not or cannot participate in learning are routinely considered to be gravely transgressing social and ethical expectations (Gerrard 2014; see also Gewirtz 2008). We often take for granted the practices, institutions, obligations and desires for education and work. Importantly—as with Weeks' conceptualisation of the work ethic—the learning ethic does not operate as some sort of monolithic oppressive force. As with work, education and learning are often at the centre for claims to equity, justice and empowerment. The dynamic capacity of the learning ethic, in other words, is that in the multifarious claims to it, overarching moral attachments to learning are enhanced and expanded.

This is particularly so for the emergent importance of entrepreneurial identities, practices and work experiences in contemporary society. Entrepreneurialism requires an orientation towards creation, development and accrual that inks not just work practices and experiences, but the self: the 'enterprising self', as Nikolas Rose put it in 1992 (see also Peters 2001). This enterprising self rests on a work ethic and learning ethic imbued with the projection of capital accrual and the projection of self as a form of capital. It is, as Peter Kelly suggests, a form of selfhood underpinned by a restless reflexivity in which individuals take ownership and responsibility for their choices and the apparent outcomes of these choices (2013). In this highly reflexive form of the 'good citizen self', there is a high demand on aligning work with an expression of self. Learning becomes an agent of this accrual: it is the means to ensure that oneself is always orientated to the needs of the market. There are, therefore, important and complex relationships between entrepreneurialism and learning that extend beyond formal training and education, but go to the very practice of work—and life—itself.

In Foucauldian terms, the emerging and now proliferating entrepreneurialism, has crafted the self as entrepreneur. This entrepreneurial dynamic is a key way in which the work ethic and learning ethic intersect. The 'economic' status of self is defined by an entrepreneurial energy based on a premise of human capital, and the need for constant accrual and production of value on the self. Foucault writes they are "an entrepreneur of themselves who incurs expenses by investing to obtain some kind of improvement" (2008: 230). As Kelly et al. explore (2015), new forms of entrepreneurial work targeting those marginalised by formal education and work (such as social enterprise) are premised on the need for self-transformation in the image of the skills required for a highly precarious labour market (see also Kelly and Harrison 2009).

Thus, modern citizenship practices are shaped by the need for entrepreneurial mobile citizens, capable of flexible skills renewal across their life course (see du Gay 1996; Appleby and Bathmaker 2006). In this way, educational initiatives produce understandings and practices of the citizen 'self', as active, constantly developing, learning, productive and participatory. In part, this turn to learning can be attributed to the perceived need for citizens to adapt to the increasingly globalised labour market, characterised by high-paced technological innovation and the withering of older forms of work associated with an industrial economy. At the same time, it also reflects a perception surrounding the cause—and possible solution to—economic downturns and unemployment, as individuals are expected to develop the dispositions and skills capable of responding to fluctuations in market needs. Indeed, for those who teeter on the edge of, or who are excluded from, formal practices of work and education such as homeless street press sellers, practices and understanding of productive citizenship have sharpened importance.

For instance, across nation states, governments demonstrate deep concern to transition 'unproductive' citizens into productive roles (e.g. McDonald and Marston 2005). And where structural inequality means that this transition is highly tenuous through persistent unemployment levels, governments fall back on creating the experience of productivity in order to ward off idleness and the perceived demons of welfare dependency (Dean 1995). Work for the dole initiatives and compulsory education and training are arguably less about providing skills and more about inculcating particular dispositions of the productive citizen self and a deep fear of idleness: a work and learning ethic. Yet, it is not just governments who intervene in this space: there is a clear authority within international contemporary politics to create and encourage non-state educational, work and social initiatives. These comprise a complex of education/work spaces, having particular significance for those marginalized from formal and traditional work and education (see also Seddon et al. 2001).

Importantly, however, this understanding of the intersecting operation of the learning and work ethics, does not presuppose that *all* work and learning is limiting, oppressive or problematic. Indeed, the conceptualisation of the ethic of work and learning rests on understanding work and learning as fundamental life activities—having varying effects, meanings and practices and giving rise to different experiences. This is not about uncovering an authentic version of work and learning in juxtaposition to that which is oppressive and limiting, but to approach the sociological experience of work as invariably shaped by, and impacted upon, the contemporary dynamics of the work ethic and learning ethic. Understood as dynamic and shifting, the practices of learning and working are shaped, but never fully encapsulated by, the imperative of capital accrual and the social relations that are formed around this.

It is in this way that the practices of homeless street press are invariably steeped in the contemporary dynamics of the work and learning ethics and, at the same time, represent an attempt to claim agency, power and productivity in different ways. Connected to activist, self-help and entrepreneurial intentions, homeless street press has attempted to create a different form of work practice (or income generation practice). As such, the learning that takes place as sellers carry out their work and cultivate their own approaches to this very fluid and flexible work is deeply connected to *both* the need for entrepreneurial capital accrual and commodity exchange, and a sense of—at times powerful—agency, capacity and independence. Unsurprising, as this chapter now explores, sellers' experiences of learning is multifarious, sometimes ambiguous, and inextricably tied to the everyday challenges of managing and negotiating precarious poverty whilst working.

The Hope of Learning/Working

When *The Big Issue* was first established, it hoped that it would provide a transitional space: a practice by which the sellers could gain confidence, work habits and skills, before moving onto more mainstream or formal employment (see Swithinbank 2001). This transitional aspiration emphasised the informal educational possibilities in working as a seller, and remains central to the organisation. Even whilst many within *The Big Issue* now acknowledge that many sellers do not understand their work as transitional, but see it as a job for life (as is explored in Chap. 8), the hope of self-transformation still mobilises educative and learning goals within *The Big Issue*. Having a 'self-help' ethos at its centre, *The Big Issue* is founded on the premise of the power of self-transformation. As a work practice, this model of self-help is connected to the core dispositions and character of work generally, and of the work offered by *The Big Issue* in particular.

To put it simply, for *The Big Issue* the power of work is paramount. The notion that work is the agent by which self-transformation, esteem and independence are made possible is central to the purpose of the magazine. Megan, a Melbourne *Big Issue* staff member, put it this way:

> *Cause I guess with The Big Issue, creating a work opportunity for someone is the biggest thing you can do to help someone lift themselves out of poverty. So for us it's not about running a program for homeless and disadvantaged people to help them: it's about giving them the actual thing that they want, which is a job. And then from that all the other stuff can flow on. Which is one of the things that draws me to this; is that I do believe that. Employment is the greatest thing that someone can have because from that you get self-esteem, increased self-confidence, ability to address your own health issues because you've got the financial means and you often have the confidence to be able to do that as well.*

In both Melbourne and London, *The Big Issue* staff place significant emphasis on the potential for selling to provide opportunities to develop self-management and self-reliance in association with connecting to community. In London, when I ask Brett what he hope sellers will learn from the experience, he suggests two things. First, a trust in the community and knowledge that there are people who care about them and their wellbeing, and, second, he says, "I hope they can learn to manage themselves."

Importantly, work is understood to be the conduit to this learning: the practice by which sellers can develop self-confidence and -reliance, by turning up to their pitches day in, day out, and persevering to get sales. It is through this practice that staff at *The Big Issue* hope sellers learn the skills and habits of work, whilst connecting with the community with dignity, afforded by the legitimacy of *Big Issue* work (as opposed, for instance, to begging). In Melbourne, Peter, who was involved in *The Big Issue* when it was established, links the centrality of work to the profundity of setting up the magazine in the late 1990s:

If you can think of the paradigm shift we were making then, saying 'homeless people are the architects of their own salvation'. They don't rely on us to change them. They actually are capable of being front and centre of their own salvation, of their own future. Salvation sounds a bit religious doesn't it? But what we were saying was 'homeless people are the most valuable asset of the business'. Nobody had ever thought of it like that before. The most valuable asset of The Big Issue is homeless people. It wouldn't operate without them!.

I ask Peter if he thinks the experience of being a seller has some sort of educational and learning basis to it, and he responds:

Oh yeah. You know, communication—just learning how to say 'good morning'. Learning how to be on your pitch because your regular customers are going to come along. Learning to understand how another person feels. ... Yeah—so there's that kind of learning.

The centrality of work for *The Big Issue* is in stark contrast to the intents and aims of the *Street Sheet*, which as discussed in Chap. 3 is more activist in orientation through its connection to the grass-roots campaign organisation Coalition on Homelessness. When talking to the Coalition's Natalie, she is clear that the solution to homelessness and poverty for sellers lies not with selling the *Street Sheet*, but in activist campaigns:

What we do here at the Coalition is that we organise homeless people to create permanent solutions to homelessness and we fight to protect the civil and human rights of those who are forced to remain on the streets. And so we have kind of a community organising model where we do a ton of outreach then we have these open workgroups where we fight for more housing and more access to treatment. A whole variety of different poverty abatement strategies to try alleviate the crisis.

Nevertheless, others at the Coalition do suggest that becoming a seller can be a powerful experience of agency and independence. Indeed, staff, volunteers and sellers talk to me about the many seller 'success stories': people who utilise *Street Sheet* to support significant life transformations, from moving away from drug and alcohol dependency, to creating a much-needed income stream in order to relieve the intensive material pressures of being poor in San Francisco. In this way, *Street Sheet* is touted as a potential avenue to a multitude ends, rather than as a work practice premised on the empowering potential of entrepreneurial practice, as in *The Big Issue*.

Learning to Labour

Organisationally, both *The Big Issue* and *Street Sheet* offer some sort of induction for sellers. For the *Street Sheet* this comprises a brief introduction to the rules of the seller contract, which stipulates that sellers do not: consume alcohol or illegal drugs whilst working; behave aggressively or make sexual or bigoted remarks to staff or volunteers of the Coalition, potential buyers or other sellers; and sell or give *Street Sheets* to other sellers. When interviewing volunteers Guy, Allan and Max at the Coalition about the *Street Sheet*, they explain:

> Guy: *It literally it takes fifteen minutes. It's just your standard little minor contract. It states that okay, even though this is not a job and you don't necessarily work nor represent the Coalition, you are kind of our face out there so there are certain rules you're going to need to congregate by. Don't be getting trashed on the job. Don't be s.moking weed or doing other kinds of substances.*
> Max: *Try to refrain from controversial behaviour.*
> Guy: *Exactly, try not to curse or get aggressive—it's basically just standard politeness rules.*
> Allan: *And also first come, first served on things like vending turf. If somebody else is working your spot just find another or wait for them to go away. Don't beef over it, don't beef in public. That's the main thing.*

The Big Issue, whilst still brief, has a more concerted training model. In London, staff explain that this happens over a week, and involves sellers being first issued with a provisional seller badge. The focus here is on sales and on treating the work as a sales job. The London *Big Issue* office hosts sessions on how to boost sales in which sellers are encouraged to attend. In addition, other than having to see sellers for issues surrounding breaking the code of conduct, staff monitor sellers' sales and actively check in with sellers if they have noticeably bad sales. All of this initial and ongoing orientation is framed by the work practice of *The Big Issue* as being a highly flexible entry point into the labour market, tailored to the needs and personality of the seller. Brett, a staff member at The Big Issue London, explains the induction process:

> *They get talked through the code of conduct which is the basic framework that people have to operate in selling the magazine. But then there's just a general chat about trying to turn up to your pitch at the right time of day because some*

pitches work well in the morning, lunchtime, evening. And you'd be wasting your time standing there at the wrong time of day. So you try and look at the sellers, see what skills they have, see whether they'd be suited to a very busy pitch or maybe a low busy pitch. See what sort of area they'd be more suited to, and try and offer them support for the pitch, and just to get the basics right. 'Cause it's not rocket science selling the magazine it's doing the basics. Being on the pitch, having a smile, trying to get eye contact. Again as I've said interpersonal skills. So you try and encourage people to sort of come out of themselves a bit but without stepping over that line. Because some people will take it too far. There's always someone that will do so. It's really trying to bring what's working in people, bring it out of them.

In Melbourne, when I talk with *Big Issue* staff member Megan about what she hopes sellers will get out of the induction process, she responds:

It's not a huge amount. It's about the ability to communicate with other people. Most of the sales training is about effective sales techniques, making eye contact, being able to speak to people, appropriate things to talk to people about, appropriate manners and things like that, basic cash handling skills in terms of the mathematics of six dollars, budgeting their money. So part of it is about talking to them about- if you're going to buy ten now, the new magazine's released tomorrow, are you going to sell ten or do you just want to buy three maybe and then come back. So educating them about, you know, risk taking and purchasing and things like that.

Importantly, the "basic stuff" of learning to be a *Big Issue* seller is ultimately the skills required for entrepreneurial sales job: how to manage the risks of buying products in order to sell them; how to develop sales techniques; and ultimately, how to develop skills to self-manage this flexible form of work. Megan explains:

There was a seller that wanted to sell magazines at 7am at Parliament Station because he wanted to get all the peak traffic, but he kept saying things like "I keep sleeping in, I wake up and it's eight o'clock." And so the life skill was "if you bought an alarm clock you could set it for six thirty and then you could be there by seven." And that was something that hadn't occurred to him. So it's that kind really basic stuff. We have to step back and think about what's happening in their lives that aren't making them do what's immediately obvious to everyone else, that alarm clocks are a really good investment. ... Really basic life skills stuff, like 'you're going to write down when you're going to come to work at your pitch. Where are you going to write it?'

There is, therefore, an educative underpinning to homeless street press: a hope for small everyday learning that could possibly make real differences to the quality of life of the homeless and poor. In this way, self-help, self-development and self-transformation are representative of work-based learning, linked to the specificities of homeless street press work but also to a broader desire to ease the experiences of poverty and homelessness.

Lessons of the Trade: Sales, Smiles and Self-Reliance

I feel awkward, and a little uncomfortable. I had come in to interview and speak with *The Big Issue* London staff earlier in the morning, and they suggested I spend some time in the seller area to see if there are any sellers who might want to be interviewed. I am sitting by myself in the large bare space on one of a couple of plastic tables presumably there for sellers to sit and rest. Sellers come in an out; some grab a hot drink at the corner vending machine. I chat with a few, but most are in a hurry and are keen to buy their magazines and get back to their pitches quickly. Roland is the first to agree, and we head to a side room to talk away from the steady stream of sellers coming in.

Roland has been working as a seller off and on for around 20 years—starting just a couple of years after it first began. He is 70 and works as a seller every day of the week. When I ask him why he first decided to be a seller, he chronicles his early years of drug experimentation that led to him 'dropping out', in his words, after starting a history degree at a reputable UK university. Having busked before, Roland explains that the transition to becoming a seller wasn't much of a stretch. Roland talks of the long days he puts in—getting up at 6:30 am to make sure he gets to his first pitch early, and usually working through the day and well past the evening peak hour.

I ask him if he has a particular sales pitch and he immediately breaks into his sing-song market-style sales line: "Big, big, big, big, big—Big Issue! A good read, a good deed!" He explains, "That kind of thing. Because the whole principle is an amazing principle, it means that traders on the outskirts like me can do something that helps others and helps themselves and is not dependent on government subsidy." I ask him what *The Big Issue* has helped him with most, and perhaps unsurprisingly, he replies, "Well it gives me a regular income. That's the first and basically most single thing, and from that I've been able to find a flat."

When I ask Roland if he has learnt anything from *The Big Issue*, he answers:

> *Well first of all you have to have a certain amount of self confidence to stand up there in a crowded place and try to sell magazines to people. And the second thing is, yes, the wonderful thing about it is that you meet the kind people in society. Nobody stops to buy a Big Issue unless they have some kind of motivation like 'I'd like to do this, I would like to help someone' and those kind of people I want to meet all day every day… What else have I learned? Well you learn—you get more self-confidence, more self-worth. I know, you see, really not external things.*

Dignity runs deep in Roland's work practice. The ability to create an income stream and have work that is literally always there when he needs it is incredibly important to him. Nevertheless, it is a struggle. We talk about the frustrations he has on living on the low income that selling provides, and how he supplements his *Big Issue* earnings with busking.

I ask Roland if, given that he is low on cash, he feels frustrated when people walk past him on his pitch and don't stop to say hello or buy. He says,

> *No it doesn't bother me at all. I remember a man once said to me 'it's a numbers game Roland, there's a principle, the principle of emptiness and fullness'. That which makes itself empty attracts things. It's a principle of the virtue of modesty. If you're modest you attract people. If you're immodest, boastful, arrogant, you push people away.*

Roland's approach, therefore, is to ensure that he makes himself as open as possible to potential sales through this virtue of modesty. Roland explains this as "self-cultivation", crafting himself as modestly as possible so as to preserve his dignity in the face of feeling frustrated by a lack a sales, or belittled by the odd derogatory comment by people passing by.

Across the three cities, as with Roland, sellers routinely talk about the need to learn how to orient themselves to get sales. Many talk about this in terms of gaining confidence and gaining the ability to express themselves. In Melbourne, Oli (49 years old) tells me what he likes about working as a *Big Issue* seller: "Yeah. Little things, sort of, gives me a buzz, like, the sun comes out, the street suddenly looks a little bit less hostile… And yeah, I've learnt to express myself—in work skills and stuff like that, you need to be able to communicate." Similarly, Julia (51 years old), also in

Melbourne, places *The Big Issue* at the centre of her self-transformation and developing confidence. She says, "It brings you a lot of confidence which I didn't have when I joined *The Big Issue*. I was a little bit mentally ill when I joined *The Big Issue*, so it's bought me out of me shell and overtime things have got better and better. So yeah it's been good for support of that yeah." She goes on, "Vending, I think it's something good to learn you know. Once you've learnt it, it's good experience for you."

Another seller in London, James (58 years old), puts his experience down to being mentored by another seller. When talking about how he found the training provided by *The Big Issue*, he reflects:

> *The training was good, but I really feel that you need to be put in the right direction. And I was lucky that I met someone who was a really great guy and he helped me out. You might not think it but I'm actually a very shy person. And we've got a sign underneath The Big Issue badge 'I am a seller not a beggar' and one of the no-no's is you don't stop a man and say 'excuse me have you got any small change?' That's begging in my eyes and that's a no. 'Excuse me sir/young lady would you like to buy a copy of The Big Issue on this beautiful day. Puts a smile on your face guaranteed' and then they break into a smile and I say 'it's working already'. And the amount of people that actually come back and buy a copy of the magazine, honestly it's a great experience.*

James and Roland's experiences highlight the ways in which the inductions provided by the homeless street press coalesce with 'on the street' learning: the tacit processes of learning within which they cultivate their approaches to their work. Interwoven across both processes of learning is an emphasis on the need to create sales and self-management skills for the challenges of sales work.

Importantly, this learning occurs in and through the institutional frameworks enforced by the homeless street press. Many sellers talk about the significance of the code of conduct or seller contract when reflecting on how they have learnt their craft. Steve (41 years old, Melbourne), for instance, laughs when I ask him if he has learnt anything from working as a seller, and after a pause, says, "Well, don't beg that's why you've got a uniform. I have heard of a few sellers get caught begging while they've got their uniform on, not actually wearing it but on their bag. I have seen a few get caught, I have heard of a few more getting caught doing it." Here, the stipulations and rules established by *The Big Issue* code of conduct provide powerful and resonating learning experiences.

Of course, there are many other sellers who hold a very ambivalent view of *The Big Issue*, its training and the sorts of work skills that might be possible to develop in working. When I asked the sellers if they think they learnt something by working as a seller, many shrug their shoulders, laugh and scoff, or just give an outright "No!" When I ask Frank (57 years old, Melbourne) if he thinks he has learnt anything from being a *Big Issue* seller, he laughs and replies, "No—all this fantastic charming personality I had before hand! I am just naturally fantastic! Ummm. It's hard to say." Frank reflects that the main skill required for homeless street press work is getting people to stop. He says, "A lot of people, as soon as you make eye contact, they put their head down. And that used to annoy the shit out of me. Because once you've got their eye contact you've usually got 'em. But, you've just got to give it a go." This speaks to the tacit learning that relates to common overriding experience of pride for 'giving it a go' and keeping at it, and learning what it takes to persevere and getting sales. For sellers this is about learning how to market themselves as much (if not more) as it is about how to market the paper.

In San Francisco, I am sitting on a ledge just outside the popular tourist destination Fisherman's' Wharf. I had met Joel earlier that day, and he asked if I could meet him at the Wharf once he had made some sales. He is eager to share his story, and is particularly proud that he has been a seller of six different homeless street presses across North America. He is turning 54 in about a week, and sports a long bushy beard and a cowboy hat. When I ask him if he has learnt something from being a seller, he replies:

> *I like being around people. I've had people tell me—well you're really good at being with people—you're a real good people person. I've had friends tell me, have you ever thought about getting into sales, like cars, or something like that? I don't think I'd like to do that because you'd have to lie to people! I just like being around people—I like talking to people. I have conversations with total strangers about the weather, and I get to know the people. ... It's the little things, it's people walking past and saying, 'hello, god bless, have a good day.' It's the little things that matter.*

For Joel, this connection to, and social relationships with, buyers and people is an important part of his work. His strategy is to work everyday for his needs that day, and it is through that work that he has developed a community. Joel relies on the help of others, and lists a number of people who drop by to see how he is going on a regular basis. He recounts enthusiastically how a friend gave him $5 to buy a pair of pants after Joel mentioned to him that he was trying to save up for a pair he saw in the shop next to his shelter. "No questions asked!" Joel exclaimed, "And he told me when I see him, if I need anything, if I don't quite make enough for the day, I just tell him and he'll do what he can. Because he knows that I am actually trying to do something to better myself. I am trying to get off the streets, I am trying to better myself."

Here, for Joel, the tacit learning of his enterprising work is enforced in and through the interactions he has with buyers and other people on the street. This particular encounter strengthens the ways in which he has cultivated sales techniques, and at the same time, strengthens the notion that by working as homeless street press seller, he is demonstrating that he 'is trying to do something better for himself'.

Just like Joel in San Francisco, Ralph (44 years old) in Melbourne found one of the most resonant experiences of working as a seller is connecting with people. I ask him, "Do you think there are any particular skills to be a good *Big Issue* seller?" and he replies, "It's like any job. If you are dedicated you can do well at it. There are no specific skills." But when I ask "Do you think you have learnt anything from being a *Big Issue* seller?" he thinks and replies:

> *No. Ah well .. No. Well I have to think about that one. ... Of course! Yeah—of course. I've learnt something. I've learnt that people really care about each other, and there are some really nice people out there. For me that's a bridging stone for me. It gives you a licence to meet people—to be outdoors. It gives you a reason to be there. So that's really impressive. And people are generally really nice."*

In San Francisco, Ray (in his 50s) also emphasises the ways in which his work creates social relationships and connects him to others who want to change society, and who care for him and other homeless people.

> *You kind of learn about the maker of the situation of what the person is in. Like what causes a person to be in a situation, it gives you an idea of how many people are interested in fixing society. And that is kind of what I have learned from it, you see how many people are interested in that.*

It is important to recognise that these experiences of connection—and ultimately recognition of the injustice of sellers' experiences of unemployment poverty and homelessness—often occur in the context of an extensive period of isolation, despair and loneliness. Learning that others care has profound impact in such circumstances.

Yet, despite the significance of social relationships, the lessons of becoming a seller are inflected with the prerogatives of work: the need for income and, ultimately, the need to manage oneself and develop skills so as to create sales. Roland, for instance, described his work practice as "soldiering on"; he has to keep up his hours and sales so as to ward off potentially being homeless again. Learning to entrepreneurially labour, in other words, is both an expression of, and mediated by the demands of 'caring for the self', to put it in Foucauldian terms in highly precarious circumstances. Here, the work and educative underpinnings of selling homeless street press is invariably reflective of much wider notions of individualised responsibility for poverty, and the material necessities of getting by as a homeless or poor person in advanced capitalist cities.

Joel, for instance, lives well below the poverty line, surviving on general assistance and food stamps. With the vast majority of his general assistance money going on paying for shelter accommodation each night, he sells the *Street Sheet* in order to get by on a daily basis: to pay for meals, essentials and the odd clothes purchase. Work for Joel therefore also needs to be managed alongside his shelter requirements. For a while he was sleeping on the streets but, more recently has been staying in a shelter in the Tenderloin. He has to check into the shelter between 2 pm and 5 pm, and then be back for the evening curfew at 7 pm. If he's not back by 7 pm, he loses his bed for the night.

"What I do", Joel explains, "is I sell the papers to meet my daily everyday needs. My food, cigarettes, maybe I will go to a movie every now and then, or do something nice for myself." Usually Joel makes around $10–20 a day, and he stretches "it out and that will get me through the day." He—like many of the city's homeless—is on the waiting list to get a much-coveted permanent single-room occupancy ('SRO'). SROs are usually converted hotels, in varying levels of condition, offering occupants a room with shared facilities.

Sales, therefore, is about ensuring that Joel has enough money to pay for his daily needs. But getting sales is not simply a matter of selling the product—the magazine or paper. As a product premised on the care of the buyer for the homeless, sellers must also learn how to market themselves. I explore in more detail the experience of self-marketing in Chap. 7. Here, I want to highlight just how often sellers talked of having to learn new ways of looking at themselves in order work as a seller. Learning to labour entrepreneurially, in other words, involved the cultivation of new ways of being, and ultimately new ways of understanding themselves, based on the projection of a happy and positive attitude that can attract sales—or an 'emptiness', to put it in Roland's words.

Joel explains the balance that he has had to learn as a seller—learning to shake off frustrations of people not wanting to buy the paper, and being the right amount of friendly. He says:

> *It all depends on how you project yourself to the people. If you have the wrong attitude, if somebody doesn't want to buy a paper, and you think—'Ah! Pfft, whatever, I don't need you!' It's a negative attitude, you get, like I say, you attract more flies with honey than you do with vinegar. It's the same with people! If you have a positive attitude, if you are friendly, but not overly friendly— if you are polite and nice to people, they will remember that.*

Thus, the practices of self-work that occur in learning to be a seller occurs with sellers' awareness that they are visible and judged on their appearance, behaviour, words and looks. The necessity for smiles, pleasant appearances and outward attitude are all part of learning to work.

This is certainly the case for Tony, a *Big Issue* seller in Melbourne. Tony, 45 years old, has been a seller for around nine years, and for him, as with many other sellers, work is something that requires constant reflection on the performance and representation of self. He says:

> *If you look like cracking the shits or you're having a bad day, it's very hard to sell The Big Issue. I think it's like going fishing with my father when I was young, you know? It's like you've got to be patient- they're not going to come all at once.... It's a waiting game.*

A little later on in this interview Tony returns to the question of public visibility and the tensions of being visible—yes, he wants people to notice him to get the sales, but equally he does not want people to notice him for the wrong reason. He says:

> *Sometimes I work out there without my smiley face on. Sometimes I feel I have to be there, so that I can pay the bills. ... And I think as soon as you look like you're not right people notice you.*

As with Tony, many sellers I spoke with were acutely aware that their selves were literally on display in their work (something I explore further in the next chapter). Underpinning all of this is the daily grind of a form of social regulation that teaches you, as Tony says, that you can rely upon yourself—you cannot rely on your customers, or your sales, but you can rely upon yourself to tough it out, and to be patient. He says:

Because even when I sell The Big Issue they don't have to buy it. So I'm not angry if people don't buy it and you just get used to um doing a lot on your own. You get used to relying on yourself more. And the Issue does teach that, that you can rely on yourself.

For Tony, therefore, being a seller is about being self-reliant, even if this self-reliance is insecure in its returns, in terms of sales. Curtis (59 years old) in San Francisco echoes Tony's reflections on learning the entrepreneurial lessons of self-reliance. For him, this is a form of work that represents his attempt at self-development and social mobility, mediated by the experience of precarious poverty. These sellers' experiences point to the inevitable intersections of learning and working that occur when working entrepreneurially on the margins. When I ask Curtis if he thinks he has learnt anything from selling the *Street Sheet*, he replies:

Yeah. I learnt how to make money! [Laughs] I've learnt that a person ain't going to lie down on the ground just because they're homeless. A person can get up and try and do something for himself, even if it's just selling papers, or doing interviews! Any time and I can make something for himself you should take advantage of it.

Jessica: What about your sales skills?
Curtis: My sales skills? You know I play poker to right? And if I didn't think that I was any good I wouldn't play. If I didn't believe that I could sell I wouldn't sell. You got to have faith, you've gotta have faith in everything that you do. Faith in God, in yourself, in your woman, in your son, in your kid. You've got to have faith. I have faith.

Here, then, Curtis's faith intersects with the required perseverance to work day in, day out, the development of sales tactics, and the ability to 'sell himself'—making the most of opportunities. In the contemporary age of entrepreneurialism and enterprise, homeless street press sellers' experiences point to the everyday realities of attempting to get by whilst engaging in incredibly precarious and morally charged work. Entrepreneurial ethos are embedded in their experiences of work, which emphasise both individual possibility and individual reliance. Their learning/working, in this sense, can maintain, rather than disrupt, the problematic notion that they themselves are the cause of their unemployment and poverty. Learning to work is also connected to the very powerful experience of working: when exclusion and marginalisation from work is deemed such a failure, the opportunity to work is important.

Here, the educative underpinnings of homeless street press—most particularly *The Big Issue*—are linked to the hope for work to provide an effective, and positive, intervention in the lives of the poor and homeless. This immediately links homeless street presses to moral judgements of worthiness and deservingness, and thus to the moral presumption that to work, and to be learning to work, is better than not: the work ethic and the learning ethic. For sellers across all the three cities, these ethics operate in and through their particular experiences and contexts of unemployment, poverty and homelessness, and their necessity to work and make money. Working has a multitude of meanings: it is a means to generate income in the context of chronic poverty and unemployment and for some homelessness; it is a powerful demonstration of 'bettering' and 'helping' themselves; it is an avenue to identify as a worker—or at the very least as willing to work. Learning becomes the means by which sellers work, as they negotiate the entrepreneurial labour required of them: precarious and reliant on their 'enterprising' capacities.

References

Appleby, Y., & Bathmaker, A. M. (2006). The New Skills Agenda: Increased Lifelong Learning or New Sites of Inequality? *British Educational Research Journal, 32*(5), 703–717.

Biesta, G. J. J., Field, J., Hodkinson, P., Macleod, F. J., & Goodson, I. (2011). *Improving Learning Through the Lifecourse*. London/New York: Routledge.

Dean, M. (1995). Governing the Unemployed Self in an Active Society. *Economy and Society, 24*(4), 559–583.

Devos, A., Farrell, L., & Seddon, T. (2010). Disturbing Work, Workspaces and Working Lives: Three Australian Case Studies. In T. Seddon, L. Henriksson, & B. Niemeyer (Eds.), *Learning and Work and the Politics of Working Life* (pp. 69–83). London/New York: Routledge.

Du Gay, M. (1996). *Consumption and Identity at Work*. London: SAGE Publications.

Eichhorst, W., Rodriguez-Planas, N., Schmidle, R., & Zimmermann, K. F. (2015). A Road Map to Vocational Education and Training in Industrialized Countries. *International and Labour Relations Review, 68*(2), 314–337.

Ferguson, K., & Seddon, T. (2007). Decentred Education: Suggestions for Framing a Socio-Spatial Research Agenda. *Critical Studies in Education, 48*(1), 111–129.
Foucault, M. (2008). *The Birth of Biopolitics: Lectures of the College de France, 1978–79.* Hampshire: Palgrave Macmillan.
Gerrard, J. (2014). All That Is Solid Melts into Work: Self-Work, the 'Leanring Ethic' and the Work Ethic. *The Sociological Review, 62,* 862–879.
Gerrard, J. (2015). The Limits of Learning: Homelessness and Educating the Employable Self. *Discourse, 36*(1), 69–80.
Gewirtz, S. (2008). Give Us a Break! A Sceptical Review of Contemporary Discourses of Lifelong Learning. *European Educational Research Journal, 7*(4), 414–424.
Hutchinson, J., Beck, V., & Hooley, T. (2015). Delivering NEET Policy Packages? A Decade of NEET Policy in England. *Journal of Education and Work, 29*(6), 707–727.
Illich, I., & Verne, E. (1976). *Imprisoned in the Global Classroom.* London: Writers and Readers Publishing Cooperative.
Kelly, P. (2013). *The Self as Enterprise.* Furnham: Gower Publishing.
Kelly, P., & Harrison, L. (2009). *Working in Jamie's Kitchen: Salvation, Passion and Young Workers.* Basingstoke: Palgrave Macmillan.
Kelly, P., Campbell, P., & Harrison, L. (2015). 'Don't Be a Smart Arse': Social Enterprise-Based Transitional Labour-Market Programmes as Neo-Liberal Technologies of the Self. *British Journal of Sociology of Education, 36*(4), 558–576.
Lee, A. (2010). What Counts as Educational Research? Spaces, Boundaries, Alliances. *Australian Educational Researcher, 37*(4), 63–78.
Livingstone, D. W. (2005). Expanding Conception of Work and Learning: Recent Research and Policy Implications. In N. Bascia, A. Cumming, A. Datnow, K. Leithwood, & D. Livingstone (Eds.), *International Handbook of Educational Policy* (pp. 977–995). Dordrecht: Springer.
Livingstone, D. W., & Guile, D. (Eds.). (2012). *The Knowledge Economy and Lifelong Learning.* Rotterdam: Sense Publishers.
McDonald, C., & Marston, G. (2005). Workfare as Welfare: Governing Unemployment in the Advanced Liberal State. *Critical Social Policy, 25,* 374–401.
Milana, M. (2012). Political Globalization and the Shift from Adult Education to Lifelong Learning. *European Journal for Research on the Education and Learning of Adults, 3*(2), 103–117.
Peters, M. (2001). Education, Enterprise Culture and the Entrepreneurial Self: A Foucauldian Perspective. *Journal of Educational Enquiry, 2*(2), 58–71.
Rambla, X., & Veger, A. (2009). Pedagogising Poverty Alleviation: A Discourse Analysis of Educational and Social Policies in Argentina and Chile. *British Journal of Sociology of Education, 30*(4), 463–477.

Robertson, S. (2016). Picketty, Capital and Education: A Solution to, or Problem in, Rising Social Inequalities? *British Journal of Sociology of Education, 37*(6), 823–835.

Rose, N. (1992). Governing the Enterprising Self. In P. Heelas & P. Morris (Eds.), *The Values of Enterprise Culture: The Moral Debate* (pp. 141–164). London: Routledge.

Seddon, T. (2004). Remaking Civic Formation: Towards a Learning Citizen? *London Review of Education, 2*(3), 171–186.

Seddon, T., Billett, S., & Clemans, A. (2004). Politics of Social Partnerships: A Framework for Theorizing. *Journal of Education Policy, 19*(2), 121–142.

Seddon, T., Henriksson, L., & Niemeyer, B. (Eds.). (2010). *Learning and Work and the Politics of Working Life*. London: Routledge.

Solomon, N. (2005). Identity Work and Pedagogy: Textually Producing the Learner-Worker. *Journal of Vocational Education and Training, 57*(1), 95–108.

Swithinbank, T. (2001). *Coming Up from the Streets: The Story of the Big Issue*. London: Earthscan.

Tuschling, A., & Engemann, C. (2006). From Education to Lifelong Learning: The Emerging Regime of Learning in the European Union. *Educational Philosophy and Theory, 38*(4), 451–469.

Weeks, K. (2011). *The Problem with Work: Feminism, Marxism, Antiwork Politics and Postwork Imaginaries*. Durham/London: Duke University Press.

Williams, J. (2011). Raising Expectations or Constructing Victims? Problems with Promoting Social Inclusion Through Lifelong Learning. *International Journal of Lifelong Learning, 30*(4), 451–467.

Willis, P. (1977). *Learning to Labour*. Hampshire: Gower.

CHAPTER 7

Working in Public: Value, Exchange and Performance

To work in public on the streets of cities in rain or shine and attempt to attract sales from people walking by, going to work, or on a shopping trip is undoubtedly challenging. Through a series of longer extracts from the research, this chapter explores two principal dimensions stemming from the public nature of homeless street press work: the value of the exchange and the performativity of the work. In this discussion I outline the ways sellers attach value to the moment of exchange with buyers and people passing by—including building social relationships with customers—in ways that go beyond, but still connect to, the need to accrue income. The value of these moments of exchange must be understood in the context of what are often harsh work conditions, including feeling isolated and ignored and managing stressful and negative interactions with the public. Connected to the value—and hope—for the moment of exchange is a deeply performative practice of work. In cultivating their work selves, sellers must both negotiate public space and consider the sorts of versions of themselves that are most conducive to sales. I start the discussion with an interpretation of a research encounter with two *Street Sheet* sellers in San Francisco—Amber and Jeffrey—in order to open up this consideration of working in public.

Amber and Jeffrey

I meet Jeffrey seconds after chatting with Amber. I am in San Francisco, and walking towards the subway entrance when I see a man with a stack of *Street Sheets* standing at the top of the escalators that lead down to the subway. I ask him if he is selling the papers and he shakes his head, mumbling something about his friend being back in a minute. I can't quite hear him and ask again about the *Street Sheets*, and he points back in the direction from where I have just walked. I see Jeffrey bounding down the street: a tall Black man in his 50s wearing worn, torn and dirty jeans and a loose sweater that hangs off him. He walks with confidence and with purpose, grinning at me as he approaches with his hand outstretched ready to shake mine.

I tell him about my research and he says he knows all about it: he has just been talking to Amber. I have become used to news about me and my research travelling faster than I can walk in a city, but this seems like a record seeing as Amber is the first seller I have met in San Francisco since arriving just a few days prior. She is an Anglo-American also in her 50s, softly spoken, and she is one of the only three women sellers I meet while I am in San Francisco. Across cities, by far the majority of sellers are men, and there are invariably gendered dimensions to this work practice in which notions of 'decency', 'deserving', and 'worth' are etched with gendered assumptions that mark women and men differently (see Adair 2002). Indeed, the sorts of performative work practices cultivated in selling homeless street press are inflected with both gender and race.

Like most (though not all) women sellers, Amber takes a quiet approach to selling the magazine. She does not attempt to take up lots of space or call out: she stands quietly on the street holding the *Street Sheet* out in front of her smiling as people walk past. She tells me in our interview, "I don't push it, I'm not an aggressive seller." Amber mainly works around the concert halls in the evenings, trying to get sales from the theatre, opera, and concert clientele with excess money to spend. She tends to stick to one spot so that her regular customers know where to find her, and does not walk the streets of the city with the paper like many of the other sellers in San Francisco. Whilst *The Big Issue* sellers have to stick to their stipulated pitch, in San Francisco sellers are free to walk and sell in public spaces as long as they keep a distance from banks and ATM machines.

Unlike all of the other sellers I meet in San Francisco, Amber has secured a much-coveted SRO (single resident occupancy) room. She is almost apologetic about selling the *Street Sheet* now that she is no longer rough sleeping or in a shelter, despite the fact that SRO housing is far from adequate. SROs are often converted hotels, crowded, small with conditions attached (see Gillem et al. 2007). In Amber's building, for instance, she has shared kitchen and bathroom facilities but is not allowed to have any cooking equipment—such as kettles or microwaves, or guests, in her room. Amber, who used to work as a waitress, now manages financially by getting some government assistance, selling *Street Sheets* as well as earning the odd $10 for watching the cars of people who go to the concerts in the area around her pitch. When I ask Amber if she ever feels unsafe working as a seller she mentions that she knows most of the people on the street in this area, and—like many other women sellers across the three cities—that she has quite a few men who look out for her which makes her feel safe. I wonder if Jeffrey is one of them.

Jeffrey introduces me to Winston, and explains that they are business partners. Winston is clearly the more nervous and shy of the two, immediately moving away from the conversation and me as soon as Jeffrey arrives, positioning himself on the other side of the square. Jeffrey and I chat for a while—Jeffrey is careful with his words and is a bit of a wordsmith, quoting and weaving lyrics from Leonard Cohen and Tom Waits as we talk about the weather, the city, *Street Sheet*, the homeless. He tells me proudly that there is already a YouTube video of him made by someone who interviewed him a few years ago and urges me to look it up. He explains that in addition to selling *Street Sheets* he also does a range of odd jobs, including regularly helping to unload flowers and fresh produce for the famers' market. We agree to meet the next week early in the morning after he finishes up at the famers' market.

The next week Jeffrey does not turn up. I spend the rest of the day chatting to other sellers, walking the city with them as they attempt to get enough sales for the day. After a long day I see Jeffrey at the subway entry again late in the afternoon. I ask him what happened in the morning, and he explains that his week has been a little "off-kilter" as in the early hours of Sunday morning the police raided the area around the subway station—the area where he always sells his *Street Sheets*, and the area that is also his home: he sleeps at the bottom of the escalators of the subway station. He tells me he wasn't around at the time of the raid, but everyone who was there split up and they left his stuff. The police took it all, and he has got no way of getting it back, as he has no ID and no way of proving that it is his.

I am taken aback by his story. I shouldn't be. I have read plenty of research that documents similar accounts (e.g. Kennedy and Fitzpatrick 2001; Kennelly and Watt 2011; MacLeod 2002; Lynch 2002), and I have now heard dozens of stories of the struggles and injustices of being homeless and poor. Yet, each story does not dull or blur the others. Rather, each new tale brings further amplification to the brutality of poverty and homelessness: the harsh reality of everyday life on the streets.

It is around 4.45 pm and he suggests that if I come back at 6 pm we can do a taped interview after he has set up and while he is selling left over flowers from the market and *Street Sheets*. I feel exhausted after a day of walking the streets, but I am keen to talk more with Jeffrey so I agree. I head to the large shopping centre down the road to grab a snack. I am marvelled and frustrated that it is a shopping centre that offers the only space for me to sit quietly. In all three cities shopping centres are a central part of my research experience. Across San Francisco, Melbourne and London, the lack of space to sit in relative peace amongst the city hustle and bustle ironically means that I often retreat into the garish shopping centres in order to eat my lunch or grab a coffee. When I first started the research in Melbourne, shopping centres were also often where I conducted my initial interviews with sellers. We would sit in food courts, and on the few couches and benches provided for shoppers, leaning in to hear each other over the sound of crying babies, laughing groups of shoppers, and office workers talking loudly on their phones whilst waiting for their lunch orders.

I quickly worked out, however, that for some sellers shopping centres are not a part of their spatial experience of the city. Or, rather, shopping centres constitute one of the many spaces in the city from which they feel excluded. Lined with shops filled with products far out of their purchasing grasp; gleaning glossy white with bright light; comprising towering interiors with ever-climbing escalators and brash ceiling sculptures or chandeliers dramatically dripping down into wide foyers underneath; and policed by private security guards: for some shopping centres are unwelcome and uncomfortable spaces. These sorts of spaces are kinds of spectacles of consumer capitalism, in which pristine and gated pseudo-public (but ultimately private) spaces come to be understood as public practice and space (for some) (MacLeod 2002). They work not only to create particular practices, desires and meanings of consumption: they also demarcate the apparent 'refuse' of their existence: the absences of these spaces—the homeless and poor—are as important as what is present.

Spectacular consumer capitalism cultivates "an idealised citizen archetype, engaged in meaningful consumption, and the work and social practices that support this" (Gerrard and Farrugia 2015: 2226). In doing so it also cultivates the so-called 'others' "who transgress or appear to reside outside this archetype": the homeless, the poor, and those who appear to be failing in their role as citizens to be consuming and working (*ibid.*). As I have written (*ibid.*) elsewhere,

> ... 'the culture of consumption', becomes melded to notions of 'community' and 'civility', and in turn frames anything 'outside' of the activities of consumption as problematic to the vitality of urban public space and life' (Ranasinghe 2011: 1939). Distinctions between 'us and them' assist to construct homelessness as a glitch in an otherwise functional system, a malfunction or abnormality.

For people who are homeless, this is experienced as "profound disempowerment" (Farrugia 2016: 95). As Farrugia's research on homeless young people powerfully reveals, homelessness is affectively embodied and characterised by sensations of shame, objectification, and displacement. Homelessness involves being excluded from both the private and public realms, and managing appearances to 'pass' as not homeless or knowing full well that they are 'read' as homeless and are unwelcome (*ibid.*).

The issue here is how homelessness becomes deemed as problematic whilst consumer capitalism and its inequalities remain unproblematised. As Robert Desjarlais writes in his 1997 ethnographic account of homeless shelters, "A common problematic vision is apparent in many accounts: the homeless live in an underworld; they are a ghostly, animal-like brood who threaten the peaceful, artful air of cafes, libraries and public squares" (1997: 2). Put simply, the homeless can appear as troublesome interruptions in an otherwise functional world. Yet in actuality poverty and homelessness are central to the dysfunctionality of the inequality and injustice perpetuating contemporary social relations.

At times even for those selling directly outside shopping centres, when I would suggest to go inside to centre couches visible from the street, they would look at me puzzled, and exclaim, "Oh! In there? Sure. I've never really gone in there." This is particularly the case in San Francisco, where the shopping centre I am grabbing my snack from is part of a new gentrification push of the area in an attempt to attract, and cater for, the growing tourist market. Most sellers I speak with in San Francisco had some sort of altercation with the expanding private security force connected to shopping precinct development. Many spoke of being 'moved-on' by private security not just from the shopping centre itself, but also from the area around it.

The city has 23 municipal codes that effectively criminalise the daily activities of the homeless. There are codes that criminalise standing, sitting, and resting in public places, camping and lodging in public places (including inside vehicles), as well as begging and panhandling (see Fisher et al. 2015). According to a recent review of the city's laws and its enforcement, every year San Francisco city issues over 3,000 citations for violations of these codes (*ibid.*). San Francisco is, in other words, far from hospitable when it comes to its homeless residents. During my time spent at the Coalition on Homelessness in the week prior, organisers told me about the Homeless Bill of Rights' campaign, running in conjunction with a number of other groups across California. Connected to similar campaigns in Colorado and Oregon, the "campaign strives to ensure that all people have the basic right to live where they choose without fear of harassment and criminalization at the hands of the police" (Western Regional Advocacy Project n.d.).

As already noted, as with San Francisco, in Melbourne and London begging is also illegal, and a range of city codes and gentrification projects have similar effects. In London for instance 'anti-homeless spikes'—metal studs implanted into the ground designed to discourage homeless people from sleeping in the area—caused significant public outcry and debate (Petty 2016). In Melbourne, the recent growth in visible homelessness across the city has prompted the City Council to take an 'aggressive outreach' approach that includes the dismantling of squats and rough sleeping camps (Dow 2016).

I get back around 6.15 pm and Jeffrey has already set up his stall outside the subway entrance. All around the subway are about a dozen other homeless people. They are starting to set up stalls from their carts, selling second-hand clothes, shoes, and other cheap goods, laid out on the street. I am struck by the patent differences between the emerging market that is forming on the streets around the subway entrance and the shopping centre four minutes' walk down the road. Jeffrey stands right at the top of the escalator and subway entry amongst a dozen buckets filled with slightly drooping bunches of flowers, left over from the farmers' market. Jeffrey's selling approach couldn't be more different from Amber's. He is beaming, smiling and loudly greeting as many people as he can as they stream past him and onto the subway escalator. His voice fills the air as he calls out, "Good evening Ma'am! Good evening Sir! Two bouquets for a dollar! Make someone happy tonight!"

I stand next to Jeffrey and we chat. He tries to keep up the conversation with me while still touting sales. Every minute or so someone comes up to buy some flowers, and occasionally someone also buys a *Street Sheet*. Many are clearly regulars, greeting Jeffrey by name and chatting with him about their day. Jeffrey is unmistakably flirtatious: the gendered figure of the macho, charismatic, entertaining, and complimenting male seller was one that I encountered again and again, and indeed I often found myself on the receiving end of these flirtations. Some sellers, such as Al in Melbourne whose experiences are discussed later in this chapter, purposefully target women buyers, as he has greater success in establishing regular customers and getting sales from women. For the most part, these charismatic men are the most successful sellers financially. Their experience of being a seller is manifestly different to sellers (including many women) who stand or sit silently holding the magazine desperately hoping for sales, but not commanding or taking up the city space in the same way.

At one point Jeffrey and Winston argue about whether or not they should give a bunch of flowers away for free to a woman (Jeffrey wants to, Winston does not), and one of the regulars who is waiting to buy some flowers, leans in to me. "They are always arguing," she says with a smile and a chuckle, "every time I come they are arguing about something!" Eventually, Jeffrey and I agree that it is too hard to chat whilst he is also working, and we make a time to meet the next day.

When we eventually do meet we sit out in the sun in a courtyard of the San Francisco Public Library. Like many others of San Francisco's homeless, Jeffrey uses the library throughout the day as a space to refresh and rest. Libraries are common public 'safe spaces' for the homeless: they are often open for longer than day centres, are more accessible, have less surveillance, and are not "stigmatized spaces" (Hodgetts et al. 2008). He tells me that all the staff know him here and that he has become expert in knowing hidden away spots that do not get checked very often: he often uses the library to catch up on much needed sleep, but sleeping is prohibited in the library so it is a matter of trying to find a spot out of the way from the library staff and security.

Jeffrey is a passionate supporter of the *Street Sheet* for the news coverage that it brings on issues surrounding poverty and homelessness. He is also a consummate salesman. He started selling the *Street Sheet* around two years after becoming homeless and, in his words, "I tried panhandling but it didn't work for me." When I ask him what the difference between selling the papers and begging is, he answers:

> From my point of view I'm in the same league as Hearst. Do you know who Hearst is? He's a big publisher in the United States. Well, he used to be in newspapers. I am a seller: I am selling a product. Well I am selling information, but this is an information age. It's no different from the [San Francisco] Chronicle or the [San Francisco] Examiner. It is a narrow focus paper, but it's just another magazine newspaper. It's a specific interest.

My time the evening before with Jeffrey showed me that he has an exceptional talent for attracting sales and engaging people in the street, and so I ask him what his selling technique is. "Basically, it's not brain surgery", Jeffrey responds, "Anyone who sees me with a stack of newspapers kind of can work out what I'm doing." He explains,

> My approach is just to make me them aware that I am there. I don't ask for money and I don't ask them to buy the paper. You know it depends. Sometimes I play one against the other. But my regulars, I never ask—I just say, 'Happy evening! Happy day!' And I find that people actually respond much better to that. The number of times, you know, I say 'happy evening' and say 'have a good weekend' as they are going down the escalator, and then they realise what I'm doing. And then they come back a minute or two later and say—'Oh you know, I have to come back and get it.' And the number of times that that happens, it makes me feel really good about myself. I must be doing something right. Begging is just begging. It's just intruding upon someone. And it puts them in an awkward situation I think. I like what I do. It's more me. Because I'm not really a salesman, but I am good at it.

Here, Jeffrey is keen to distinguish his work as offering another product or service in the city, not an intrusion to the everyday culture and rhythm of the city. The importance of the legitimacy of this work is paramount: Jeffrey does not want to be, in Erving Goffman's words, a "destroyers of worlds" by being awkward or disrupting the tacit everyday order (1961: 72; see also Gerard and Farrugia 2015). Begging, according to Jeffrey is an interruption—not offering anything and creating 'awkward' situations; the sorts of situations Desjarlais describes when he talks of homelessness disturbing the city's 'peaceful' air (1997).

Jeffrey's interaction with the public is of paramount importance to his sales technique, but also to his sense of worth and purpose in his work. Social relationships are core to the value of homeless street press work. He tells me, "I try to establish a personal contact rather than a business one, I tell people it's not about the money if I'm out here long enough I'll get the money its not about that. So the other part of the equation is the people that I meet. I've made some really nice friends and I've met some really truly beautiful people." Selling the *Street Sheet* alongside selling flowers is something Jeffrey sees as "giving back to the community." "The community is very generous," he says, "very supportive. You know, people stop by and say I haven't seen you are you okay have you been sick? It makes me hold my head up a little higher. You know, it makes me feel a little better about myself. You know I like my life."

THE VALUE OF EXCHANGE

Like Jeffrey, sellers in all cities discussed the moment of exchange as holding particular importance and worth. The opportunity to speak with locals and tourists, to meet people, and perhaps even make some friends, is central to the meaning and significance of working as a seller. What is important here is that the exchange moment's significance goes much further than any potential use-value of the newspaper or magazine. The exchange value is defined by the social relationships between sellers and buyers that are created in the moment of exchange. From the shortest of exchanges when buyers try and quickly stuff the money into sellers' hands and make little eye contact, to the longer exchanges that involve buyers pausing in their day to stand with sellers while catching up on each others' news, these relational moments are what furnishes the feelings of worthiness—a core affective dimension—of sellers' work.

British sociologist Beverley Skeggs (2004a) writes powerfully on the ways in which we make ourselves in and through the values attached to our personhood. Making the self, Skeggs writes, is an undeniably classed process and morally charged, tied to presumptive norms surrounding the good and proper self. Work is, of course, central to the making of self. In the context of homeless street press, both buyer and seller engage in acts of self-making in the moment of exchange. In other words, exchange is central to cultivating the 'self'. For buyers, it is both an expression of 'ethical consumption' and an act of care and judgement, in which consumption is interpellated into a political or ethical event (see Barnett et al. 2005; see also Zizek 2009). Homeless street press is a product premised on the value of an experience shared (the exchange) with an 'authentic'—and deserving—homeless person.

This is a spatial and embodied act in that it brings sellers and buyers into closer proximity and creates the potential for moments of relational intimacy: the locking of an eye gaze, the return of a smile, the touch of skin in the exchange of money, the sharing of names, stories, views on the weather or the latest city or political controversy. Luc Boltanski writes about the ways in which contemporary media representations of suffering evokes a highly constrained politics of pity, which buttresses divisions and the apparent void between the 'viewer' and the 'suffering' (2003). In this regards, homeless street press could be understood as one response to the apparent moral and political vacuum for personal action around poverty and homelessness (Barnett et al. 2005). It is, nonetheless, personal action that relies upon a performance of productivity and deservingness on the part of sellers, and a marketised politics of care on the part of buyers.

Zizek (2009) writes on the new level of contemporary consumption as a "new spirit" of "cultural capitalism". "We primarily buy commodities," he suggests, "neither on account of their utility nor as status symbols; we buy them to get the experience provided by them, we consume them in order to render our lives pleasurable and meaningful" (2009: 52). Or, to put it as Skeggs does, "Experience is the only thing left to buy for those who are materially sated" (2004b: 106). Homeless street press sellers are acutely aware of this dynamic. Like Jeffrey, they know that they are partly selling a commodity, a product with potential use-value, but that ultimately they are also selling an experience that is created in the moment, and value, of the exchange. Importantly, it is a moment that they too value.

It is particularly important, for instance, for Rachel. Rachel has been a seller for around 8 years in Melbourne and is in her 50s. She has a regular pitch outside a shopping centre—it is not a particularly busy pitch, but there is generally a constant slow stream of people coming in and out of the shopping centre throughout the day. Like Amber, she is not an assertive seller. Rachel stands with her back against the wall with her red *Big Issue* vest on, holding up the magazine in front of her. When she is working I notice that most people ignore her, walking past her as if she is not there. Rachel's approach, however, is to continuously actively search the faces of the people walking past to try and catch someone's eye. This means that most people have to purposefully not look at her in order to avoid her. Occasionally they sneak in a sideways glance as they go past when they think the possibility of eye contact has passed.

Rachel vehemently endorses *The Big Issue* and sees herself as an ambassador for the organisation. Unlike the vast majority of sellers I speak to, as with Jeffrey Rachel downplays the importance of money in her work. She loves to talk with people as they come through her pitch, and says that it is this that keeps her going, not the money. She is immensely proud that she has a number of 'regulars'—buyers who are committed to buying the magazine each fortnight from her. She explains that this is probably because she is not so focused on the sales. "It's not just like I'm saying here's the magazine, give me my money and see you later," she says. "I will sit and chat to them and I've done that always. And I think I do it more because I don't spruik and that's part of my thing. I will sit and say, 'How's your day been, what have you been doing?', or they'll ask me how I am."

I end up catching up with Rachel regularly over the course of a year. We meet at her pitch and I buy her a coffee at the nearby café, where we sit and chat for an hour or so. She spent years rough sleeping and then in and out of refuges before finally—a few of years ago—securing a public housing unit. Rachel is on the government's job seeker allowance 'Newstart', which means she has to regularly report on her job searching activities to the commonwealth government. She also has multiple chronic and ongoing mental and physical illnesses, and over the year was in the process of trying to secure disability payment so that she wouldn't have to be looking for work whilst also working as a *Big Issue* seller.

Rachel's identification with being a *Big Issue* seller is underpinned by a valuing of the interactions and social relationships she has with buyers, and is also heavily woven with judgements about the 'right' way to sell. Talking about Gabby, whose experiences were discussed in Chap. 5 and who sells close to Rachel's pitch, she expresses annoyance that Gabby sells *The Big Issue* in such a way that emphasises the material necessity of the work, rather than relationship building. She says,

> When I walked up there was one of my customers, and I could hear Gabby going—'Oh, I really need the money', and it's just like, why are you saying that?! We all need the money but you don't need to beg for the money. My attitude is if the customer wants to buy it they'll buy it. To me, if I wasn't a seller and I heard someone going—'Oh, I really need the money, please buy it'—I'd go, 'Well—no, because you're too forceful. I'd prefer to give the money to someone who is just being quiet about it, or being happy about it.' She's too pushy. And I get heaps of my customers tell me that. It's not a good look the way she is sitting there.

For Rachel, being 'quiet' and not 'pushy' is a way of cultivating respectable relationships with buyers. These are her tactics for ensuring that she is not viewed as disruptive or troublesome in the public spaces and practices of the city.

Regardless of what sorts of judgements made and approaches taken with regards to sales tactics, sellers talk often about the value of the exchange moment circumventing bad sales. Building rapport with regulars and having exchanges with people who bought the magazine, or even those who just smiled as they walked past, are what make the badly paid work palatable. When I ask Tom (48 years old) in London, for instance, what would make a good day in sales, he answers:

Tom: Oh my god. My—I'm an abysmal seller. My sales targets are poor.
Jessica: So what would you be happy with? What would you be happy with at the end of the day?
Tom: I'd be happy meeting the same customers I've always met. Making more customers. Making more contacts. And five a day: if I can do five magazines a day that won't be too bad.

Here, the importance of meeting and talking with customers intermingles with the overarching concern of making money—for Tom his aim amounts to £6.25 a day.

But it is also important because these more 'positive' exchanges occur within a common overarching experience of feeling ignored, or negatively targeted, by members of the public, something I explore further in the discussion below. For many sellers, the difficulty lies in watching people walk by again and again, for hour after hour, and not making a sale. In this context, 'positive' exchange moments—material or not—are a welcome relief. As put by London seller Margo (37 years old), "If someone nice stops it makes up for twenty idiots, oh yeah it's good."

For Al (41 years old), Melbourne *Big Issue* seller, the worth of being a seller is connected to both his ability to independently earn money, having been unemployed for a long time, and the social connection. Like Jeffrey, Al is a charismatic and energetic seller, and is one of the most financially successful sellers I came across in the research. He works tirelessly on his pitch, calling out, and leaning in to target people as they walk past. In his best hours he makes just over the minimum wage in Australia, as I explored in Chap. 4. When I ask him what he likes about being a *Big Issue* seller, he doesn't hesitate to answer:

I like the independence it gives you financially and mentally as well, the social connection you have. Even if they don't buy, people will stop and give you their time and talk to you.

Jessica: I have noticed that you're quite social at your pitch.
Al: Yes, yes, I actually crave that. I look forward to the next encounter and being able to catch up with someone, to find out what's going on in their lives. I've built up relationships with customers and even people that don't buy and those people can surprise you at Christmas and December coming up. It's the best month of The Big Issue earnings wise because you get tips. And the people that don't usually—who will say hello and talk but don't give you a cent or

buy the magazine, at Christmas time they might give you twenty dollars. I have quite a few of those to look forward to.

Al's response highlights the complex interconnections of the value within relationships with buyers. Having the opportunity to talk, and build social relationships is paramount, but the significance of this is never far from the opportunity to earn more money. For sellers, whose income is precarious, the need to earn is never far from their minds. The lead up to Christmas seemed to particularly compound these dynamics: many sellers talk of the need to be seen selling in the weeks and months leading up to Christmas, so that when Christmas came regulars have them in their mind to give gifts of money—something sellers rely upon to buy gifts for their own children and families.

Within this kind of work practice, a sale signifies both income and a break in the stream of people, seemingly unconcerned or uninterested, passing by. When talking with Jenna, a San Francisco seller of about 2 years who immigrated to the US from South America, about how she felt about the neighbourhood she regularly sold in, she replied.

Yeah, well, people pass and sometimes they say they refuse to buy it. They come up with different excuses. They say, 'I am very busy', 'I have not time to read', 'I don't read newspapers'. And I say, 'I don't believe that. I don't believe that! You are going to say to me that you don't know how to read!' I say, 'I know how much money you have in your hands! You've got a $20 bill, are you going to say that you can't read it!' And sometimes, they have the cookies or the peanuts. And I say, 'Oh you are eating peanuts and chocolate do they taste good'! And then they laugh.

Like Jeffrey, Jenna takes an assertive, rather than quiet, sales approach. She says, "It's the same as if you were going to sell an orange or an apple. Or if you are standing at the front of your café and you are trying to get people to come in. You need to make a speech, to make your restaurant full, you know! To bring the customers inside!" Yet Jenna takes the approach of pointing out the uncomfortable, the pretences, and the unsaid in the moments of exchange. She knows, and the people who walk past know that they can read, that they probably read newspapers, and that they have $1. Rather than accept and smile at their responses like most vendors, Jenna is more brazen: pointing out the deceits and pointing out the realities of her poverty: she does not have cookies or peanuts to snack on.

Performing for the Public: Working in Urban Spaces

If the value of the exchange—for both sellers and buyers—is imbued with a sense of worth in connecting with each other, then part of the sales job that sellers undertake involves "selling themselves", as put by one of the organisers and ex-seller of *Street Sheet*. Sellers develop selling practices to enable them to project particular images of themselves to the public so as to attract sales. This is a deeply performative work practice. As explored in Chap. 2, this is not simply a matter of sellers having experiences of being watched and surveilled by an amorphous or faceless 'public': the performativity of sellers' experiences occurs in and through sellers' own judgements, concerns, and experiences of the city.

Nevertheless, sellers' 'in public' work, requiring the attraction of sales through a morally charged demonstration of 'helping' and 'bettering' themselves, creates a particular experience of work that is framed by the practices and spaces of the city. For some, managing the public nature of their work involves a careful analysis of the sorts of representations of themselves they need to craft in order to attract sales. Troy (69 years old, San Francisco), for instance, views his *Street Sheet* work as an extension of his 'people person' personality. "I've always been a people person", he tells me,

> And I try to understand what people want. You've got to understand what people want and what they want to see before you get involved with them in order for them to give you something. Because a piece of paper with a newspaper, you know, they might give you twenty dollars for it, that's saying something. So you must be doing something right. They must like you. *[Laughs]*. That's the way I see it. I love them for it. They bless me and I give them all the blessings in the world for putting out for me. You know when they see a lot of other stuff that kind of makes them doubt that's when it doesn't work. So I like giving people something.

Here, Troy's "giving people something" occurs through the careful management of his image as a clean, respectable man. Troy puts a lot of effort into ensuring that his clothes are neat and clean, and that he is always smiling and approachable.

In addition, sellers' work, carried out on the street, is a competitive enterprise. Sellers feel like they are competing for the attention and custom of city-goers with buskers, charity workers, beggars, and of course other sellers. Adrian (in his 40s, Melbourne), for instance, reflects, "I think there's a lot of us, and we're in competition. And you hear most people when they walk past, 'I just saw one of you up there on the corner.'" For sellers in Melbourne and London, who unlike the San Franciscan peers are assigned pitches and cannot walk the city to sell the paper, this means that they have to develop sales practices to attract customers within the boundaries of ostensibly small urban spaces.

To explore these public performative dynamics, I start here with an extended reflective extract from my field notes and interview with Andrew, a Melbourne *Big Issue* seller in his 50s. (The photo discussed here can be seen in Chap. 4).

> *I arrive back at my university office after a day of interviewing and hanging out with sellers. After parking and locking my bicycle, I enter the austere and corporate foyer of my campus building that gives minimal information about the teaching and research activities that lie within. As I travel up the elevator I fumble in my bag for my staff card, which doubles as a security pass. I 'beep' myself in and make my way to my cubicle. My cubicle in the open plan office is noisy and awkward, rendering all work public, in view of colleagues moving in the space.*
>
> *But upon return from my day with sellers, I am reminded that the surveiling quality of my open plan office occurs within a bounded space: a space that is accessed only by university staff and students, and a space that is literally gated from the 'outside world' through security cards. For sellers, their work occurs on the street: also an open space, but much less bounded. To add to the public nature of this, their work is based on their public visibility and is enhanced by their bright red vests and hats, provided for sellers by The Big Issue as a part of their 'uniform' when they are signed up to work.*
>
> *Today I spent some time with, and interviewed, Andrew. In this interview we discussed the photographs he had taken as a part of the research project. As I sit at my cubicle, Andrew's words keep rolling over again and again in my head as I look again at copies of the photos. I had asked him to take photos of a 'typical day's work', and we were going through them one by one. The first few were relatively self-explanatory. There was a photo of his coffee mug taken on the pavement outside his flat where he has his breakfast every morning, and a photo of his local tram stop.*
>
> *We got to a dark photo of a non-descript doorway on a city street. I say: "This is a bit of a dark one", to which he replies, "That is the doorway, that's my phone booth."*
>
> *Jessica: Your phone booth?*
> *Andrew: In the way of relating it—that's where I turn into the Super-Big-Issue-Man.*
> *Jessica: [laughs].*
> *Andrew: Superman has a phone booth: I have a doorway.*

Jessica: And you go here every day?

Andrew: I don't know if this has a urine smell to it! Sometimes I've got to get changed out of there because someone's had a bit of an upchuck from the night before sort of thing. But yeah, that's where I put me stuff down there and I get changed.

Jessica: Yep.

Andrew: And um, it's amazing how the process of putting a uniform on you can actually physically change how you become, you know, your voice is going to change, your demeanour's going to change and I go from being a very serious person to a very—kid with too much red cordial sort of thing. I do that in the process of putting a uniform on and by taking my jacket and my jumper off, you know. I'm taking off the person—the guy from [home town] to when I put the jacket and that on, I'm putting on all the quirks and idiosyncrasies of a 'Big Issue' guy that you would be able to see on a regular basis.

Jessica: How does that make you feel when you're doing it?

Andrew: I enjoy the process, I enjoy it. I enjoy being someone else more than I do myself. That's without a shadow of a doubt. And I think you'll find most creative people whether they tread the boards or in front of the camera, say the same thing. It's a lot easier—becoming someone else gives you a lot of freedom. You're not stuck by the norms of Andrew, I'm the norm of the Big Issue guy. He doesn't have a lot of things in play. Because of the person he is I enjoy becoming him because he's a nice person. He's a genuinely nice person, so I enjoy the process of becoming him.

Jessica: How does it feel when you take the uniform off?

Andrew: Ah, highly financially dependent, but if I've had a good day, the process of changing back into the normal state of old Andrew from [home town], he's totally different 'cause I know financially I'm secure for the next little while, I know I'll be having a bed, I know I'll be having to think what I eat, I know I've got money for the phone, I know I've got power, I know I've got assuredly that comes with financial security....

Jessica: And what about if you haven't made enough that day?

Andrew: Well then I've got to re-evaluate what I've got to do. Am I going to have to come into work and do an extra shift the next day? Am I going to have two-minute noodles with sausages rather than homemade lasagne? They're the decisions you've got to make sometimes. I mean I can run on the smell of an oily rag if I need to. I can guide my way financially around things quite well. I know as long as I've got magazines in the bag and the health to be able to stand out there and sell it, I can always make money. And if not, well I know okay it's time to go into the safe mode, okay I'm not going to have that extra cigarette after dinner, I'm only going to buy two

litres of milk and I'm not going to have the extra bowl at ten o'clock at night and the bananas aren't going to go on it either! They're going to be saved for breakfast. So yes it's just readjusting.
[...]
Jessica: What are the main differences between The Big Issue guy and Andrew?
Andrew: The main issue, I'm prepared to smile. I get told a sneer a lot [laughs].
Jessica: [laughs].
Andrew: It's not that I'm sneering, it's just that I see people doing things and I just—my disappointment shows, I can't hide my disappointment in, whether it's the individual, whether it's in society, whether it's in an organisation, you know I don't hold back. If someone's being rude on the bus I will get up and I will say 'you're being rude sit down shut up 'cause you wouldn't say that if your grandma was there.' It gets me into a lot of trouble, a lot of confrontations. It's the only way I can get through those.
Jessica: And when you're in the uniform, you're just...?
Andrew: In uniform I will take a certain amount but don't spit on me and don't touch me. Spit on me or touch me, that's assault and the legal preamble's going out quicker than the punches are. ...

This reflective research note and transcript is an unavoidably insufficient slice of an important research moment. It doesn't capture the changes in tone and tenor as Andrew and I make our way through what has now become (being our third 'formal' interview) a familiar combination of research 'Q and A' and general chatting. Nor does it capture the rhythm of our conversation, or the clangs of our coffee cups and the hum and horns of the traffic behind us as we sit at an outdoor city café. It also doesn't capture the intersubjective relationship between Andrew and myself.

Yet, Andrew's account of his shape-shifting from his 'normal' self into his Super-*Big Issue*-Man 'self' powerfully describes the performative demands on the work practice of being a seller. In the first stance, the shape-shifting Andrew undertakes in 'becoming' his *Big Issue* self points to the navigations that are made between the private self and the public— *The Big Issue*—self. For Andrew this distinction is of profound importance. Later in the interview Andrew explains that he is not working at the moment because he is unable to 'spruik'—to call out to advertise *The Big Issue*—owing to have a cold and a sore throat. Spruiking is for Andrew a fundamental part of his *Big Issue* performance and self, and for which he has a reputation. He is worried that if he works without spruiking people might approach him and ask him if he is okay, and he does not want to have to explain that he is unwell as that would reveal too much about his 'normal' self.

Of course, performativity is something that underpins our conduct in most of our work and social activities. As Erving Goffman (1959) suggests, each social interaction or role we undertake requires a performance of a kind. Such performances are often driven by a desire to represent ourselves in a particular way, in an effort to be understood in a particular way. To, in other words, "convey an impression to others which it is in [their] interests to convey" (1959: 4). For Andrew, the need to convey a particular version of himself as a *Big Issue* seller means creating a range of work routines in order to become a seller: shape-shifting from 'normal Andrew' to '*The Big Issue* Andrew' in the pocket slither of privacy provided by a shadowy street doorway. Here, the transition between private and public/work self occurs with high levels of public visibility. Spatially and socially sellers must eke out a space on the street for selling homeless street press. They must do so whilst the vast majority of peopling passing by are concurrently using the space—spatially and socially—as a transitional passage to consumption, employment and leisure.

As discussed above, Andrew's shape shifting and performance occurs within a moral economy. For the most part, consumers purchase *The Big Issue* because they are motivated by the organisation's goal of helping 'the homeless through a process of empowerment' (Hibbert et al. 2005). The purchase of *The Big Issue*, whilst at some level motivated by an interest in the commodity itself, is invariably steeped in morality: the moral imperative to act in response to homelessness. Sellers are, in this sense, not only publicly visible as sellers of a magazine, but also publicly visible as 'homeless' people 'helping themselves'. Indeed, purchasers are influenced by the representation of sellers, and tend to buy magazines from those who look particularly 'needy', whilst also having grievances surrounding those who have too 'assertive' or 'aggressive' sales techniques (Hibbert et al. 2005). For Andrew, being the charismatic and energetic '*Big Issue* guy' is key to his work practice. Being sick or ill means that he cannot work, because he does not want his performance or his image to be put under threat.

Like Andrew, other sellers also manage, navigate—and at times embrace—being constantly open to the public gaze in order to make sales.

Some who are not homeless, who have either secured public housing or who are in the private rental market, are ambivalent about possible judgements of them as homeless, as long as it got them more sales. These sellers embrace a work practice that effectively requires them to enterprise the margins. Many talk about need to have their 'happy face' on or needing to have thick skin in order to manage being ignored, and at times being openly snubbed or derided. Sellers also worry about the possibility of members of the public complaining about their behavior and activities, and many have been suspended or reprimanded by *The Big Issue* in particular as a result of this.

Andrew's shape shifting is a powerful reminder of the ways in which sellers must manage their marginality in and through a highly morally charged performative work practice. How sellers manage this is of course varied. Gabby (33 years old, Melbourne), for instance, attempts to embrace 'getting a laugh' out of people walking past in her work practice. It is worth quoting her at length from my third tape-recorded interview with her. By this time she views herself as an accomplished seller, reflecting on her journey to learn the work practice. Gabby mentions that she feels that she has improved as a seller. So I ask:

> *Jessica: What do you think you have improved at?*
> *Gabby: Um, self-confidence, my personality, um what else…? I mean I am shy, don't get me wrong, but I'm not as shy as I used to be.*
> *Jessica: And have your selling techniques changed over the time, have you changed that?*
> *Gabby: That's also what I was going to say, my selling technique has changed a lot, you know, so that's why it's working out better for me. Before I just didn't have a certain way of selling, I just said, "Oh yeah this is The Big Issue blah, blah, blah", nothing exciting. Now I've actually got a trait and it's spruiking and it makes people laugh, it makes me feel funny and it's good. Like the best medicine is laughter and if you can laugh at yourself, you've succeeded and that's what I do.*
> *Jessica: So how do you make people laugh?*
> *Gabby: I just do silly things like of course I read what's in the thing, like that sheet of paper they [The Big Issue] give us what to say about the edition. I don't just go 'Oh it's this, this, this'. For example when they say, 'Oh you know the spring racing carnival's coming up', I make silly noises like a horse, or I pretend I'm riding a horse.*

And I read a few lines of someone's poem and that's what gets them, if you want to know more find out. Just silly little things like that or you know—'cause as you know I have muscle spasms and seizures—I can't help it so I say, 'Come and watch my chicken dance!', that's what I call them, the chicken dance and I'm just mucking around, and people just laugh.

Or if I'm not—you know how people have good days and bad days obviously anywhere. So when I have bad days, I try not to let it out in public or let myself go down too much, so I just think of positive things that I could do to turn it around to make it good.

It's like being an actress. That's how I put it. I'm like an actress and I'm like, okay cover that up, who cares that you've said you're sad, angry or whatever? And so what I do is I go, no I'm not going to be depressed or angry. I mean I can be crying in the bathroom and no one will know 'cause I come out with a big smile on my face and I just make fun or whatever of myself or this or that and you know I just make it turn around.

Gabby's discussion of the performative expectations, which occur in all workplaces, but which are heightened when the workplace is on the street (and when you are managing a host of health issues and the everyday reality of poverty), highlight the ways in which self-development, self-management, and morality are imbued in these work practices. Goffman's (1959) discussion of the presentation and performativity of self, and the dramaturgical dynamics of everyday life, is helpful here to understand the sorts of roles and practices created by homeless street press work. Goffman suggests we deploy 'defensive and protective practices': strategies and tactics in order manage the reception of ourselves, and to avoid embarrassment, shame. Gabby is involved in a whole range of preventative practices in order to cultivate her practice as a sales person, and to avoid discrediting herself or her work, including using her seizures as a means to cultivate 'playful' sales techniques and a way to engage people as they pass by. Like Andrew, Gabby places principal importance on maintaining her performance. Yet, this performance takes its toll: it is exhausting and painful at times. For Gabby, this involves taking time out—crying in the bathroom—and gathering her strength and confidence to keep working.

Significantly, Gabby's improvement and development is an important and welcome part of her work as a *Big Issue* seller, as it has made the job far more manageable. In our first interview, she talked at length about how she could not bear to stand on the street trying to sell the magazines, and every ounce of her body and mind was screaming to give up. However, the development towards being a more confident seller does not lead to any neat resolutions within herself and nor does it eradicate the challenges of working publicly, constantly attempting to perform deservingness and worth. Work helps sellers like Gabby feel more like full, worthy and productive citizens. But there is a brutality at the centre of its practice, it is not *quite* work, and it both exposes and hides the realities of the experience living in poverty. It requires sellers to both lay bare their lives and stories, at the same time as holding back that which might make them 'unsellable'.

Another difficulty for sellers' performances of productivity and deservingness, are the many 'negative' exchanges that occur as a part of their work. "Get a real job!" is a regular cry targeted at sellers, as are sniggers and smirks as people walk past. Sellers manage these events differently, though most are keen to highlight their resilience and ability to withstand being called out at: a skill learnt from their experiences of selling homeless street press, but also of being homeless and/or begging.

Stacey (33 years old) in Melbourne, for example, says that when people tell her to get a real job, or blatantly ignore her, she pretends it does not bother her. "I don't worry about it at all," she tells me, "'Cause I mainly focus on when a big crowd of people come across the road, that's when I start showing off the mag and stuff." Rodney (in his 50s) in San Francisco, explains that in response to people calling out to him he prays. "Some guys sometimes they tell you, 'you shouldn't be selling it!' A couple of times, you know, I just say, 'you prick,' and I walk away." When I ask him if it happens often he says maybe once a week, but the thing that really bothers him is when people don't acknowledge him. "They are sitting down reading something, and I say, 'Excuse me, how are you doing today?' And they just kind of sit there. And they don't acknowledge me. That's what gets me."

Even for Rachel (in her 50s), for whom the sociality of work is so important, being ignored to the point of being pushed around on her pitch, gets her down. She tells me:

> *It's like I think to myself, oh my god, I stand virtually in your way and you don't do anything, I'm sitting here back away from everyone and they still cut straight across and still give me a dirty look because I'm in their way. It's like how much footpath do you need!? I just don't understand people sometimes. I just shake my head. And I think that's why I have my days where I don't want to talk to anyone. It's like, nah I've got coffee and sugar and milk at home, cat's got food, I don't want to go out, I don't want to face people because they're just idiots.*

Like so many sellers, the necessity to feel good within themselves—to feel strong enough to withstand working in public—is a necessity for the work. On days when they feel down, or worn down, working as a seller becomes too difficult: better to stay at home despite the lack of food in the cupboard or coins in the purse.

The necessity to be strong and positive inside is a response to the potential difficulties of public nature of sellers' work. In addition to aching feet, bad backs, feeling the cold or suffering in the sun, sellers' work in the city is characterised by the experience, and fear of, violence. In the context of violence against homeless people, and of the physical vulnerability that homelessness—and working on the street—brings, the potential for violence is never far from sellers' minds. This includes the potential for people passing by to shout abuse, or the fact that working on the street makes them more accessible to people they are trying to avoid.

As already noted, this is inevitably felt differently for women and men. Andrew, for instance, is prepared to respond to potential physical threat with his fists and his knowledge of the law. Many sellers across of the three cities also talk of potential physical threat, and many brought up recent or not so recent cases of homeless people being assaulted in public. For women, this threat is imbued with the reality (and sometimes personal experience of) gender-based violence.

Jan (48 years old, Melbourne) for instance refuses to work as soon as it gets dark and is constantly aware of her vulnerability whilst working on the street. She tells me,

> *Women are more vulnerable on the street. I have to be honest with you, I have had guys come up to me and try and pick me off the street. In other words they want to take me somewhere, give me money in return for sex and that's not good. I won't work after dark. A lot of women sellers that I know won't work after dark, because as a woman you are more vulnerable on the street. You shouldn't have to feel like that, but that is the way the world has become. It's just not safe to be walking the streets at dark, so I will not sell in the dark. Because if that sort of things is happening in the light, you would be much worse after dark.*

Like Andrew and Rachel, Jan has to navigate this concern whilst also engaging in a work practice that is welcoming for potential buyers to approach her. She explains her approach to attracting sales as she stands on the street, "Sometimes I try and catch people's eye, and trying omiling at people goes a long way. Because if you're frowning you're not going to attract any people—you're just going to look like another beggar."

At times, judgemental comments from people passing by have deep impact on sellers, provoking introspection on their life. For example, when I ask Mick (30 years old)—a seller in Melbourne—if he gets any unwelcome comments when working as a seller, the first thing he mentions is people commenting on him being overweight, suggesting to him that he should go for a walk. When talking about this Mick immediately reflects that he is trying to "get motivated again" to "improve" himself, and talks about wanting to walk more. The publicness of Mick's work makes him exposed to the judgements and thoughts of people passing by, which then become wedged in his own reflections on himself. In the hours he has waiting for sales, he turns these comments over and over in his mind.

In this same exchange Mick relays what he describes as a "bizarre" discussion he had with his employment consultant at a job agency. The consultant advised him not to put his *Big Issue* work on his resume as this would hinder, not help, his chances of getting a job. Mick is genuinely confused by this advice and what more he can do to improve himself, as all other messages he had received about *The Big Issue* focused on the possibility of this work to lead to more secure (and hourly paid) work. The promise of homeless street press as a pathway into other employment is discussed in the next chapter. Here, I want to highlight how significant the public exchanges are for sellers. Exchanges are the point of income, but it is also the means by which sellers cultivate relationships, develop understandings of themselves as workers, and through which they performatively demonstrate their willingness to try and lift themselves out of poverty and unemployment. For Mick, this work opens him up to judgements that hurt and which ultimately appear to thwart his hope for a better job.

The significance of the public space as a site of work cannot be overestimated. Melbourne-San Francisco-London: each of these cities provides the context, and material and social worlds, for sellers engaging in their work. The 'publicness' of sellers' work is felt in their performances on city streets, carried out with a constant knowledge that they are visible and viewable, and through their exchanges and interactions with 'the public'—sometimes positive, sometimes negative. The performative work cultures of homeless street press—create a range of practices for sellers: from deep self-reflection surrounding the need and expectation to 'be better', to physically managing themselves in the face of abuse, and feelings of rejection. These performances are connected to sellers' affirmations that they are workers, engaged in legitimate work. Yet, they also reveal the core tensions of a work practice that requires a moral judgement of 'worthiness' and 'deservingness' of people who are poor and homeless. Here, the moment of exchange is heavy with meaning surrounding charity, dignity, and entrepreneurialism, which sellers must then negotiate in their attempts to generate income to buttress the effects of poverty.

Sellers embrace many of the social and relational aspects of working, occurred alongside difficult negotiations stemming from the public nature of their work. Performances of themselves as 'authentic', 'productive' and charismatic occur with the express purpose of attracting sales from people passing by, and of therefore cultivating the 'right' kind of image of themselves. This involves hiding as much as it does revealing, and it involves image management. Sellers, of course, interpret and respond to this differently. From macho charisma to quiet respectability, sellers are involved in deeply performative practices of work that may be extensions and reflections of themselves, but which is ultimately created for the sale.

REFERENCES

Adair, C. (2002). Branded with Infamy: Inscriptions of Poverty and Class in the United States. *Signs, 27*(2), 451–471.

Barnett, C., Cloke, P., Clarke, N., & Malpass, A. (2005). Consuming Ethics: Articulating the Subjects and Spaces of Ethical Consumption. *Antipode, 37*(1), 23–45.

Boltanski, L. (2003). *Distant Suffering: Morality, Media and Politics*. Cambridge, MA: Cambridge University Press.

Desjarlais, R. (1997). *Shelter Blues: Sanity and Selfhood Among the Homeless*. Philadelphia: University of Pennsylvania Press.

Dow, A. (2016, July 18). The Homelessness Crisis Gripping Melbourne. *The Age*. http://www.theage.com.au/victoria/the-homelessness-crisis-gripping-melbourne-20160715-gq6yog.html

Farrugia, D. (2016). *Youth Homelessness in Late Modernity: Reflexive Identites and Moral Worth*. Singapore: Springer.

Fisher, N., Miller, N., & Walter, L. (2015). *California's New Vagrancy Laws: The Growing Enactment and Enforcement of Anti-Homeless Laws in the Golden State*. Berkeley: Policy Advocacy Clinic, Berkeley Law, University of California.

Gerrard, J., & Farrugia, D. (2015). The 'Lamentable Sight' of Homelessness and the Society of the Spectacle. *Urban Studies, 52*(12), 2219–2233.

Gillem, M. L., Croll, S., Brown, K., Gilmour, P., Kimball, T., Maulhardt, C., Mershon, S., Ruben, K., Schaible, S., & Vasepallo, R. (2007). Housing with Dignity: A Post-occupancy Evaluation of Single Resident Occupancy Units. In J. M. Bissell (Ed.), *Proceedings of the 38th Annual Conference of the Environmental Design Research Association* (pp. 73–78). Edmond: The Environmental Design Research Association.

Goffman, E. (1959). *The Presentation of Self in Everyday Life*. New York: Anchor Books.

Goffman, E. (1961). *Encounters: Two Studies in the Sociology of Interaction*. Middlesex: Penguin University Books.

Hibbert, S. A., Hogg, G., & Quinn, T. (2005). Social Entrepreneurship: Understanding Consumer Motives for Buying the Big Issue. *Journal of Consumer Behaviour, 4*(3), 159–172.

Hodgetts, D., Stolte, O., Chamberlain, K., Radley, A., Nikora, L., Nabalarua, E., & Groot, S. (2008). A Trip to the Library: Homeless and Social Inclusion. *Social & Cultural Geography, 9*(8), 933–953.

Kennedy, C., & Fitzpatrick, S. (2001). Begging, Rough Sleeping and Social Exclusions: Implications for Social Policy. *Urban Studies, 38*(11), 2001–2016.

Kennelly, J., & Watt, P. (2011). Sanitizing Public Space in Olympic Host Cities: The Spatial Experiences of Marginalized Youth in 2010 Vancouver and 2012 London. *Sociology, 45*(5), 765–781.

Lynch, P. (2002). Begging for Change: Homelessness and the Law. *Melbourne University Law Review, 26*, 690–706.

MacLeod, G. (2002). From Urban Entrepreneurialism to a "Revanchist City?" On the Spatial Injustices of Glasgow's Renaissance. *Antipode, 34*(3), 602–624.

Petty, J. (2016). The London Spikes Controversy: Homelessness, Urban Securitisation and the Question of 'Hostile Architecture'. *International Journal for Crime, Justice and Social Democracy, 5*(1), 67–81.

Ranasinghe, P. (2011). Public Disorder and Its Relation to the Community-Civility-Consumption Triad: A Case on the Uses and Users of Contemporary Urban Public Space. *Urban Studies, 48*(9), 1925–1943.

Skeggs, B. (2004a). *Class, Self, Culture*. London: Routledge.

Skeggs, B. (2004b). Exchange, Value and Affect: Bourdieu and 'The Self'. *The Sociological Review, 52*, 75–95.

Western Regional Advocacy Project. (n.d.). *Homeless Bill of Rights* http://wraphome.org/what/homeless-bill-of-rights/

Zizek, S. (2009). *First as Tragedy, Then as Farce*. London/New York: Verso.

CHAPTER 8

Moving On?: Aspirations, Pathways and Stasis

Carter (San Francisco, 50s): There's no way I'm going to be doing this for the rest of my life.
Jessica: Okay.
Carter: I would rather be dead. To tell you the truth, there's a good side of this and then there's also another side: I could do better, I could do better, you know? I could be useful somewhere else. There's other people also doing it, but I appreciate that they probably won't be doing it for the rest of their lives. It's not that type of thing. It's temporary, because there are days when if you don't get busy you won't be making any money anywhere that day.

Jessica: What about your plans?
Nick (Melbourne, 40s): I'll probably do this for maybe for another couple of years, I don't know. Maybe. Or I will find myself full time work, because there are days when I get sick and tired of what I am doing. But, I keep saying I am going to stop selling The Big Issue, but I never do. I never do. But I will find full-time work in the next year, maybe couple of years. But I will find full-time work.
Jessica: What sort of work would you like?
Nick: Just in sales, like what I am doing now.
Jessica: What sort of sales?
Nick: Um. Anything. Something in sales. I don't know what it will be. Something. Anything.

© The Author(s) 2017
J. Gerrard, *Precarious Enterprise on the Margins*,
DOI 10.1057/978-1-137-59483-9_8

We are routinely told we should aim higher. A key political, institutional and policy response to inequality and poverty is to suggest that individuals should aspire to do better and work more on their personal project of social mobility. As Adkins writes on unemployment, "Unemployment now buzzes with value-producing activity, including the anticipation of events to come" (Adkins 2012: 637). Linked to the potential for self-change, aspiration is deeply imbued with educative assumptions surrounding self-development and growth. As discussed in Chap. 6, the linking of homeless street press to the learning of work skills, habits, and dispositions is fundamentally about an aspiration for sellers to 'move on' into more formal employment. In this chapter, rather than offer neat explanatory conclusions, I approach the ending of this book with the purposefully open ended question of what comes next for sellers of homeless street press. I explore how the overriding concern to 'move on' is lived and felt by sellers, and the sorts of aspirations they have about their futures. Many of their experiences are characterised by intense stasis, in which they manage the expectation to 'move on' and aspire higher, despite residing and persistent inequality and poverty in their lives past, present and seemingly into the future.

This chapter therefore considers what it is to live in a relatively 'stable' state of poverty, characterised by precarity and insecurity, whilst also holding the aspiration of moving out of this poverty. For many sellers, work is release enough from the drudgery of homelessness, poverty and unemployment. These women and men see homeless street press work more as an arrival point, than a transition on to other things. For others, such as Carter and Nick, it is part of a wider aspiration to fuller employment, less poverty, stable housing, and an easier existence less overridden with concerns about where the money for the next meal or rent is going to come from. Thus, in what follows I examine not only the multitude of aspirations, but also the ambiguities and tensions contained within these aspirations, in the context of a lack of supposed pathways into employment or out of poverty. Indeed, it is important to take very seriously the real lack of employment opportunities and the residing impact of long term unemployment, underemployment and low paid employment (see Shildrick et al. 2012; Kwon and Lane 2016).

I suggest that for many, working as a seller is like living within a state of perpetual transition, ironically characterised by enduring experiences of poverty and stasis. For many, however, the arrival of what is next appears ever elusive. For these sellers, living in precarity and poverty, and awaiting a pathway to move on involves living endlessly in a hope for transition, yet never actually moving. This is what Lauren Berlant describes as 'cruel optimism' (2011). There is a symbolic violence in the heralded capacity of 'moving on' when this never arrives, or arrives so partially, and when the struggle to survive does not recede but takes on new qualities and challenges. In other words, selling homeless street press does not eradicate poverty, and nor does it provide income security.

Thus, part of this consideration of aspiration and 'moving on' is a reflection on what work and education does. Work and education have long been knotted into collective and individual aspirational claims. The formal institutions of work and education are markers of social inclusion, of economic capacity (though not necessarily economic security), and are powerful practices in which we make ourselves in the everyday (see Weeks 2011; Gerrard 2014). Aspiration is often linked to these institutions, and to the promise of social mobility (see Raco 2009; Allen 2014; Sellar 2015; Morgan 2006). Yet, the embedded inequalities of these institutions—the competitive meritocracy of education, and the stark distinctions in employment opportunities, pay and conditions—create aspiration's sharp underbelly: the lack of work opportunities, the failure of education to translate into work, and most importantly the inevitable exclusion of many from these formal institutions. At a time when individuals are deemed responsible for their successes and failures, and for making their aspirations a reality, the sharpness of these exclusions cannot be underestimated.

Yet more broadly, informal and tacit associations with—and claims to—work and education reflect a desire to make or do, and to 'grow'. These are not necessarily linear or even rational desires. But they are deeply social and cultural, as much as they are individual. Such aspirations are impossible to disentangle from social and economic position and context. In the case of homeless street press, the self-help and activist intentions intertwine with sellers' needs and desires to work and to accrue income. This more expansive understanding of aspirations, and aspirational capacity, points to ambiguity about what is actually meant by aspiration. As many have pointed to, despite an enthusiastic policy take-up of the notion of aspiration, there is often a lack of clarity surrounding what is actually meant for people to aspire (see Stahl 2012; Sellar 2015). Within the contemporary context, even these more informal aspirational claims, whilst never fully determined from, are still connected to the emergence of the flexible, adaptable, precarious citizen self.

Micki McGee (2005), for instance, links the proliferation of the self-help industry in the US to the operation of the contemporary work ethic. McGee outlines how following one's 'calling' (as Max Weber put it) is iterated in new modalities of gendered work in the new economy. As Raco suggests, this is an existential form of politics. Post-Keynesian governance heralds the importance of "the *essential characteristics* of human nature, well-being, responsibility, and virtue" (2009: 436, original emphasis). It is also affective, tapping into our desires and evocating an optimism that is never truly fulfilled (see Berlant 2011; Sellar 2015). In the ultimate blurring of work/education/life, work-on-the-self and the-self-in-work are brought together in aspirational pulses of self-fulfilment and worth.

For anthropologist Arjun Appadurai, the capacity to aspire must be understood as framed by the material realities of inequity and poverty. He writes (2013: 189),

> *If the map of aspirations [...] is seen to consist of dense combinations of nodes and pathways, relative poverty means a smaller number of aspirational nodes and thinner, weaker, sense of the pathways from concrete wants to immediate contexts to general norms and back again. Where these pathways do exist for the poor, they are more likely to be more rigid, less supple, and less strategically valuable, not because of any cognitive deficit of the poor but because they capacity to aspire, like any complex cultural capacity, thrives and survives on practice, repetition, exploration, conjecture and refutation.*

Importantly, the capacity to aspire is thwarted—not unleashed—in the narrow affordances provided by individualised socially mobile so-called 'pathways'. In such narrow conceptualisations aspiration becomes a symbolic marker for surviving contemporary inequalities. In contrast, the capacity to aspire, as Appadurai understands it, can represent a claim to capacity, aspiration, and voice that troubles the existing status quo and its injustices. Appadurai's reflections offer a way to understand how aspiration is invariably linked to the imperatives of work and capital accrual in modern economies, but also how such imperatives never fully capture it.

I start this final chapter with these broad considerations of aspirations, as a means to prompt deeper reflection of the complex future-oriented politics of the marginal work practice of homeless street press. Aspiration is temporal: it rests on an understanding or judgement of the past and present, the lived experience of the past and present, and a proposition or hope for the future. Homeless street press organisations aspire to do something about the entrenched character of homelessness and unemployment in modern society—and ensuing experiences of poverty, inequality, injustice, exclusion, marginalisation—and to provide a different future for those who are poor and homeless. As explored in Chap. 3, these aspirations differ significantly across the organisations. San Francisco's Coalition on Homelessness' *Street Sheet* emerges from a commitment to grass roots activism, by homeless people for homeless people, as the root for social change. For *The Big Issue*, the organisational aspiration rests more within the ethos of social enterprise with the capacity to provide alternative forms of dignified work, whilst raising the public profile of the issues of poverty, unemployment and homelessness.

Sellers traverse multiple aspirations in their daily work and their hopes for the future, whilst often living for years without a real change in their material circumstances. In this chapter first, I explore the ways in which the women and men I spoke with became sellers, starting with a reflection on the thorny notion of 'pathways' and 'moving on'. Here, I extend some of the themes and experiences touched on in Chap. 5 and draw on recent critiques of 'pathways' approaches in sociology and education, to consider the entry points into becoming a seller and the ways in which this troubles much of the simplistic representations of 'pathways' into work and out of poverty. Second, I consider the ways in which sellers understand and articulate their aspirations in the context of long-term poverty. Finally, I turn to the aspirations sellers hold for their futures, ending with an extended research reflection.

'Pathways': Becoming a Seller

Jessica: So tell me, why did you first decide to work as a seller?

Sociological and educational literature is fixated on the possibilities for pathways: pathways between education and work, pathways out of poverty, pathways into housing, pathways out of unemployment. The notion of pathways is an attempt to account for biographical life-course and the significance of people's agency and subjectivity as they negotiate major life events and 'transitions' (see Farrugia and Gerrard 2016; Fopp 2009). At face value, the 'pathways' metaphor can appear relatively benign. After all, there does appear a number of key 'transitional' events across our life-course in which we are expected to move from one state to another—from primary to high school, from school to work, from living with our parents or carers to living independently, from work to retirement. When considering social inequality, pathways often come to signify the potentiality for individuals to move on, and out of, poverty, unemployment and homelessness: in this use, the metaphor indicates the move from 'exclusion' or 'marginalisation' to 'inclusion' and 'participation'.

There are two underlying problems surrounding the mobilisation of the metaphor of pathways. First, that for many the potential (or the absence of potential) to 'move on' relies upon a fundamental lack of opportunity: a lack of housing, education, secure employment, benefits that lift them out of poverty. As put by Murphy et al. (2011: 137) in their study of welfare recipients in Australia, the contemporary labour market "struggles to accommodate anyone other than the unencumbered worker in full health." Pathways can presume a stable and achievable arrival destination, not accounting for the structural inequalities that mean for so many that there is never an arrival point.

Often, attempts to address this apparent lack of movement, leads to the presumption that the 'problem' lies in decisions or moments in individual biographies. Rather than focus attention on structural inequality, individual 'risk factors' are tallied and declared as explanations for homelessness, unemployment and poverty: addiction, trauma, domestic violence, family breakdown (Farrugia and Gerrard 2016). "Poverty is not a 'culture' or a character defect", writes Linda Tirado on her experiences in the US, "it is a shortage of money. And that shortage arises from grievously inadequate pay, aggravated by constant humiliation and stress, as well as outright predation by employers, credit companies, and even law enforcement agencies" (2014: xii).

Second, and relatedly, pathways presume that the arrival symbolises a kind of resolution or progression. For many the pathway into housing, for instance, does not mean a pathway out of poverty; and nor does the pathway into more formal employment. For instance, writing on poverty in rural South Carolina in the US, Kingsolver (2016) points to the ways in which poor communities, stepped in the logics of race and racism, become productive sites of work and capitalism through the attempt to regenerate communities with low wages, anti-union policies, and poor conditions. Here, pathways do not offer a movement out of poverty, but rather entrenches it.

Moreover, these so-called life-course transitional events are currently undergoing significant change. Many taken-for-granted pathways are being re-formulated as advanced capitalist economies continue to adjust to 'post-industrialism' and as governments attempt to resolve crises. This includes the lack of pathways between education and employment for workers of all ages; the lack of housing to 'pathway' into; and new social relations of work and education that are not captured in the neat metaphor of a pathway (see Cuervo and Wyn 2011; Farrugia and Gerrard 2016; Clarke and Polesel 2013; Wright 2000). Ultimately, then, the notion of pathways emphasises individual deviancy from an otherwise unproblematised 'normative' life-course, which for many is simply unattainable (see Farrugia and Gerrard 2016; Fopp 2009).

Certainly, the biographies of sellers demonstrate the thorny navigations that characterise the lives of those in poverty; navigations which are not captured by the notion of pathways. Most often, one of my first questions to sellers was how it was that they first became a seller. Whilst each seller had their own personal story of how they ended up working selling homeless street press, collectively their journeys indicate the harsh realities of contemporary poverty and homelessness across Melbourne, San Francisco and London. Their answers reveal the impact of sustained inequality and the systemic failure to address poverty and homelessness in advanced capitalist wealthy countries trans-nationally. Alongside poverty, housing and homelessness services, the contemporary dynamics of the each city's employment market (and its race, gender and class dimensions) provide the undeniable context for sellers' experiences. As put by Tom (48 years old), a London *Big Issue* seller, when I ask him why he first started working as a seller: *"Oh god, obviously unemployment: long-term unemployment. I couldn't keep a job. Couldn't—hadn't had a job for a long time and relationship breakdowns as well on top of all that. And it's hard, yeah."*

For Stacey, at 33 *The Big Issue* offers her the only route to employment. When I ask her why she decided to start working as seller, she says,

Well I'm currently homeless. I got kicked out of home and I'm basically sleeping from place to place and I thought if I have something to do during the day that would get my mind of what I'm going through, you know, it would be good. So I decided—plus I've got a few friends that also do The Big Issue as well, so I thought why not, it's something to do. And plus I can't do any other work because I didn't finish high school so I've got no qualifications to work anywhere else and you don't need any proper qualifications for The Big Issue. You don't have to have any experience at all in anything. It would nice to have a little bit of knowledge when it comes to maths though.

Patricia, at 63 is thirty years Stacey's senior and recounts a similar employment experience. When I met her she had been working as a seller for four months. Before that she had been unemployed for twenty years, and is now on a disability pension. She recounts her experience of being on benefits and looking for work before she was on the disability pension:

I was out of work for 20 years. See, I'm disabled. A lot of people won't employ disabled people in case you have a fall. You had to ring four jobs a fortnight back then. I've been on the disability pension for ten years now. And before that

> you had to ring four jobs a fortnight and then go back for interviews at the Centrelink [government welfare] office, and they'd try and help you get work. And they all said, 'No dear'. No one wants to employ you!'
>
> Jessica: But you still had to apply for the four jobs a fortnight?
> Patricia: Oh yes. And I did mine because I didn't want to lose what money I was getting. I was in a private flat then. For 14 years, so I didn't want to lose that. So I made my calls, because they could always ring and check.

As a young woman, Patricia was encouraged to leave school, "because I wasn't getting anywhere and I couldn't do the work." After failing her nursing exam by 2 points, she then went on to work in toy factories, as a child minder, working in a fruit shop, and eventually completing a typing course.

Patricia's experience is also one of brutal poverty and homelessness. She was rough sleeping for many years, and was eventually hospitalised because she was so unwell and physically injured from being homeless, including chronic sores on her feet. She spent over a decade waiting for public housing, which she now has. Her journey to becoming a *Big Issue* seller is driven by financial necessity, as her pension is simply not enough to get by. She tries to work six to seven hours five days a week in summer, but finishes a little earlier in winter because of the cold, and makes on average five to ten sales in a day ($15–$30). She uses her walker to sit on at her pitch so that she can try and work as long as possible without putting pressure on her legs and feet.

Patricia can't speak highly enough of the staff at *The Big Issue*, and tells me again and again how significant it is to have their support, and their smiles and encouragement when she goes into the office. Reflecting on her work experience and her typing course, Patricia sees her *Big Issue* work as an accessible form of work, from which she has no intention from moving on from. She says,

> I don't think there is anything else that I am particularly brilliant at. It takes me five times longer to catch on than what it does other people, because I'm so slow. But this is alright—I can do this job. Raucous voice, and you sing out, and hold the book [Big Issue] up and people can see it. I am enjoying it.
>
> Jessica: Is there anything about selling The Big Issue that you find hard?
> Patricia: No, no! [Laughs] Thankfully! That's why I am sticking at it. I've learnt over the years how to count properly, so I can do the money

Also in Melbourne Jon's longest-term job is his work as a *Big Issue* seller. Now in his 50s, when I ask what sort of work he had done before working as a seller, Jon recounts a long list of casual, manual and insecure employment and many long and short stretches of unemployment. Jon also has a long experience of begging. In fact, after our first interview the next time I see Jon he has gone back to begging having had a "falling out" with the staff at *The Big Issue*. The falling out was him "getting caught" begging near his usual pitch. I ask him how he is going now with the loss of the work routine, which he had placed so much emphasis on when I first interviewed him. He says, "Well, I am still getting out of the house –just a bit later in the day!"

Importantly, as already noted, the gender dimensions of work play an important role in sellers' past employment experiences, and their work as homeless street press workers. Women account for far fewer sellers than men, and often worked with their male partners, or with a network of people who they knew around the city. In addition, the gendered dimensions of work—from safety to childcare—invariably shape women's pathway into working as a seller, and their everyday experiences. Like men, many women also had experiences in highly precarious labour, but then also had to manage this with their role as primary care giver for their children.

Tonya (Melbourne, 38 years old), for instance, compares her work as a seller to that when she worked in a food-packaging factory. She says, "I'm used to it [standing up for long hours] 'cause years ago I used to do it in the factory—I used to stand up all day." Tonya's factory experience was many years ago. She worked for just a couple of months, when she was in her mid-twenties. She explains to me:

I did that for six weeks, and then it was supposed to be a permanent job. But it was my sister's birthday and she wanted me to go out for her birthday, she said, 'You won't get the job', I said, 'Yeah I will' And, then they rang me up the following day and said, 'Why didn't you come to the interview?' I said, 'It's my sister's birthday,' and they said, 'Well, we gave it to someone else and you missed out.' Cause they were going to give it to me, and I would still be there now and not—and not had all me kids. I've got three kids. I've got a seventeen year-old, sixteen year-old and now a seven year old.

Jessica: They must keep you busy.
Tonya: My parents have got the seven year old, and then my ex-husband's got the other two. Thank goodness that the child support finishes for the older one, it will give me some money.

Like Tonya, most of the women I speak to struggle to 'juggle' parenting responsibilities and precarious low-paid labour, including their current work as sellers.

Mary (Melbourne 50s), for instance, has one daughter in care who she visits regularly and another in her twenties. She constantly feels the desire and pressure to give them money and gifts. Every time I see Mary she speaks of trying to keep up with the costs of her own medical and medication bills, owing to a number of complex illnesses, and also providing for her daughters. Yet, for Mary and Tonya, as with many of the sellers across the three cities—both male and female—the opportunity to have continuous employment is also marred by on-going illnesses and physical and intellectual disabilities. A large proportion of the Melbourne sellers, including Tonya, Mary and Patricia, for instance are on disability pension, rather than job seekers allowance. They are, in other words, excused from having to look for work and are awarded a very basic welfare cheque. Yet, the drudgery and boredom of unemployment, a desire to work, and material realities of welfare poverty drive these women and men into becoming sellers.

In addition, the significance, and continued presence, of physical injuries from past employment arose again and again for sellers, particularly for men who had worked in manual labour. From lost fingers to back injuries, these past injuries were often brought into the present as sellers managed their bodily pain, and the frustration of not being able to obtain mainstream employment. At one point, Ryan (44 years old), a seller with whom I spent many hours in Melbourne needed a complicated surgery arising out of an old work injury. Every time I see him for the few months before the surgery he eagerly lifts up his shirt grabs my hand and pushes my fingers into his spine so that I can feel the bones out of joint. Ryan works mostly with his partner Susan, taking it in turns throughout the day or working side by side. Every time I see him I see the physical pain he experiences from standing for long stretches at a time, jumping from foot to foot. He speaks of the agony of standing and the little relief he gets from sitting on a crate when standing gets too much. Ryan's employment history is a long list of highly precarious mostly manual labour: shelf stacker at a supermarket, factory work making car components, laundry work and fruit picker.

Jon's last job before becoming unemployed and then a seller, was working in garbage collection over ten years before I met him. He quit this job after his supervisor refused to let him make a complaint against a fellow co-worker, and in his words, he decided "I'm not going to cop this, so I left." Before this—over twenty years ago—Jon had worked in a metal factory where he was involved in a workplace accident that lost him two fingers because the machines were not properly fitted with safety equipment. The compensation money did not last long and did not do much to compensate for the loss of potential work, or his two fingers.

In San Francisco, it is previous experiences in the military—and the difficulty of re-integrating into civilian life—that reoccur over and over in seller experiences. Many talk about needing to top up their benefits, and the need to do something with their time and energy after returning from military service. Here, the racial dimension and dynamics of poverty are starkly obvious. All but two of the sellers I spoke with are Black, and the vast majority of homeless people around the Tenderloin where I spend most of my time are Black. Race is, as sociologist Loïc Wacquant's (2008) research on Europe and the U.S. attests, a central vehicle by which symbolic and material power is produced and enacted in contemporary class relations, and the experiences of work and unemployment do not escape these dynamics.

Becoming a seller, therefore, is a part of a longer and far more complex narrative of poverty and struggle. There are no clear pathways in and out, but rather a multitude of experiences of poverty, precarity and stasis. Sellers have to manage the everyday effects of poverty, of having to count money fastidiously, and worrying about having enough money to pay for housing, food and medication. Keeping busy, and filling their days with something was one way to make a little extra money—though this extra money never pulled them out of poverty. It is also a way to manage the many other complex issues in their lives, as I now go on to explore.

Perpetual Transition/Stasis

For many sellers, particularly those who are older, or who entered into street press work after long stretches of unemployment, the idea of having a desire for, or a plan to get other employment seems absurd. Roland in London, for instance, is taken aback when I ask him if he has employment plans. He tells me, "I never have plans! I'm 70!" When I ask him how long he plans to keep selling, he replies laughing, "Well my plan is to die happy". Roland started an undergraduate arts degree from a prestigious UK university, before "dropping out" and travelling. Ultimately, Roland became homeless and has been a seller for twenty years. Like many other sellers, he attributes his work as a seller as the reason why he is able to cope better financially and why he was able to secure on-going housing.

Talking about his personal history Roland laments the course of his life, saying that he enjoyed university and never anticipated the life of poverty he now leads. He says, "I feel like a stranger in a strange land", like he is the odd one out amongst his homeless and seller friends, but also within society and his community more generally. *The Big Issue* therefore gives him social connection as much as it does assist with income generation. For Roland, at 70 years of age, being a seller is his arrival point. He is proud of the regular customers he has built up over the twenty years that he has been a seller, and works five or six days a week, always at the same time in the morning, because "people expect me to be there."

Other sellers echo Roland's desire not to do anything else, not to be planning another future. It is important to note that this lack of projection into the future is cultivated through life experiences characterised by plans falling through: from housing to employment. When there is, and there has been, nothing secure it is hard to imagine a future in which even one of these things are bedded down. In Melbourne Roger (49 years old) also sees no point entertaining plans. For Roger, this is part of his on-going experience of living in poverty and being homeless: "I just do day by day. I've got no plans. Because as soon as I make a plan it doesn't go according to plan. So that's why I just take each day as it comes. I don't plan, because there is no point."

For others, plans are focused on a concerted choice to continue street press work. For instance, I meet Troy in San Francisco's Coalition on Homelessness. He is an enthusiastic *Street Sheet* seller, diligently reading the paper each issue so that he can sell it more confidently, talking to his customers about the contents of each issue. He is certain that this is what he will do for the rest of his life. When I ask him if he will continue selling the *Street Sheet* he replies without hesitation, "Yeah this is it. This is it. .... It's the thing to do for me. You know, I don't know about nobody else but this is it for me."

Troy has previously worked as a cook and in the army, and sees his work as central to transitioning back into civilian life. He tells me, "I've been to prison, coming out of the army and stuff, you know, I had a hard time with that back then. Everything's straight now, everything's straight. I'm just keeping it together." Like many other sellers, it is working as a seller that has enabled him to improve his standards of living: to move from homelessness to more secure housing, and, something Troy repeats a few times when we talk, the ability to buy beyond food: toiletries, clothes, and other things so that he can "feel good". The power of this is significant and should not be underestimated. Working as a seller enables Troy to shift the feelings of despair, homelessness and being dirty, the sense of "low ontological worth" that so often characterises the experience of homelessness (see Farrugia 2011).

The here and now, in other words, represents enough of an ease in the material realities of poverty, and with no clear better alternative, working as a seller is enough. This is not to say that these sellers have no aspirations or desires for a better life, or that the material difficulty of poverty suddenly recedes. Rather, that they have made a judgement surrounding the possibility for alternatives, and have decided that their current situation is what is available to them. Sellers like this still desire, and devise a range strategies and tactics for generating more income and for bettering their conditions of living, but it is within street press work.

When I ask *Street Sheet* seller Curtis what his plans are, he exclaims,

Plans! I'm old now! I am 59 I plan to get me an SRO [single resident occupancy housing]. I've got an income now. I've got SSI [Supplemental Security Income for people with a disability], so I've got a little money coming in. I'm homeless right now- living in a shelter. That's why I'm selling the Street Sheet. But I plan on getting my own place eventually. I need somebody to help me with the applications. So I can get one-third income I hope to have a studio apartment or a one-bedroom apartment one day. That's in terms of my really future plans.

Jessica: And in terms of selling the Street Sheet?
Curtis: I do it because I like talking. So you've got to love to do it in order to do it. You've got to be able to talk to anybody anywhere at any time. You know what I'm saying? Sometimes you've just got a make people laugh. I'm just looking for a laugh. So I say, 'Hey you, you're looking really cute today.' You've just got a make people laugh. You can't be embarrassed. It's not for the faint of heart. This is not for everybody.

In this context, working as a seller is a means to manage seller's insecurity and exclusion, and a pathway to somewhere else. Or perhaps, to put it more precisely, being a seller is the 'somewhere else'. Also in San Francisco, Rodney, for instance, tells me he will keep selling *Street Sheets* because he feels lonely within the Tenderloin. "It's a bad area", he tells me, "if you don't have beer or drugs no one will talk to you. They don't want to talk to me." Here, street press work provides a means to get out of the neighbourhood, with purpose, for the day and to talk with people.

As discussed in Chap. 7, the value of social connection is substantial, particularly when this is linked also to a sense of worth for working. Rachel (Melbourne, 50s), for instance, talks about *The Big Issue* work as being an extension of her previous employment in hospitality. She has used her income to help her secure housing, and has taken up opportunities through *The Big Issue* to complete a diploma, but ultimately it is *The Big Issue* work that she wants to do:

> *I think The Big Issue to me is still kind of part of hospitality, because you're still interacting with customers. Everyone asks me, 'what are you going to do when you get your diploma,' and I say, 'I'll be selling The Big Issue!' I don't think I'd ever get away from it, as much as sometimes I think, 'Ah look I'm kind of over it, I just want to stop.' I don't think I could because I love getting out there. To me it's not about the money, it's about being out there actually having that communication with other people and letting them know we're not all sitting there waiting for a hand-out, you know we're there helping ourselves to do what we need to do and supporting ourselves. We're not expecting the government or everyone else to say you know, 'give me a dollar, give me a dollar'. We're actually doing it ourselves. And that comes to self-respect as well, I don't expect anyone to be helping me to do things and I'm probably one of the only vendors that when I get a tip I get more embarrassed than what the person does.*

For Rachel and many other sellers, the notion of moving on from the place that has generated self-respect, social relationships and connection as well as independence is jarring. Despite its limitations, what it does afford is dignity and legitimacy. It is also a work practices that emphasises for Rachel the importance of individual responsibility and agency: by working as a homeless street press seller Rachel is demonstrating that she is helping herself. Whilst she does receive government welfare support, her homeless street press work allows her to distinguish herself as being productive and worthy.

For these sellers, focus is put in particular on cultivating their craft as a seller. Stacey (Melbourne 33 years old) tells me she is "going to stick it out for as long as I can". As a relatively 'new' seller, she looks to those who have been around for longer as potential aspiration. "There's some vendors that I've seen that have actually been doing it for I would say seven or eight years," she says. "So I'm thinking I might just stick with this as my job from now on. At least that way I don't have to worry about any other qualifications and it's easy to do, like anyone can do it." Coleman (Melbourne, 46 years old) also sees homeless street press as the solution to his long-term unemployment. However, this is mitigated by the insecurity of the income homeless street press work generates and the need to attract sales from people passing by. I ask,

> Jessica: So, are you going to stick at this for a while?
> Coleman: Well I'm hoping, I'm hoping. That's why I try to work at this spot regularly. I've sold twelve here, today I've already sold twelve. So people are getting used to me. If I keep working at the pitch here, I'm going try make it my permanent stand, so people, even if they didn't buy it they will start buy it because of how I'm going. That's what I believe anyway.

Those homeless street press workers who accept, and perhaps even embrace, their work as sellers as a their only option, live in a society that heralds their efforts to move beyond their position, but which also holds an aspiration that their efforts might lead to something else. Having accepted homeless street press as an arrival point comes with a sense of accomplishment for some. But for others, it brings frustration and shame. Sitting with Mary, squeezed in together in a busy food hall, I ask her if she could get another job what would she like it to be. She looks at me, meets my eyes, and with her voice getting shakier with every word she replies, "Well, probably packing and sorting because that's the only thing I can do. Because I've been trained in packing. I've got communication—the basics, but I can't read or write properly. That's my problem. Only limited skills. So where am I meant to go!?" By the end, Mary has tears in her eyes, and talks to me about how her lack of academic ability, and no employment experience, really gives her no options. Homeless street press is her only option, and an option that involves her managing work on the street, feeling exposed and tired, with on-going depression and complex illnesses.

For sellers like Carter and Nick, who are quoted at the beginning of this Chapter, the aspiration to move on fostered feelings of frustration contextualised by a profound lack of employment opportunities or 'pathways'. Sometimes, I couldn't shake the feeling that sellers answered my questions about their employment aspirations with an answer that they felt they had to say. Nick's response about wanting to become a salesman was both ambiguous and abstract, perhaps thrown out to me as part of his demonstration that he is thinking of 'what next'. Sellers are of course aware that many judge them for their homelessness and poverty, and that there is an expectation that they might find 'a real job'.

194   8 MOVING ON?: ASPIRATIONS, PATHWAYS AND STASIS

Whilst I tried to avoid the perception that I might have this judgement, I was aware that sellers might interpret my question as a form of judgement. Nick has been a seller for over five years, and is one of the sellers who looks visibly homeless- scruffy, wearing noticeably dirty clothes, and hair greased to his scalp. His overtures towards the possibility of a future sales job, in the context of his profound poverty, highlights the disjuncture that occur in the proclaimed possibility of transition amidst a lack of opportunities, resources, time and money: of existing in a space of poverty that takes all of your energy to get by, whilst juggling the impression that you should be aiming higher.

Jeffrey's responses to my questions about plans in San Francisco, points to the both the ambiguity of the notion of plans, when you are poor or homeless, but also of the stultifying welfare system. Jeffrey is currently rough sleeping and I ask,

> *Do you plan to continue selling Street Sheet much longer?*
>
> *Jeffrey: Well I am trying to get indoors. Once I am indoors, you know, usually with the single residency occupancy—it's based on what you earn. Which doesn't leave very much. So I will probably still need to do the Street Sheets just to eat. I have nothing against the soup kitchens but if I can earn it I would rather to do that than stand in line. So yeah I am going to continue. I am going to continue.*

To plan anything beyond securing shelter, or food for the day, when living in profound poverty is understandably impossible. To expect anything else would misunderstand the nature and experience of poverty: the all-consuming worry over money, shelter, health and safety. Moreover, the welfare system effectively constrains rather than enables Jeffrey's hope for work. When wages are so low, and work is so precarious, Jeffrey makes the decision it's better to work on the margins.

Considerations of the future occur for many sellers in the context of long-term poverty and an expectation that this will not change. Kaz (Melbourne, 57) put it this in particularly desolate terms.

> *Jessica: So you said your plan is basically to keep selling The Big Issue?*
> *Kaz: Till the day I get hit by a bus or something like that or a tram. I've got no outlook for the future. I'll work until I die, I guess. They don't give away a gold watch there but so what, it suits me.*

Jessica: Would you be interested in any other sort of work or not so much?
Kaz: Yeah I would, as long as I could sit down like what I was doing, it would be good yeah.

Yet, in comparison to his previous work as a labourer, gardener and factory hand, Kaz reckons that his *Big Issue* work is the most enjoyable. "It's quite easy money if you're in that spot where people are buying it," he tells me. "All you've got to do is be nice to them for a couple of seconds, they hand over their money and you can think what you like of them after that. But I do like most of me regulars, they look after me." He is quick to qualify this, however: bad sales and people walking past giving him a look that has "get a real job" written all over it makes the work tiresome and frustrating, leaving him—in his words—"feeling like shit."

Jeffrey's comments about the limits of the welfare system, repeated to me by sellers in all three cities, also reveal the ways in which current institutional structures can hinder, rather than help them. The fear of not being able to return to their current rates of welfare, and the long bureaucratic procedures required to get onto welfare or disability payments, mean that sellers are extremely reluctant to enter into employment that could mean giving up welfare. Sellers know that whatever employment that is available to them is precarious, low paid, and insecure. They also know that in all likelihood it will not last, and they dread having the face complexities and pitfalls of the welfare system again.

Other sellers have experiences of moving back and forth, between formal employment and homeless street press. For these sellers, street press is the 'stable' part of precarious poverty: the form of work that is always available to them, and which does not involve employers. Jan (Melbourne, 48) for instance, used to work as a cleaner before it became too painful on her knees, and before then worked as a packer. Working casually, her employer was able to cut her hours at any time. When the hours became too low, she would supplement by working as a *Big Issue* seller. In her first interview with me, she explains:

> *I had like a small period when I was doing other things [cleaning and packing work]. I must have been here for a couple of years before I started doing The Big Issue. It's been a job that I've always gone to and come back from. I can do it for a while, then go away, and come back to it. That's one of the good things about it. I like that about it—it's always a job there when you want it.*

Later, however, Jan is frustrated by the lack of income her selling attracts. We stay in contact for around a year, and by the end of that year she is looking for other work, but is conflicted as she feels passionate about her *Big Issue* work, and underwhelmed by the alternative possibilities; essentially low-paid cleaning work. She says,

> In the past, to me The Big Issue has been a stepping stone job, a job for when I didn't have a job. I'll have a look around and if I get enough work I'll give it up. Because at the end of the day, as I said, The Big Issue work is commission based and as much as I like the flexibility that comes with it, I'd rather have the security of something that has a secure wage with it. But in the meantime, it's satisfying.

As with many other sellers, Jan's frustration is one that she lives with every day. She becomes increasingly despondent about the possibility of finding other work as she is never successful at getting an interview at the jobs her employment consultant puts her forward for. She is also reluctant to leave her *Big Issue* work: despite its downsides, it provides her with an accessible form of work, and some (very small) income, and a job that she finds fulfilling and satisfying. These are the realities working on the margins when the formal employment market is itself so precarious, so limited, and ultimately so exclusionary to people like her.

Dom

To end, I offer an extended research reflection about Dom, the very first seller I interviewed for this book. At 25 years of age, Dom, whose experiences are briefly discussed in Chap. 5, is one of the youngest sellers I speak with. I first meet Dom outside a major shopping centre in Melbourne. We chat, and after a while he agrees to be interviewed there and then. We retreat off the loud street and into the less-loud—but bustling—shopping centre, finding a bench to sit and talk. Dom has just arrived in Melbourne three weeks ago and he is finding it tough transitioning to a city where nobody knows him. In Sydney, where he had worked as a *Big Issue* seller for 18 months, he had regulars, a 'permanent pitch' and was doing OK in sales. Here, he feels as if he is starting new all over again.

He describes what first led him to working as a *Big Issue* seller: living in Sydney, homeless and rough sleeping, and with no food. After a week he became so desperate he went to a police station to find out where he could access support, shelter and food. They put him in touch with some youth homeless services, and through word of mouth he decided to try selling *The Big Issues* to help him get back on his feet. Recounting his first day on the job, Dom says he wasn't nervous because he desperately needed the money. "I just had to make money", he tells me, "I just stood there holding the magazines and people started coming up to me and buying."

Now he is in Melbourne, Dom is still homeless and has a highly precarious housing arrangement with a friend. Everyday he is not certain that he will have a room to go back to. Before becoming a seller, Dom was trying to finish his bakery apprenticeship to become a pastry chef. When I ask him about this, Dom's disappointment and frustration is clear as he describes his apprenticeship experience: confusing bureaucratic dealings with an employment agency; seven apprenticeships over two years; and bad work conditions:

> *I got a position at one bakery and the boss that I had was absolutely horrific. I would start at 10 o'clock at night and then I was still there at 11am. And then these guys would want to come for a few hours to have a bit of a chat, and then I'd have to turn around to clean the kitchen until about 1pm and then I drive back home at 2 o'clock in the afternoon and then get up and get over there by 10 o'clock again. The latest I think I ever got home was around 3 o'clock in the afternoon.*

Dom wants to get back to work, but right now he is concentrating on earning money and on sorting out his housing situation. When I ask him about plans for the future, he quickly quips back "No idea at this stage, I'm just trying to get through."

Dom's understandable overriding concern is making money. This means that he finds work as a *Big Issue* seller challenging. The sales are not fast enough, and he acutely feels what he views as street competition: beggars and charity workers. "Do you have a selling tactic", I ask him. Dom responds,

> *No. No spruiking. I just say hello to people. But most people—they gawk at you. They wonder what the hell you are doing. 90% of people don't even realise that it's a magazine to help the homeless. And, most—60% of the time, say there's someone selling the magazine and there's someone begging, they'll give the money to the person who is begging. ... People see beggars on the street and they just assume that someone else will buy the magazine. But everyone assumes someone else has bought the magazine. So sales just drop.*

I meet Dom one more time about three months after this first interview. Like some of the other sellers I meet, I never see him again after this second interview. Homeless street press work is undeniably precarious and transitional and whilst there are many sellers who have worked the same spot for years and years, there are many others who sell for a few weeks or months before moving on. In this second interview Dom describes in greater detail his sales strategy, which involves buying and selling magazine stock throughout the week in order to accrue a large stock of magazines for the busy crowds on a Saturday, when he can sell more. With this strategy Dom reckons he makes around $150–$200 a week. It's a Tuesday when we meet, around lunchtime, and he's been working since 8:30 am. He's only sold 3 this morning, but he's hoping for a few more before the day is out.

Dom has dogged determination in approaching his work, or, perhaps more accurately, he has dogged determination to generate income. He feels that he cannot afford the time to do courses right now, as it's time wasted when he could be making money: "Look at it this way," he explains, "if I am not getting a qualification out of it, then I am actually losing money. And that's money I can't lose. I have to be out here selling." Now, Dom's main frustration is focused on charity workers—the workers who try to sign on donations and subscriptions to major charities by stopping people in the street. Dom sees these people as his main competition, and feels annoyed that they get an hourly rate of pay for the same job he is doing. He has tried applying to work as a charity worker to no avail.

Like others, Dom tries to work to a target each day. "Are you working every day at the moment?" I ask him.

Dom: Yes.
Jessica: And how many hours are you working a day?
Dom: Until I get bored and go 'Stuff this! I'm going home'.
Jessica: And how long does that take!?
Dom: Sometimes it's half an hour to a few hours, other times it can be six, seven hours longer.
Jessica: How do you manage those long hours?
Dom: You just got to do it! You've just gotta keep going with it. That's all there is—there is nothing else you can do!.

Dom still has plans to go back to his apprenticeship, but right now he is consumed with the task of getting by. I ask him, what work would he want in an ideal world, and he's clear in his answer. He doesn't want to go back and work under someone, to be subject to the work conditions he had to do before:

> It would have to be me running my own bakery. I would go back and do an apprenticeship but not under someone. I'm about half way through, but the shit I've been through there's no way I'd continue on under someone's bakery. I'd be running it myself, and obviously there'd be other apprenticeships and bakers and they'd be doing all the work. And I'd do all the work. So you start off with doing ovens for 8 months, but I'd change it all around. But that won't happen.

'But that won't happen': at 25, Dom's aspirations are already worn down by the everyday realities of being poor, homeless, and without a qualification.

In some ways Dom's experiences are not usual. Most of the sellers I spoke with were much older than Dom, and most had been unemployed for long stretches of time—over five years. Dom's struggle to complete his apprenticeship, and his movement into homelessness and poverty, is a stark reminder of the inter-relationship between the insecure conditions of work and unemployment, poverty and homelessness. His experience also highlights the paradox of aspirations and plans when living in a space of profound ontological uncertainty. Aspirations and plans are difficult, and at times painful, when all energy is required to manage the everyday. They are also thorny when they connect to the existing inequalities of work specifically, and society more generally. Dom wants to finish his apprenticeship, but the prospect of having to endure long days or an unfair boss is distressing. Yet, aspirations and plans are also powerful: speaking and connecting to a desire and knowledge that life can hold more than the present; that this current life is not the sum of who one is. In the meantime, it is back to trying to get more sales, smiling and searching the faces of people passing by.

Sellers, therefore, navigate a complex of aspirational claims when it comes to their work: the aspiration for them to move out of poverty is undoubtedly felt by themselves, but also by customers who purchase homeless street press with the hope that it will 'make a difference', as discussed in Chap. 7. The aspiration to work, and to be a worker, is truly significant when contemporary society places so much weight on work as the marker for accomplishment, achievement and 'good citizenship'. Whilst homeless street press work offers some gesture towards these aspirations, ultimately sellers' experiences of transitions or pathways appear to be minimal.

Aspirations here can be locked into the existing social order and norms, linked to rigid (and out of reach) arrival points (see Appadurai 2013). It is here that what Berlant describes as 'cruel optimism' emerges. She writes that we have an affective attachment to 'the good life', "which is for so many a bad life that wears out the subjects who nonetheless, and at the same time, find their conditions of possibility within it" (2011: 27). Sellers, must contend with their poverty and the common judgement that they are the makers of poverty (wholly or partially), but yet nonetheless, make their own way. They are not objects of unproductivity and lack, but people engaged in enterprising work attempting to create better, or at least, management futures. This is not to under-value the importance of securing housing, or of generating income to supplement meagre benefits, or of the opportunity to work. Rather, it is to point to the prolonged experiences of living in a state of perpetual transition, whereby sellers aspire, and are told to aspire, for more, whilst structural inequalities persist and go unchecked. In this context, living in a perpetual state of seeming transition—offers release from previous experiences of absolute unemployment but also represents frustrating and wearisome constraint as poverty and precarity endures.

REFERENCES

Adkins, L. (2012). Out of Work or Out of Time? Rethinkign Labor of the Financial Crisis. *South Atlantic Quarterly, 111*(4), 621–641.
Allen, K. (2014). 'Blair's Children': Young Women as 'Aspirational Subjects' in the Psychic Landscape of Class. *The Sociological Review, 62*(4), 760–779.
Appadurai, A. (2013). *The Future as Cultural Fact: Essays on the Global Condition.* London: Verso.
Berlant, L. (2011). *Cruel Optimism.* Durham: Duke University Press.
Clarke, K., & Polesel, J. (2013). Strong on Retention, Weak on Outcomes: The Impact of Vocational Education and Training in Schools. *Discourse, 34*(2), 259–273.
Cuervo, H., & Wyn, J. (2011). *Rethinking Youth Transitions in Australia: A Historical and Multidimensional Approach* (Research Report March 2011). Youth Research Centre, Melbourne Graduate School of Education.
Farrugia, D. (2011). The Symbolic Burden of Homelessness: Towards a Theory of Homelessness as Embodied Subjectivity. *Journal of Sociology, 47*(1), 71–87.
Farrugia, D., & Gerrard, J. (2016). Academic Knowledge and Contemporary Poverty: The Politics of Homelessness Research. *Sociology, 50*(2), 267–284.
Fopp, R. (2009). Metaphors in Homelessness Discourse and Research: Exploring "Pathways", "Careers" and "Safety Nets". *Housing Theory & Society, 26*(4), 271–291.

Gerrard, J. (2014). All that is Solid Melts Into Work: Self-Work, the 'Learning Ethic' and the Work Ethic. *The Sociological Review*, 62, 862–879.
Kingsolver, A. E. (2016). Zones of In/visibility: Commodification of Rural Unemployment in South Carolina. In J. B. Kwon & C. M. Lane (Eds.), *Anthropologies of Unemployment: New Perspectives on Work and Its Absence* (pp. 118–134). Ithica/London: ILR Press, an imprint of Cornell University Press.
Kwon, J. B., & Lane, C. M. (2016) *Anthropologies of Unemployment: New Perspectives on Work and Its Absence*, Ithica/London: ILR Press, an imprint of Cornell University Press.
McGee, M. (2005). *Self Help, Inc.: Makeover Culture in American Life*. Oxford: Oxford University Press.
Morgan, G. (2006). Work in Progress: Narratives of Aspiration from the New Economy. *Journal of Education and Work*, 19(2), 141–151.
Murphy, J., Murphy, S., Chalmers, J., Martin, S., & Marston, G. (2011). *Half a Citizen: Life on Welfare in Australia*. Sydney: Allen & Unwin.
Raco, M. (2009). From Expectations to Aspirations: State Modernisation, Urban Policy and the Existential Politics of Welfare in the UK. *Political Geography*, 28, 436–444.
Sellar, S. (2015). 'Unleashing Aspiration': The Concept of Potential in Education Policy. *Australian Educational Researcher*, 42, 201–215.
Shildrick, T., MacDonald, R., Webster, C., & Garthwaite, K. (2012). *Poverty and Insecurity: Life in Low-Pay, No-Pay Britain*. Bristol: The Policy Press.
Stahl, G. (2012). Aspiration and a Good Life Among White Working Class Boys in London. *Journal of Ethnographic and Qualitative Research*, 7, 8–19.
Tirado, L. (2014). *Hand to Mouth: The Truth About Being Poor in a Wealthy World*. London: Virago Press.
Wacquant, L. (2008). *Urban Outcasts: A Comparative Sociology of Advanced Marginality*. Cambridge, MA: Polity Press.
Weeks, K. (2011). *The Problem with Work: Feminist, Marxist, Antiwork Politics, and Postwork Imaginaries*. Durham/London: Duke University Press.
Wright, T. (2000). Resisting Homelessness: Global, National and Local Solutions. *Contemporary Sociology*, 29(1), 27–43.

CHAPTER 9

Epilogue: Enterprise on the Margins

There are no neat conclusions for a book such as this. Writing about lives is messy work, and in many ways it is the mess that allows for understanding. This is particularly true when writing about those who are so often viewed as 'other' and as set apart. Mess allows us to see that there are no clear endings and beginnings between the lives 'we' have—the aspirations held, values assumed, and work practiced—and those written about in this book. Mess muddies the neat boundaries that are presumed in the proclamation of 'us' and 'others'. In writing this book, it has struck me again and again how the contemporary cultures of the work ethic, the learning ethic and of precarity prevail across context and circumstance. The current preoccupation with individual responsibility and the project of making/performing oneself, (re)born out of complex neoliberal politics over the past 30 years, is felt by homeless street press sellers, academics, government workers, hospitality workers, and the unemployed: though, of course, its effects are manifold and diverse.

The experiences and accounts written here are woven into the fabric of contemporary social relations. Homeless street press sellers are engaged in precarious enterprising work on the margins, yet this work is central to our social, employment and labour relations. Unemployment and marginal and informal work are not the unproductive waste sites of society, but are essential to the ways in which inequality (and thus capital, power, and privilege) is cultivated in and through social relations. Moreover, as this book has demonstrated, the poor and the homeless are far from unproductive or 'idle'.

© The Author(s) 2017
J. Gerrard, *Precarious Enterprise on the Margins*,
DOI 10.1057/978-1-137-59483-9_9

As I noted in Chap. 8, rather than offer resolute orderly conclusions, I ended this book with an exploration of aspirations, and the experiences of sellers whose lives—and opportunities for employment—appear to be in a 'stable' state of precarity and frustrating hopeful transition. In doing so, I want to lay bare the ambiguity and complexity of 'what next' for these sellers. In this Epilogue I do not want to walk away from this tension, but aim to leave it exposed. The Chapters within are where the substantive thinking and writing lies: here I offer some brief reflections on the writing of this book by returning to the four themes outlined in the Introduction.

First, homeless street press highlights the paramount importance of work in contemporary social relations, trans-nationally. The women and men I spoke with in Melbourne, San Francisco and London all wanted to work, to be 'workers', and felt power and agency through the act of working: working, learning to work, demonstrating the willingness to work, are all powerful ways to mark productive participation in a society that places so much value on employment and so much fear and derision on idleness and its markers (such as begging). The will to work is not simply about identification, however. It is also of profound economic importance: sellers need to generate income in order to make ends meet. The material reality of poverty is an ever-present tide having tremendous and lasting impact.

Importantly, in the age of entrepreneurialism, these sellers are literally enterprising the margins: creating an income stream out of their marginality and homelessness; wearing and making visible their poverty through selling homeless street press. In this case, both unemployment and informal labour is made 'productive' through the enterprising energies of the homeless and poor. It is also enterprising work that occurs outside the stringent and harsh conditions of the welfare systems across these nations. Many sellers decide homeless street press work is better than risking losing their welfare payments and then having invariably to deal with the slow bureaucracy of getting back onto welfare once the casual, low-paid and poor conditioned work they were potentially offered was terminated. Yet, these enterprising energies have their toll: this is highly precarious work, and it is highly exposed—occurring in public on city streets and at the whim of customer's moral judgement surrounding sellers' deservingness and worthiness. Sellers manage exhaustion, their physical and mental health, disabilities, the hustle and bustle of the city, and the need to perform particular versions of themselves in order to attract sales.

Second, homeless street press, and most particularly the transformation of some of these press into a social enterprise (such as in *The Big Issue*), must be understood within the context of broader shifts towards market-based responses to poverty and unemployment. Homeless street press are part of a long past and present tradition of the informal economy, and can certainly be seen as an extension of the many practices of informal income generation on the margins. Yet, homeless street press is also fundamentally about 'ethical consumption'. Even in the case of activist *Street Sheet*, the hope is that by buying the paper San Francisco locals will become more interested and invested in the lives of the city's poor. Homeless street press is effectively a commodity available for purchase in morally charged exchange markets.

Like micro-finance and philanthropy, homeless street press invites 'the public' to individually purchase or donate as an ethical and political act responding to poverty. This invitation cultivates exchanges and relationships with customers that many sellers value. Yet it also provokes sellers to reflect—and perform—the ways in which they are 'bettering themselves', gesturing towards the traces of learning, education and self-development expected of sellers. Indeed, this invitation occurs whilst concurrently governments have augmented their roles and responsibilities toward unemployment and poverty, establishing a range of 'mutual obligation' arrangements across national contexts, pushing the responsibility of poverty (and getting out of poverty) to individuals. There are multiplying individualising impulses that surround the response to poverty, whilst the core structures of inequality remain untouched.

Third are the intricate everyday dynamics of the city, in which homelessness is rendered more visible by homeless street press. Homeless street press attempts to subvert and counter popular narratives of the homeless: that they are lazy, scary, and incapable. As one of the most 'visible' forms of poverty, homelessness has long provoked public and political judgement, from concern to anxiety, empathy, disdain, alarm, and derision. For sellers, this means that they—and their lives—are on show. The publicness of this work involves constant self-management, as sellers navigate the knowledge that they are being judged and assessed, and the everyday challenges of working exposed in the city.

Here, gender, race and disability count. Sellers are acutely aware of the ways in which they are 'read' differently, and the ways in which they need to manage their work situations in order to be safe. There is also a cruel hierarchy in their work in the city: sellers are keen to distinguish themselves apart from beggars, despite their past (and for some present) experiences of begging. Even for most sellers of San Francisco's *Street Sheet*, which clearly states it is not a job (unlike *The Big Issue*) these points of distinction are important. Yet, frustratingly for the sellers, these points of distinction are slight, and still require managing the inevitable, 'get a real job!' yelled from a passer by.

Fourth, and finally, the experiences of sellers of homeless street press highlights the tensions between stasis and mobility: between the aspirations towards better future and the learning and working undertaken by sellers toward this, and the seemingly 'stable; poverty experienced by them. Here, the brutality of 'inclusion' is exposed. Sellers are engaging in entrepreneurial work, self-development, and various attempts to learn to work; yet formal or fully recognised work—or even a liveable welfare cheque—remains out of reach. Moreover, the experience of poverty is consuming: not knowing when or if there is going to be enough money is wearing and requires the very careful management of energy, resources and time. Homeless street press offers one means to generate further income, but it is a work practice that also involves careful management as sellers manage poor sales alongside addressing their own emotional and physical health, housing, and family needs.

Traversing across the experiences of sellers in three very different cities—Melbourne, San Francisco and London—*Enterprise on the Margins* demonstrates the trans-national significance of unemployment and poverty in wealthy nations. Despite clear differences across these cities, homeless street press marks the global experiences of poverty and work on the margins sutured into wealthy nations, past and present. This book aims to contribute to the understanding of the experience of poverty, and most particularly of the effects of individually toiling for social mobility when there are no clear pathways and no clear arrival points. I suggest the need to further interrogate the contemporary entanglement of learning and working, and their shadowy underbellies, for those who are excluded or who are on the margins. My hope in writing an account of these experiences is for renewed discussion surrounding the ways in which old tropes of deserving/underserving, productive/idle, worthy/unworthy are reiterated in and through the sorts of expectations placed on those who bear the brunt of capitalism's inequalities in wealthy nations. The women and men I spoke with carried these judgements as they attempted to craft their entrepreneurial work, and the judgements did not recede as they stood and walked the city in the hope of a sale. These experiences point to the morality and politics of contemporary poverty, but also to the activity and agency that occurs on the margins.

Index

A

Aboriginal, 17, 29, 39, 86
academia/the academy, 32, 33, 36, 44
academic knowledge, 30
activism/activist, 2, 6, 18, 20, 21, 48, 53, 57, 58, 60–7, 74, 75, 112, 113, 122, 137, 139, 181, 183
activist street presses, 19, 58, 67
Adkins, L., 114, 180
affect/affective, 9, 43, 62, 71, 82, 84, 87, 92, 157, 161, 182, 200
Allison, D., 10, 11
Anderson, B., 16
Anderson, N., 56
Appadurai, A., 182
appearances, 90, 148
  homeless, 56, 72, 79, 157
Arendt, H., 115
aspiration(s), 8, 10, 11, 16, 21, 22, 48, 66, 80, 84, 86, 98, 137, 179–200
aspire, 21, 180–2, 200

B

Back, L., 35, 41, 44, 80
beggars, 7, 21, 54, 57, 70, 109–13, 120, 124, 166, 175, 197
  (*see also* panhandlers)
begging, 20, 57, 58, 67–9, 83, 107–28, 135, 138, 144, 158–60, 173, 187 (*see also* panhandling)
Berkeley, 57
Berlant, L., 180, 200
Biesta, G., 131, 133
The Big Issue, 2, 28, 53, 64–7, 72–5, 81, 107, 131, 154, 183, 204
  code of conduct, 68, 109, 117, 140, 144
  establishment; London, 60; Melbourne, 3, 61, 68
  offices; London, 74; Melbourne, 72–5
Bird, John, 61, 64, 67
boarding house(s), 55, 86, 87, 100, 103, 125
The Body Shop, 61, 64, 65, 99, 104

© The Author(s) 2017
J. Gerrard, *Precarious Enterprise on the Margins*,
DOI 10.1057/978-1-137-59483-9

208 INDEX

Boltanski, L., 161
boredom, 81, 82, 100, 107, 120, 126, 188
Bourdieu, P., 30, 34
Boxcar: A Journal of the Women's Itinerant Hobo's Union, 59
Boxcar Bertha, 59
business model, 2, 7, 61, 65, 67, 75, 119
buyers, 3, 8, 21, 70, 72, 85, 86, 100, 104, 109, 121, 125, 126, 140, 145–7, 153, 159, 161–3, 165, 166, 175
(*see also* customers)
By No Means, 59–60

C

campaign(s), 2, 18, 56, 60, 61, 63, 65, 71, 73, 74, 139, 158
capitalism/capitalist, 1–22, 34–8, 40, 41, 49, 54–6, 69–71, 79, 80, 115, 116, 134, 147, 162, 184, 185
charitable, 13, 17
charity/charities, 44, 70, 176, 198
workers, 124, 166, 197, 198
children, 11, 12, 40, 46, 117, 125, 127, 165, 186–8
citizen(s), 5, 6, 9, 10, 54, 61, 132, 134–6, 156, 157, 173, 181
citizenship, 5
city/cities, as a practice, 14–17, 167
city space, 86, 93, 99, 159
(*see also* public space)
city streets, 3, 8, 30, 41, 95, 107, 108, 126, 167, 175
class, 1, 6, 9, 10, 27, 32, 37–9, 41, 56, 73, 80, 125, 185
Coalition on Homelessness, 2, 18, 60–3, 73, 74, 82, 122, 139, 158, 183, 190
Cockburn, P. J. L., 70
colonialism, 39, 55

commodity/commodities, 7, 8, 39, 55, 66, 67, 69–71, 74, 80, 117, 119, 137, 162, 170
confession/confessional, 19, 42–9
consumer capitalism, 15, 16, 156, 157
consumerism, 15
consumption, 70, 205
couch surfing, 3, 12, 125
cruel optimism, 180–1, 200
customers, 47, 65, 88, 89, 104, 118–21, 139, 149, 153, 154, 159, 163–5, 167, 190, 192, 199
(*see also* buyers)

D

The Daily Mail, 39
de Certeau, M., 31–2, 41
dedicated/dedication, 64, 84, 126, 146
Denning, M., 115
DePastino, T., 56, 79
deserving/deservingness, 7, 10, 39, 54, 70, 71, 85, 103, 107, 112, 114, 150, 154, 161, 173, 176, 204, 206
Desjarlais, R., 15, 157, 160
Devos, A., 133
dignified income, 67
dignified work, 67, 183
dignity, 120, 138, 143, 176, 192
Dillabough, J., 3
disability/disabilities, 22, 46, 80, 85, 86, 120, 125, 163, 185, 188, 195, 204, 205

E

earning and learning, 5, 68, 81, 87–9, 91, 93, 99, 100, 102, 104, 114, 143, 155, 197
education, 1, 3, 5, 7, 11, 22, 46, 56, 80, 98, 114–16, 132–7, 181–4, 205
Ely, L., 62
Empire, 13, 14

INDEX 209

employment, 1, 3, 6, 7, 21, 27, 28, 34, 37, 55, 63, 66, 68, 72, 74, 79, 90, 99, 107, 113–15, 117, 118, 120, 123, 127, 128, 137, 170, 175, 180, 181, 184, 185, 187–90, 192, 193, 195–7, 203, 204
enterprising, 3, 124, 126, 128, 146, 150, 200, 203, 204
enterprising self, 124, 135
entrepreneur, 136
entrepreneurial, 6, 20, 22, 53, 64, 66–72, 84, 85, 102, 104, 108, 113, 116, 123–8, 131, 135–7, 139, 141, 149, 150, 206
entrepreneurialism, 80, 84, 116, 135, 136, 149, 176, 204
Erkison, K., 31
ethical consumption, 70–2, 161
everyday, concept of, 6, 8–9, 11, 17, 20, 36, 40–2, 45–7
exchange, 7, 8, 21, 30, 34, 67, 70, 72, 91, 117, 137, 153–76, 205
excluded, 2–5, 27, 36, 64, 68, 70, 82, 107, 116, 117, 136, 156, 157, 206
exclusion, 5, 6, 27, 36, 37, 99, 102, 134, 135, 150, 181–3, 191
exploitation, 27, 127
expulsion, 19, 37, 38

F
failure, 3, 5, 6, 10, 35, 45, 46, 49, 84, 115, 181, 185
family violence, 12, 18, 40
Fanon, F., 32–3
Farrguia, D., 157
Felski, R., 42
feminist, 36, 41, 115, 134
Ferguson, K., 133
fieldwork, 53, 72
First Amendment, 58, 69
flexible/flexibility, 1, 83, 124, 136, 137, 140, 141, 181

food, 29, 45, 59, 87, 93, 95, 97, 111, 147, 156, 174, 187, 189, 190, 193, 194, 196
formal education, 5, 27, 34, 132, 133, 136, 137
formal work, 5, 34, 67, 80, 114, 133, 136, 137, 206
Foucauldian, 136, 147
Fox, C., 54

G
Gale, T., 44
gaze, 30, 33, 104, 161, 170
gender/gendered, 1, 5, 6, 8, 10, 12, 27, 32, 37–9, 55, 93, 125, 154, 182, 185
getting by, 9, 81–9, 114, 147, 198
Global Financial Crisis, 1
Glucksmann, M., 115
Goffman, E., 160, 170, 172
Golden Gate, 59
Gowan, T., 15, 20, 58, 125

H
Havemann, P., 39
health, 7, 16, 22, 46, 47, 88, 172, 184, 194, 204, 206
Hibbert, S. A., 72
Higbie, F. T., 55
Highmore, B., 16, 40
hobo, 19, 54, 55, 59, 79
"Hobo News", 56, 57
Hobo World, 57
Hobsbawm, E., 13, 55, 57
Hogg, G., 170
Homeless Bill of Rights, 158
homeless/homelessness, 1, 27, 53, 79, 107, 131, 153, 180, 203
criminalisation of, 108, 157
diversity of, 39, 72
enumeration (problem of), 12, 34
hidden, 12, 39, 125

homeless/homelessness (*cont.*)
  judgements of, 30, 35, 55, 102, 150, 171, 205
homeless street press, establishment of, 48
The Homeless Times, 59, 60
housing, 7, 12, 28, 39, 44, 45, 55, 58, 61, 65, 73, 88, 90, 97, 103, 125, 155, 180, 183–6, 189–92, 197, 200, 206
  public, 87, 97, 163, 171, 186
Howley, K., 60, 66

I
identity/identities, 1, 9, 12, 16, 32, 37, 54, 83, 86, 100, 104, 105, 107, 121, 123–8, 133–5
idle/idleness, 6, 10, 20, 21, 79, 114, 116, 117, 136, 203, 204, 206
illegal/illegality, 57, 112, 121, 140, 158
Illich, I., 132
immobility, 9, 17, 101
inclusion, 5, 6, 125, 134, 135, 181, 183, 206
income, 6, 7, 21, 37, 46, 47, 56, 59, 60, 64, 66, 67, 69, 75, 84, 85, 88, 89, 112, 114, 120, 121, 126, 127, 137, 139, 142, 143, 147, 150, 153, 165, 175, 176, 181, 190–3, 196, 198, 200, 204–6
Indigenous, 32, 39, 55, 86, 125
individual responsibility, 114, 124, 147, 203
inequality/inequalities, 1, 4, 6, 9–11, 16, 19, 22, 27, 32, 34–8, 57, 127, 134–6, 157, 180–5, 199, 200, 203, 205, 206
informal economy, 5–7, 14, 49, 53, 67, 69, 75, 114, 116, 125, 205
informal labour, 67, 204
injustices, 17, 34, 38, 66, 127, 146, 156, 157, 182

insecure income/work, 2, 9, 55, 127, 149, 195, 199
itinerant work/workers, 53–6, 59, 79

K
Kelly, P., 135, 136
Kennelly, J., 3
Kingsolver, A. E., 184
knowledge economy, 1, 5

L
labour/labouring, 1, 5, 9, 21, 37, 53, 55, 64, 67–9, 72, 80, 85, 98, 108, 112, 115, 116, 131–50, 184, 187, 188, 203, 204
lack/lacking, 3, 4, 34, 115, 200
laws, 17, 41, 69, 98, 121, 158, 174, 184
lazy/laziness, 10, 54, 79, 83, 104, 205
learn/learning, 1, 2, 4–6, 11, 15, 20, 21, 40–2, 45, 46, 49, 65, 73, 80, 98, 114, 115, 131–50, 171, 180, 203–6
learning citizen/s, 5, 6, 134
learning ethic, 6, 80, 131–7, 150
learning society, 5, 134
Lee, A., 133
Lefebvre, H., 40
legal, 57, 60, 65, 69, 113, 117, 122
legitimate income, 2, 75, 112, 126
legitimate work, 64, 75, 113, 117, 126, 176. *See also* legitimate income
Lindemann, K., 72
liquid modernity, 9
London, 2, 4, 11–19, 21, 43, 47, 48, 53, 60, 61, 65, 68, 72, 74, 75, 82–4, 89, 107, 109, 112, 113, 117–21, 123, 138, 140, 142, 144, 156, 158, 163, 164, 167, 175, 204, 206

M

marginalised, 2, 4, 5, 27, 36, 38, 42, 44, 48, 49, 67, 75, 117–23, 136
marginality, 1, 2, 19, 28–49, 99, 171, 204
marginal work, 6, 21, 37, 182
margins, 2–6, 13, 19, 27, 32, 34, 36–40, 69, 70, 72, 99, 107, 112–17, 131, 149, 171, 194, 196, 203–6
Marx, K., 36
McGee, M., 181
Melbourne, 2, 4, 11–21, 28, 30, 43, 47, 48, 53, 61, 65, 68, 72, 73, 75, 81–7, 89, 91–3, 95, 97, 100, 103, 107–9, 111, 112, 117, 120, 121, 123, 124, 127, 138, 141, 143–6, 148, 156, 158, 159, 162, 164, 166, 167, 171, 173–5, 179, 185, 187, 188, 190, 192, 194–7, 204, 206
microfinance, 7, 71, 205
migration, 17, 39
mobility, 4, 8–11, 22, 149
(*see also* social mobility)
money, 9, 46, 65, 67, 79–105, 107, 109–11, 117, 119, 121, 122, 126, 147, 150, 154, 160–2, 164, 165, 179, 180, 184, 186–9, 191, 192, 194, 195, 197, 198, 206
monotony, 9, 82
moral, 4–6, 8, 11, 35, 10, 54, 55, 67–72, 79, 80, 114, 121, 132, 134, 135, 150, 161, 170, 176, 204
    economy, 170
morality, 4, 8, 71, 170, 172, 206
morally charged exchange, 67, 205
mundane, 9, 41, 42, 47, 80, 91
Murphy, J., 184

N

neoliberal/neoliberalism, 7, 13, 34, 37, 40, 116, 134, 205
North American Street News Association (NASNA), 60

O

Occupy movement, 1
O'Donoghue, L., 39
opportunities, 17, 63–4, 66–7, 82, 118, 125–8, 135, 138, 149, 150, 161, 165, 180, 181, 184, 188, 192–4, 200, 204
Orwell, G., 21, 113, 114
'other'/'othering'/'otherness', 3, 4, 10, 15, 19, 20, 27, 33, 35, 42–4, 49, 104, 156, 203

P

panhandlers, 54, 62, (*see also* beggars)
panhandling, 60, 67, 69, 113, 121, 122, 158, (*see also* begging)
pathways, 5, 21, 22, 68, 117, 175, 179–200, 206
Peel, M., 9, 35
performative/performativity, 153, 166, 170, 172
performs/performing, 8, 21, 72, 85, 115, 166–76, 203–5
perpetual transition, 180, 189–96, 200
perseverance, 84, 85, 101, 104, 149
philanthropy/philanthropists, 7, 66, 72, 205
photos/photographs, 8, 46, 47, 57, 89–91, 94–102, 167
    typical day's work, 20, 47, 80, 81, 89, 98
Picketty, T., 1
police, 57, 66, 74, 111, 121, 155, 158, 196

poor, 1, 2, 4, 7, 9–11, 17, 21, 32, 35, 37, 38, 41, 42, 44, 46, 58, 61, 63, 64, 70, 71, 73, 85, 99, 114, 127, 128, 139, 142, 147, 150, 156, 157, 176, 182–4, 194, 199, 203–6
post-colonial, 19, 32, 36
poverty, 1–22, 35, 39, 42, 44, 46, 49, 53, 56–8, 60, 62–6, 75, 80, 84, 87, 104, 105, 107, 112, 124, 126, 132, 137, 139, 142, 146, 147, 149, 150, 156, 157, 159, 161, 165, 172, 173, 175, 176, 180–6, 188–91, 193–5, 199, 200, 204–6
precariat, 9, 37
precarious/precarity, 1, 2, 4–11, 19, 21, 34, 37, 38, 46, 47, 55, 67, 69, 72, 80, 82, 84, 85, 88, 116, 118, 123, 125–7, 134, 136, 137, 147, 149, 150, 165, 180, 181, 187–9, 194–7, 200, 203, 204
work/labour/employment, 9, 55, 84, 203, 204
productive citizenship, 6, 114, 136
productive/productivity, 3, 5–8, 10, 11, 20, 21, 54, 69, 72, 80, 82, 83, 98, 107–28, 136, 137, 161, 173, 176, 184, 192, 204, 206
public space, 4, 8, 45, 125, 132, 153, 154, 163, 175 (*see also city space*)
pseudo-public space, 15, 156

Q
Quinn, T., 170

R
race, 1, 6, 27, 37–9, 55, 79, 80, 86, 113, 125, 154, 184, 185, 205
racism, 29, 55, 86, 184
Raco, M., 182

refuges, 3, 18, 86, 163
reinventing self, 9
research reflexivity, 42, 43
risk, 9, 99, 121, 141, 204
risk factors, 3, 45, 49, 184
risk society, 9
Roddick, Gordon, 61, 64, 66
Romani, 39
Rose, N., 124, 135
rough sleeping, 12, 18, 86, 98, 104, 121, 154, 158, 163, 186, 194, 196
routines, 8–10, 20, 41, 46, 47, 80–3, 89, 93, 95, 115, 131, 132, 134, 135, 143, 170, 180, 187
Roy, A., 71

S
safe/safety, 44, 84, 93, 125, 126, 155, 187, 194, (*see also* unsafe; violence)
sales, getting, 87, 119, 145, 147, 159
sales job, 140, 141, 166, 194
sales tactics/techniques, 3, 90, 91, 117, 141, 146, 149, 160, 163, 170, 172
  assertive, 165, 170
  gender, 12, 80, 86, 125, 154, 187, 205, (*see also* performance/performativity)
  quiet, 95, 124, 125, 154
  race, 154, 185, 205
San Francisco, 2, 4, 11–21, 38, 43, 47, 48, 53, 57, 64, 69, 72–4, 82–4, 88, 107, 108, 112, 121–3, 125, 139, 145, 146, 153, 154, 156–9, 165, 166, 173, 175, 179, 183, 185, 189–91, 194, 204–6
Sassen, S., 15, 37–8, 69, 70
Seddon, T., 5, 133

INDEX 213

self-development, 6, 10, 21, 46, 114, 116, 133, 142, 149, 172, 180, 205, 206
self-help, 20, 21, 53, 60–7, 75, 137, 138, 142, 181
self-management, 84, 133, 138, 144, 172, 205
sexuality, 27, 37–9, 55, 80, 125
shame/less, 10, 11, 107, 126, 157, 172, 193
shelter, 12, 15, 46, 58, 59, 146, 147, 155, 157, 194, 197
shopping malls/centres, 14, 15, 45, 81, 156, 157
single resident occupancy (SRO), 147, 154, 155
Skeggs, B., 34, 43, 44, 161, 162
skid row, 18, 57, 58, 73, 79
skills, 65, 80, 121, 131, 132, 134, 136–8, 141, 143, 145–7, 173, 180, 193
Smith, D., 31, 41
social enterprise, 2–8, 14, 20, 21, 48, 53, 60–7, 73, 75, 136, 204
social mobility/socially mobile, 9, 132, 149, 180–2, (*see also* mobility)
social relationships, 21, 37, 82, 118, 146, 147, 153, 160, 161, 163, 165, 192
Solomon, N., 134
Sontag, S., 8
Spare Change, 57, 58, 64
spatial, 17, 38, 41, 156, 161, 170
Spivak, G. C., 19, 36
Standing, G., 9, 37
stasis, 4, 8–11, 16, 17, 22, 179–200, 206
stigma, 3
Street News, 60, 61, 64
Street Sheet, 2, 6, 18, 20, 21, 53, 60–64, 66, 67, 69, 72–5, 82, 84, 112, 113, 122, 131, 139, 140,

147, 149, 153–6, 158–60, 166, 183, 190, 191, 205
code of conduct, 68, 121
establishment, 48, 62
offices, 73–4
streets of cities, 153
StreetWise, 2, 60
studying, 15, 18, 39, 45, 98, 184
Suleri, S., 40
swagmen, 54
swagwomen, 55
Swithinbank, T., 60, 64

T
Teasdale, S., 66
Telegraph Avenue Liberation Front, 57
temporal, 16, 41, 47, 79, 81, 83, 92, 182
Tenderloin, 18, 58, 73, 147, 189, 191
Thompson, E. P., 80
time, 20, 43, 65, 79, 80, 93, 101, 181, 189, 194
tips, 29, 87, 93, 119
Tirado, L., 184
tired/tiring, 94, 111, 126, 179, 193
training, 114, 115, 124, 135, 136, 140, 141, 144, 145
transition, 17, 93, 136, 142, 170, 180, 183, 194, 199, 200, 204
transnational, 13, 14, 16, 71, 117, 206

U
under-employment, 114
undeserving, 54, 103, 107
unemployed, 2, 3, 9, 10, 38, 41, 56, 72, 99, 109, 114–16, 126, 164, 203

unemployment, 1, 20, 21, 34, 44, 53, 75, 81–5, 107, 114, 115, 117, 120, 124, 128, 132, 136, 146, 150, 175, 180, 182–5, 187–9, 192, 199, 200, 204–6
unproductive/unproductivity, 3, 6, 20, 79, 83, 104, 112, 114, 116, 136, 200, 203
unsafe, 155 (*see also* safe/safety; violence)

V
value, 21, 34, 58, 69–72, 82, 114, 117, 134, 136, 153, 160–3, 165–6, 180, 192, 203–5
violence, 34, 40, 46, 57, 66, 93, 125, 174, 181, 184
visible/visibility, 3, 4, 8, 17, 30, 33, 44, 57, 71, 95, 108, 125, 148, 157, 158, 167, 170, 175, 204, 205

W
Wacquant, L., 9, 16, 38, 189
Watson, J., 125

Weber, M., 79, 134, 181
Weeks, K., 2, 21, 80, 114, 134–5
welfare state/s, 4–8, 13, 38
welfare system, 10, 30, 98, 194, 195, 204
Williams, R., 10, 14, 16
Willis, P., 5, 133
work ethic, 5, 6, 20, 64, 107, 115, 132–7, 150, 181, 203
workfare, 114–16
working lives, 4, 19, 20, 28, 41, 42
worry/worrying, 9, 87, 88, 107, 111, 171, 173, 189, 192, 194
worth/worthy/worthiness, 3, 6, 8, 9, 70–2, 79, 82, 87, 88, 107, 111, 113, 134, 150, 154, 160, 161, 164, 166, 173, 176, 182, 189, 192, 194, 204, 206

Y
young people, 12, 40, 125, 157
youth, 132, 197

Z
Zizek, S., 7, 71, 162

Printed by Printforce, the Netherlands